THE PROFESSOR

AND THE FOSSIL

THE PROFESSOR

AND THE FOSSIL

by MAURICE SAMUEL

SOME OBSERVATIONS ON

ARNOLD J. TOYNBEE'S

A STUDY OF HISTORY

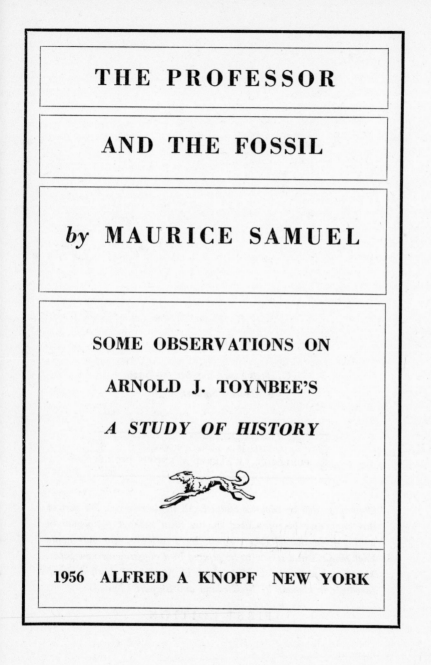

1956 ALFRED A KNOPF NEW YORK

L.C. catalog card number: 56–8929

© Maurice Samuel, 1956

THIS IS A BORZOI BOOK,
PUBLISHED BY ALFRED A. KNOPF, INC.

FIRST EDITION

ACKNOWLEDGMENTS

The author wishes to thank the following for the use of material from their books:

Beacon Press, for excerpts from Pieter Geyl, *The Pattern of the Past*, 1951, 21, 36 ff., 107, 111.

The Christian Heritage Press, for excerpt from Justin Martyr, *The First Apology*, 1949, chapter 21 (translation of T. B. Falls).

Harcourt, Brace, for excerpt from Lewis Mumford, *The Conduct of Life*, 1951, 139.

Harper and Brothers, for excerpts from Chaim Weizmann, *Trial and Error*, 1949, 11, 224, 258, 404 ff.

Jewish Frontier Association, New York, for excerpt from Chaim Greenberg, *The Inner Eye*, 1953, "Letter to a Christian Clergyman."

Jewish Publication Society, Philadelphia, for excerpts from Cecil Roth, *Personalities and Events in Jewish History*, 1953, 3, 4, 7; for excerpts from Leon Poliakov, *Harvest of Hate*, 1954, 41, 113, 122 ff., 124, 131 ff., 182 ff., 198.

Macmillan and Co. (London), for excerpt from Samuel Dill, *Roman Society from Nero to Marcus Aurelius*, 1920, 67.

Oxford University Press, for excerpts from *The Legacy of Israel*, edited by Charles and Dorothea Singer, 1927, xxxix, 174, 182 ff., 247; for excerpts from Herbert J. Muller, *The Uses of the Past*, 1952, 14, 19, 67, 186, 197, 206, 226 ff., 289 n., 192 ff.; for excerpts from the *Survey of International Affairs*, 1939–46: George Kirk, *The Middle East*, 1945–50, 1954, pp. 251–72; for excerpt from *The Middle East and the War*, 1952, 250 n.; for excerpts from Arnold J. Toynbee, *A Study of History, passim*.

CONTENTS

CONTENTS

THE PROFESSOR

AND THE FOSSIL

CHAPTER ONE

THE STARTING POINT

THE CIRCUMSTANCES under which I made acquaintance with Professor Arnold J. Toynbee's *A Study of History*—more exactly the first six volumes of it—furnish me with the introduction to my comments on it.

In August 1939 I was commissioned by the *New York Post* to proceed to Europe and find my way onto one of the boats that were carrying Jewish refugees illegally to Palestine. I undertook the assignment uneasily, with the knowledge of my emotional unfitness for it, with a foreboding that the horrors I would witness—were all preceding reports but half-true—would make me inarticulate. I was, moreover, oppressed by the probable futility of the enterprise. It will be remembered that in those days the democratic Powers had hung out a sign for the benefit of the little peoples engulfed or about to be engulfed by Hitler: "Do not scream while the alligator is devouring you: it will only infuriate him unnecessarily"; and of all the little peoples so adjured none was heard with more impatience and distaste, none was more frequently accused of self-centeredness and effrontery, than the Jews. But it was urged on me that one more firsthand description of conditions on a crowded, unseaworthy, unsanitary cattle-boat, dodging, with its load of men, women, and children, the gunboats of the Royal Navy in the Mediterranean, might touch a chord of pity here and there and get us a few more visas into other lands than Palestine. I accepted.

I arrived in Paris on the day of the publication of the Nazi-Soviet Pact, and my assignment was over. Now the world's newspapers would not have even a ten-line filler on the tenth page to spare for the peripheral tragedy of the Jewish refugees. Moreover, the traffic in rescue was temporarily disrupted, to be resumed later under more desperate circumstances. Not that war was considered quite certain; nor, when it was declared, was its continuance considered quite certain. (Let the incredulous reader consult the newspaper files for the early days of the "phony war.") But the pact itself was a tremendous event; and if war was uncertain, both before and after the declaration, the wild maneuvering was now being conducted on the very edge of the abyss.

From Paris I made a dash for Geneva to take in the closing session of the Twenty-second Zionist Congress. I had no intention of reporting on it. I was impelled in part by panic, by the feeling that I would there take a last farewell of old friends and acquaintances I had met at earlier conferences, representatives of Jewries to which my heart had been drawn for many years. From Geneva I went by way of Paris to London, recalling how, twenty-five years earlier, I had made the same journey after the Battle of the Marne; and in London I waited some three weeks before I managed to get passage for New York in the *Manhattan*.

They were three weeks of bewilderment, of general and special fears, of endless talk, feverish surmise, maddening helplessness. I attended meetings of large and small groups who discussed the necessary changes in the techniques of rescue, legal and illegal; but the rapid changes in the picture made each day's proposals obsolete the next; for while the war was "phony" in the West, ghastly events unrolled in the East, not so much a war as an annihilative invasion. Here is their order:

On September 1 Poland was invaded and Warsaw bombed; on the 3rd, British fliers dropped peace pamphlets on Germany. On the 6th, Cracow was occupied; and on the 7th, the Germans were reported seven miles from Warsaw. On the 12th, a few British planes raided German territory with trifling results. On the 12th, Russia announced her annexation of two Polish provinces. On the 15th, Hitler declared his agreement with Russia's ambitions in Poland; and on the same day Nazi and Communist envoys met to arrange the details of the complete partition of the country. On the 20th, the day I sailed for New York, the Mayor of Warsaw sent out a wild, unanswered appeal for help.

Then I went out of the world into darkness. No daily bulletins, such as are customary on trans-Atlantic liners, were issued during the crossing. We sailed in a complete blackout, and for ten days the *Manhattan* did not use its radio. When we arrived in New York, we learned that Warsaw had fallen, and Poland was lost.

And still to many people it seemed possible that France and England would come to terms with Hitler; what had happened after Austria and Czechoslovakia would happen again; the world would settle once more into a stupor of acquiescence. Nor was there any comfort in the alternative; that which had been done to Austria and Czechoslovakia and Poland could only be undone by a world explosion; and if for those countries the explosion could still come in time, for Polish Jewry it would be too late.

I ask the reader to believe that my friends and I had not lost our bearings; we were not blind to the threat that overhung the world at large; we had not forgotten the perils and problems that faced our respective countries. But has not the issue shown that as Jews we were justified in the sick foreknowledge that ours was a special case, that for us was reserved a limbo of suffering in depths not to be plumbed by other peoples?

That weird phantasmagoric time in London, when millions walked the streets with gas masks slung over their shoulders, and the barrage balloons hung over the city like parodies of Macy floats on Thanksgiving Day, and the English weather took on a bewitching radiance, and hundreds of men and women sat or lay in the grass of Hyde Park and St. James's Park through the long afternoon hours! It was like the pageantry of a charming ritual memorializing a national danger long past, or like lifeboat drill on a calm, sunny day in mid-Atlantic. Or so it was for others—not for us. We did not suspect then that the German conquest of Poland was the prelude to the systematic extermination of that nine tenths of Polish Jewry which had not fled into the Russian area. We only understood that Polish Jewry was done for. Two prospects, and two only, lay before it, as we then saw things: the first meant the brutalization and then the fragmentation of the Jewish people, the rapid, relentless, defiant, and cynical demolition of a great social organism carried out in sight of all the world; the second meant the hypocritical—perhaps even more cynical—repression of the soul of a people by forcible assimilation labeled "democracy." Do not reproach us with perverted sentimentalism if we did not know whose destiny to lament more bitterly, that of the ninety per cent of Polish Jewry which fell into German hands or that of the three hundred thousand or three hundred and fifty thousand who fell or fled into Communist keeping.

There was no likelihood that the criminals who had formulated the Nuremberg race laws and had organized the November (1938) Burning of the Synagogues, who had ex-

torted a communal fine of two hundred and fifty million
dollars for the murder of a German official by a crazed Jewish boy and had infected no small portion of the world with
their diseased anti-Semitic fantasies, who had reduced German Jewry to rubble and were now applying themselves to
Czechoslovakian and Austrian Jewries—there was no likelihood that these frantic sadists intended to leave to their
new Jewish victims that minimum of free psychic energy
without which man degenerates into a talking beast. There
was as little likelihood that the criminal fanaticism of the
Communists would relax its hatred of Judaism and of traditional Jewish culture or make exceptions of its new Jewish
subjects. It is true that before the lifting of the curtain
on the apocalyptic satanism of the gas chambers and crematoria we took it for granted that on the animal level the individual Jew would fare better with the Russians than with
the Germans. Neither body nor soul would be spared by
the Germans; the body of the Jew was offered survival in
Russia if divorced from the soul. But the Germans offered
another relative "advantage": they were eager to be rid of
their Jews; they, unlike the Russians, would not prohibit
emigration; at worst they would impede some of it to extract
blood-money from Jews abroad. On the other hand the four
and one-half million Jews they would be ruling with the
annexation of the better part of Poland (Romanian and
other Jewries were to raise the number to some seven million) would not find admission into the democratic countries within the foreseeable future, and thus life under Nazi
domination loomed before a huge segment of the Jewish
people—more than half of world Jewry outside of Russia—
as a nightmare of indefinite duration.

We weighed the competing horrors in the balance, and
now the right scale, now the left, affrighted us more. It was
"good" to hear of the remnant that escaped from the Scylla

of Germany into the Charybdis of Russia, as it is "good" to hear that someone who is threatened with total extinction has at least been reprieved from the tortures of the flesh; while concerning him who was trapped in the torture chamber there was consolation in the thought that he had a remote chance of escape.

Two other aspects of the tragedy struggled for the priority in our emotions: the straightforward physical tragedy of millions of individuals and the programmatic doing to death of a living civilization. We talked despairingly of men and women known to us from contacts in Jewish movements, or by their reputations: "What's going to happen to old Simon Dubnow? Did Gottlieb get back to Poland? Where are Segalovitch and Prilutsky? . . ." [1] And then we talked of institutions, communities, traditions, which were about to be erased from the face of the earth. In those September weeks our talk reverted daily to the successive amputations that the twentieth century had performed on the Jewish body spiritual. We remembered in a ritual of our own (how ancient *this* one was!) all the great communities, Kiev and Odessa and Pinsk and Berdichev, cities and mothers in Israel, as well as the *shtetlach*, the townlets, the Pereyeslavs and Belzes and Motteles and Svislovitzes, numberless and precious, whose Jewishness had been asphyxiated by Communist rule. We remembered the types—the scholars, the householders, the coopers and tailors and butchers and fishmongers and shoemakers, the students in the Talmudical academies of Mir and Volozhin and Zhitomir and Slobodka, the Tevyes and the Menachem Mendels, the Bonches and

---

[1] Simon Dubnow, the historian, in his eighties, perished in the Riga ghetto between 1941 and 1943. Joshua Gottlieb, the journalist, was arrested by the Russians in 1939 and was never heard from again. Zalman Segalovitch, the poet, escaped through Soviet Rusia to Israel (then Palestine). Noah Prilutsky, the journalist and politician, a member of the Sejm from 1922 to 1928, was killed by the Nazis in 1941.

the Rabbis of Nemirov, the hearty wagoners, the humble shopkeepers and peddlers; we remembered their synagogues and their festivities, their folk songs, their weddings, their burials; and we saw it all shot through with a radiance streaming from an ancient land and an ancient faith. We will be forgiven—will we not?—if in such an hour we turned our eyes away from the failures and defects, the squalor and meanness, that were to be found in old Russian Jewry. God knows we had throughout the years acknowledged and published these with perhaps more than the necessary frankness.

And of German Jewry, which we had so often denounced for its bourgeois complacency and its cowardly assimilationism, we remembered now only its brilliant achievements even in the Jewish field, its *Jüdische Wissenschaft*, its Graetz and Geiger and Zunz, and more recently its Franz Rosenzweig, its Martin Buber, its Leo Baeck, and its Gershom Scholem.

To these two vanished Jewries of our day a third was about to be added, larger than Russian Jewry by a million or more, and six times as large as the German Jewry of pre-Hitler days. Now it would be Warsaw and Cracow and Lemberg and Lodz among the great communities, and, among the *shtetlach*, the Kutnovs and Zamosches, the Abts and Szeberzhins. And there was no escape, no hope —and not even the right to complain.

Poland's was a tremendously vital Jewry. Impoverished throughout the nineteenth and twentieth centuries by a gradual shrinkage of its old economic functions, hounded in the last few decades by a government-abetted boycott, leading a marginal existence without prospect of improvement, it struggled to keep alive the values it had inherited from a brighter past. It was a divided and unhappy Jewry, pursuing conflicting ideals in the midst of universal want;

but the conflicts bespoke an energy of soul which in such
adversity moved one to astonishment and admiration. Po-
lish-nationalist Jews—that is, assimilationists—fought with
Jews determined to continue into the far future the religious
and cultural identity inherited from the millennia. Those
who acclaimed the minority rights granted Polish Jewry
under the Treaty of Versailles were themselves divided as to
the use of them. Religious groups founded religious schools;
secularist Yiddishists founded secular Yiddish schools; Zionists supported a modernized Hebrew educational system and
preparation for emigration to Palestine. The orthodox and
the super-orthodox, the Chassidic, the Musarist (moralist),
the Bundist (revolutionary), the Communist, the Nihilist,
and the bourgeois forces tugged in their respective direc-
tions. It was a highly literate Jewry, with its Polish, Yiddish,
and Hebrew presses and publishing houses. It had its distinguished novelists and its hacks, its agnostic thinkers and
its Talmudic commentators, its poets, its pietists, and its
universalists. A Polish Jew, Nahum Sokolow, had been one
of the great leaders of Zionism, and another Polish Jew,
Zamenhoff, had been the creator of Esperanto.

I had learned to know Polish Jewry at first hand during
my two months' service with the Morgenthau Pogrom In-
vestigating Commission in 1919. I had seen the squalor of
the Nalevkis and the Franziskaner in Warsaw and of the
Baluta in Lodz. For hundreds of hours I had interpreted to
the commissioners the stories of the survivors of pogroms in
Vilna, Grodno, Lvov (Lemberg), Warsaw, and Cracow. I
had begun to feel the deep-rootedness of Polish anti-
Semitism. I had also begun to learn something of the inner
being of Polish Jewry. I attended, in unofficial hours, gather-
ings of intellectuals and idealists. I witnessed performances
of the brilliant Vilna Theater Group. I read, through half
the nights, the works of Peretz (then but recently dead) and

of the generation of younger writers who had come under his influence; I continued the reading in later years, and I was always haunted by the impulse, only imperfectly followed, to help uncover to the English-speaking world some of the treasures of a *terra incognita*. I thought it an injustice to my people, and a loss to all others, that beyond the inner circle nothing, or next to nothing, should be known of the Chassidic and Folk Tales of Peretz, of the early novels and stories of Sholem Asch, the realistic panoramas of I. J. Singer, the lyrics of Segalovitch, the religious epic of Menachem Boraisha.

These are only a part of the treasury of Polish Jewry, itself only a part of the larger Jewry that included Russia. There, still waiting for English translation from the Yiddish, were the stinging satires of Mendele the Bookseller and the sly and loving portraits of Sholom Aleichem; and, from the Hebrew, the prophetic exaltations and homely tendernesses of Chaim Nachman Bialik, the sensuous and fiery songs of Zalman Schnaiur, and the dramatic and close-knit tableaux of Tchernichovsky. The very names were unknown to the West forty years ago; today enough of them have broken through the barriers of difficult languages and a still more difficult setting to alert the Western World to the existence of a neglected spiritual experience.

The fountains of Russian Jewry had been stopped up; those of Polish Jewry were being stopped up before our eyes. It will help the reader to understand the frustration that gave a bitter edge to our wretchedness if he recalls why we had not the right even to complain. In the days when we were the practice-target of Nazism in a far wider sense than Guernica, our warnings were cried down as the dangerous talk of special pleaders; and how ingrained this aversion to understanding us was, how profoundly we were affronted, the later years have testified. Even Winston Churchill, with all his warmth and magnanimity, with all his shrewd foresightedness, did not and does not understand. I have looked in vain through his memoirs for the suggestion that when the Germans elected to leadership the author of *Mein Kampf*, with its patently demented ravings on the Jews (see below, pp. 246 f.), the rest of the world should in self-protection have withdrawn its representatives from Germany. He mentions various stages at which the power of Hitler could have been broken by drastic but uncostly action: the remilitarization of Germany, the occupation of the Rhineland, perhaps even the threat against Czechoslovakia, though that came very late. Nowhere does he hint that the moment should have been Hitler's accession, which was proof enough that Germany had passed into a maniacal condition uncontrollable from within. He speaks with contempt of Hitler's anti-Semitism, and records with good humor and wit how Hitler, hearing of his views, refused to meet him. Of the deeper nexus there is no hint of perception.

A last word concerning my state of mind—our state of mind—in those September weeks of 1939. I was thinking of American Jewry, as well as of European Jewry and Palestine. To whatever extent we have been a special creative factor in the West, we owe it to the continuity of our tradition, transmitted by east European Jewry. The history of American Jewry does not begin, except in the purely formal sense, with the twenty-three refugees who arrived in New Amsterdam in 1654. If American Jewry is once more seeking contact with its heritage, to the enrichment of American life, the immediate sources of the need, as well as of the satisfaction, must be sought no farther back than the immigration of the last seventy years. The strain of those few who arrived in the first two hundred years has died out. Our connection with Ur of the Chaldees and Sinai and Jerusalem, and with the two thousand years of creative exile experience, unique in human annals, leads through the east European Jewry —Russian, Polish, Romanian, Galician—which began its tidal movement westward after the assassination of Alexander II of Russia in 1881.

The character of the Jewish Homeland too, until the founding of the State, and even after, owed and owes more to east European Jewry than to all other elements combined. American Jewry and Palestinian Jewry were in desperate need of more carriers of the tradition. We wanted to save individuals, men and women; we also wanted to save from extinction—but this was hopeless— a great segment of a civilization.

CHAPTER TWO

WE ARE
IDENTIFIED

I

On a sunlit afternoon shortly before I left London for Southampton, I came away, heavyhearted as usual, from a meeting at Zionist headquarters in Great Russell Street, and wandered past the British Museum and down Oxford Street toward my hotel. At Bumpus's bookshop I saw on display the first six volumes of Professor Toynbee's *A Study of History*, and thought: "This is the time for it."

I had been hearing of him since 1933, when he published the first three volumes. His name, I understood, was in high repute among the learned and the near-learned, but it had not yet achieved the general acceptance that followed on the publication of the one-volume condensation after World War II. I had formed the vague, attractive, and imposing picture of a new polyhistor who stood above his time and place "with wide eyes calm upon the whole of things," inviting perplexed and troubled spirits to share his ordered reconstruction of the confused secular panorama. For the dreary days of the crossing I could unreservedly accept the invitation. I anticipated from it a helpful restoration of perspective in worldly, if not cosmic, terms. It was an encouragement to know that in this feverish age one man at least was pursuing undistracted the Vision of the Whole; and by his side, or at his feet, I would rediscover the sense of historical pattern which the day's psychotic distractions had numbed.

Well, it was not quite like that. During the long isolation from world news I surrendered myself to Professor Toynbee, and, indeed, he took me to a mountaintop and showed me the kingdoms of the world all in a moment: twenty-odd kingdoms, or rather Societies, or Civilizations —besides some bits and pieces—living and dead, covering the globe from the Arctic to the southernmost of the South Seas, their births and the deaths of most of them, their "Apparentations" and "Affiliations," where such were demonstrable, their differences and their common features. At the same time he did not maintain a uniformly Olympian pose. He would sweep down from the peaks for an anecdote about an Italian Senator lecturing in America, or the story of a personal encounter on a railroad trip in the Balkans; and then, in an instant, without loss of poise, he was back on the heights, twirling the globe this way and that. His wide eyes did seem to be on the whole of things, but calm they were not; for he issued frequent judgments along the way, now as a historian, now as a prophet, now as a scientist, now as a mystic, and now as an Englishman, and the judgments were often marked by asperity and even violence. His universality was stupefying, the range of his references encyclopedic. He called in myth and poetry from many languages and ages to elucidate the mysteries of prehistoric beginnings. He evaluated and put into their proper places the Chinese, the Hindus, the Eskimos, the Babylonians, the Sumerians, the Japanese, the Mayas, the Romans and the Greeks, the early and modern Irish, the Turks, the Byzantines, Christianity, Judaism, Mohammedanism, Taoism, Zoroastrianism, industrialism, Marxism, nationalism, with copious quotations from the Greek, the Latin, the French, the German, from the classics and from contemporaneous writers, from Lucretius and Aldous Huxley, from the *Zend-Avesta* and Lord Acton, from Plato and Paracelsus.

I found the going heavy. His style was a curious blend of dignity, colloquialism, and Gongorism, and I was cowed at first by the sheer pyrotechnics of information. But before long, and thereafter quite frequently, I was jolted into a critical alertness that sent me scurrying back to earlier passages for comparisons; and as I proceeded, an extraordinary impression gained on me that I was "being had," that I was being pushed around by someone with a vast amount of miscellaneous information. But this was utterly inadmissible. Here was a distinguished if not yet famous work; there could certainly be no intention to confuse; the confusion was undoubtedly (so I thought) of my own making, the result of my incapacity to retain simultaneously and in an ordered framework a large number of facts.

Let me at once make clear that I am not speaking now (as I will be later) of facts that I challenged as facts. I was quite willing, for the purposes of Professor Toynbee's argument, to accept most of his facts as he presented them. It was after I had accepted them that I could not make sense of the thesis they were intended to support. I remember being angry with myself for not being able to concentrate, and I was ready to believe that worry had affected my mind. It was only when I had begun to make systematic notes that I recovered some degree of self-assurance; and it was only recently—that is, many years later—on a rereading of my notes and of *A Study of History* (now supplemented and concluded by four additional volumes) that I felt justified in setting forth the conclusions which will be found in this book.

II

A special factor in my initial uneasiness was my disagreement with Professor Toynbee's views in a field with which I am familiar: that of the Jewish people, present and past. Here my disagreement was with the "facts" and the spirit; that is to say, I suspected that this work was both biased and inaccurate. Here, above all, I refused for some time to trust myself, for my emotions (that is, my prejudices) were engaged, and it was probably impossible to keep check on them. I must therefore advise the reader that my criticisms of A *Study of History* are of three kinds. In the first I shall challenge its intelligibility in some areas, and this challenge has nothing to do with its bias and inaccuracies; it is directed at the essential meaninglessness of much of the work, at the complete self-obfuscation that it achieves by a peculiar method and that remains complete self-obfuscation regardless of the validity of the facts. In the second I challenge, wherever I feel competent to do so, the historic facts themselves; and here of course the reader must take his choice between my account and Professor Toynbee's. In the third (this chiefly in my last chapters) I challenge the account of certain contemporaneous events in the Jewish field and indicate where he has omitted from the record material which he had at his disposal, *and which in fact he helped to prepare,* so that there emerges a distorted picture.

The first kind of criticism stands by itself. In a way it is not concerned with history, but with logic or, to be less pompous, with ordinary common sense and the use of the English language. It can be applied—and I do apply it—to passages that I also subject to the second and third kinds of criticism, but it operates independently.

I also use a fourth approach, which is only an indirect form of criticism. I devote a large part of this book to an extended picture of Jewish life as I see it today and as I believe it to have been in the past. It is my hope that the general reader will find here a corrective to the impressions created by Professor Toynbee's treatment of that subject.

III

My troubles began quite early. I was just becoming accustomed to the rather exacting style when, on page 35 of Volume I, after the listing of the living Societies or Civilizations of mankind, this passage occurred:

> On a closer inspection, we can also discern two sets of what appear to be fossilized relics of similar societies now extinct, namely: one set including the Monophysite Christians of Armenia, Mesopotamia, Egypt, and Abyssinia and the Nestorian Christians of Kurdistan and Malabar, as well as the Jews and Parsees; a second set including the Lamaistic Mahayanian Buddhists of Ceylon, Burma, and Siam, as well as the Jains in India.

"How quaint!" I thought. I could not speak at first hand of the Mahayanian Buddhists of Tibet, or the Monophysite Christians of Armenia, or the Jains of India; but "fossilized" as applied to the Jews was, I took it, a touch of facetiousness. Knowing that I am not responsive to professorial drollery, I could not be sure of the point, so I surmised that this was an intramural, ironical little side-swipe at certain fossilized writers on the Monophysites, the Parsees, the Jews, and the rest. I continued to read, and was once again caught up in the vast rhythms of his codifications and reminiscences.

But a little farther on he repeats the witticism without furnishing a clue to its target—the same list, the same words: ". . . fossilized relics of societies now extinct" (I, 51); and once more: "The Jews and Parsees are *manifestly* [my italics throughout unless otherwise indicated: M. S.] fossils of the Syriac Society in the state in which this society was when it was developing under the Achaemenian Empire, before its normal development was suddenly and violently interrupted by the intrusion of the Hellenic Society in the wake of Alexander the Great" (I, 90 f.). And in succeeding volumes: " The Zionist legatees of a fossilized Syriac Civilization" (III, 49); and: "*We need not doubt* that we have discovered what are *unmistakably* fossilized fragments . . . of the Syriac Civilization in the Parsees and the Jews . . ." (V, 7 f.). And so on, and so on.

It began to dawn on me that, incredibly enough, the man was quite serious. It was odd that, without adducing new evidence—actually he had not offered any to begin with —he should be rising from level to level of assurance; he did, to be sure, intersperse the successive advances with deprecatory statements like: "*In principle* we have already conceded that an extinct society may leave fossilized remains of its fabric behind. We have identified a number of fossil remnants of two extinct societies—the Syriac and the Indic— in the world of our own day" (I, 136). But this is only the classic technique of *reculer pour mieux sauter*.

Let me assure the reader that I am not boggling at a mere word, or at a purely technical classification on a special and esoteric plane. I am not dealing with a misunderstanding that a restatement on another plane would instantly remove. This assurance is necessary because a general impression seems to exist, particularly among those who have not read A *Study of History* carefully—and of course careful readers are always rare—that the word "fossil," which has attracted a good deal of attention in this connection, refers merely to the rigidity or spiritlessness of Judaism as Professor Toynbee sees it. It refers to that, of course, but also to a great deal more. Whatever Professor Toynbee may mean with regard to the other specimens in his showcase, he means that the Jewish people is spiritually and intellectually a fossil, an inert and petrified form devoid of any living juices, a lifeless and unproductive, though perhaps instructive, curiosity, a simulacrum of genuine peoplehood. He is not referring to the age of the Jewish people or to individual Jews in their capacities as individuals at large or as members of other groups. Nor does he imply directly that the Jewish people is necessarily a fossil because it is small (though that implication does offer itself now and again), a miniature, a reduced version of a once widely distributed force. Let this be absolutely clear: he is referring to the corporate personality and to the specifically Jewish element in the Jewish people, and he means that this Jewish people is completely dead as a spiritually functioning entity. It is evident throughout the six volumes (and in fact throughout all the ten) that he knows of no moral, intellectual, spiritual, or any other kind of superior value that the Jewish people has created since ancient times; and the implication is that if the world does not mention it we may safely assume that it does not exist. We shall see that he is undecided, by six or seven centuries, as to the approximate date when the fossilization set in or was completed, but that the condition has now existed for more than nineteen hundred years is to him an unchallengeable fact.

To prove an *is not* is often difficult, sometimes impossible. It is in the nature of Professor Toynbee's case regarding the fossildom of the Jewish people that it must rest on an absence rather than on a presence. And yet it seemed to me that he might at least have indicated that many scholars are under the delusion that during the last two thousand years the Jewish people has been very much alive and has made important spiritual and intellectual contributions to Western civilization. He might at least have touched on certain Jewish names that have been given, however un-justifiably, considerable standing in the Western World, if only to dismiss them for what they were worth. I quote, for instance, from *The Legacy of Israel* (Oxford University Press, 1927) a few passages which are representative of a widespread view among distinguished scholars:

Such influence on thought, other than religious thought, as can be called specifically Jewish was exercised mainly in the period that preceded the great classical Renaissance. It is in the earlier 'Revival of Learning', that of the thirteenth century, that this influence may be most clearly discerned. Without Jewish aid this earlier Renais-sance would have been long delayed and would have as-sumed a different form. . . . The Western mind had sunk into ineptitude during the centuries that preceded the scholastic revival. Systematic thought had ceased to be; philosophy had wholly vanished; science had perished; even the love of nature was submerged; the very instinct for intellectual consistency was languishing. But still be-yond the sunrise trickled the ancient spring of Hellenic wisdom. From these healing waters man could still renew his youth, and it was the Wandering Jew who bore west-ward the magic draught. . . . Arabian philosophy thus had a profound effect on Latin thought, which seized many of its most characteristic ideas and used them as generally and with as great avidity as it did the texts of Aristotle. Of the Arabian authors whose ideas were thus incorporated into the body of Christian thought, the most important were Averroes, Maimonides, Avicebron, and Algazel. Two of these, Maimonides and Avicebron, were themselves Jews [Charles and Dorothea Singer, pp. 174, 182 f., 247].

Professor Toynbee might have asked how a fossil could bear westward, or in any other direction, a magic draught, even if that draught was (and this is debatable) entirely prepared by some other, and living, organism. Or he might have paused for a moment over the views expressed by A. D. Lindsay, late Master of Balliol, on Spinoza: "What I have tried to indicate as the peculiar qualities of his greatness are not found in anything like the same degree outside Jewish thought, and the achievement of these combined qualities, whether in the Book of Job or the Ethics of Spinoza, seem to me no small part of the legacy of Israel" (p. xxxix). But Professor Toynbee does not seem to have heard of these cultural aberrations among Western scholars, and the names of Maimonides, Avicebron (or, to give him his Jewish name, ibn Gabirol), and Spinoza do not occur anywhere in the ten volumes. Nor is this because he avoids philosophers; Kant and Hobbes and Descartes are there, but not Spinoza. Nor Yehudah ha-Levi. Nor is there any allusion, even by way of denigration, to the Talmud, or the Mishnah, or the Midrashim; or to the singular Yiddish literature that has lately made something of a stir among non-Jews. Chassidism, which is being widely recognized as a religious episode of high importance, is not mentioned. Professor Toynbee has ransacked the world for stories, myths, and sayings of the Uzbeks, the Eskimos, the Shilluk, and the Kushans, and some of his quotations from these sources are not very interesting or enlightening. The legends and laws of the Talmud, the profound moral aphorisms of the Mishnah, the parables and interpretations of the Midrashim (to speak of certain features only), the mystical wisdom and loving example of the Baal Shem, the parables of the

Magidim, the penetrating moral insights of the Musarists
(and again I touch only on some of the high points of these
phenomena) have no place here.

It would have been a relief if he had merely said, in one
of his statelier moments: "In that Schism of the Soul
which in the Modern Western World is known as Wilful
Esotericism, and has its analogue in the dichotomy between
the triumph of Shi-ism as a political force and the concom-
mitant spiritual victory of Sufi-ism, as well as in the sustained tensions which we may observe in the combination
of Cyclopeanism and Baroque in the ruins of the Mayan
Civilization, the names of Maimonides and ibn Gabirol
survive as curious examples of the Persistence of Attitude."
Or: "The extraordinary regard in which Wolfgang von
Goethe held Benedict d'Espinoza (*floruit circa* 1670)
marks the climax of that affectation of the rationalist form
as a disguise for a basically fallacious mysticism which in
nineteenth century Germany parallels, though with inverted
values, the rigidity of doctrine concealed behind the apparent fancifulness of utterance characterizing the literature of the Ugaritic Kingdom." We should then have
known where Professor Toynbee stands on these matters.
As it is, the informed reader is left with the suspicion that
though the author has certainly heard of Maimonides, ibn
Gabirol, the Mishnah, the Talmud, Spinoza, and Chassidism, he either does not know what to say about them or
prefers not to mention them, while the uninformed reader
is left with the impression that the last two thousand years
of Jewish history have been a spiritual blank; and, of course,
if the Jews have not produced a Talmud and Chassidism,
a Maimonides and a Spinoza, they *are* a fossil people.

If it be objected that Professor Toynbee has already al-
lotted too much space to the Jews in a review of all mankind's history I should, while not disagreeing, suggest that

by removing some of the repetitions he could have put in a great deal about medieval and recent Jewish life and still have saved time and paper. Or if it be objected that he is not bound to know so much about the small Jewish people, I would suggest that he is also not bound to devote several hundred pages to it and to express himself on the subject with such devastating finality.

IV

Of the values in contemporaneous Jewish life Professor Toynbee knows only the Zionist movement, to which he makes frequent reference—usually with contempt. Yiddish literature, as I have noted, is never mentioned, and the Yiddish language, to which I devote a chapter *à titre d'information*, rates nothing more than a footnote: ". . . the Jewish dialect of German known as Yiddish (*Jüdisch*)" (VI, 70). It took me some time to get over this extraordinary verdict, and I was glad to find, years later, a parallel to my astonishment. Professor Pieter Geyl, the distinguished Dutch historian, refers thus to Professor Toynbee's cavalier dismissal of another language: "There is in particular a passage in which Afrikaans as a cultural language is belittled in comparison with Dutch: V, 493–4. It is amusing to see so completely misinformed a statement delivered so positively" (*Debates with Historians*, 1955, p. 127 n.). Professor Geyl continues in a general strain: "Of course not even Professor Toynbee can know everything. It is useful, nevertheless, quite apart from the considerations built upon it in the text, to note such mistakes. The conclusion may be drawn that it is not imperative to believe him unreservedly when he speaks with the same assurance about peoples or ages unfamiliar to us and constructs his towering conclusions on facts which we cannot so easily check."

Professor Toynbee has sought to forestall the challenges of those who know more than he in a particular field by hanging out a "Hands Off" notice at the beginning of his immense opus. He directs it at the parochialism of the historian specialists whose information is confined to "insignificant" areas of man's historical experience, and he cites as a horrid example the reception accorded to H. G. Wells's *The Outline of History:* "Mr. H. G. Wells's *The Outline of History* was received with unmistakable hostility by a number of historical specialists. They criticized severely the errors which they discovered at points where the writer, in his long journey through Time and Space, happened to traverse their tiny allotments. They seemed not to realize that, in reliving the entire life of Mankind as a single imaginative experience, Mr. Wells was achieving something which they themselves would hardly have dared to attempt—something, perhaps, of which they had never conceived the possibility. In fact, the purpose and value of Mr. Wells's book seem to have been better appreciated by the general public than by the professional historians of the day" (I, 4 f.).

Mr. Wells's history was, indeed, enormously successful. In its various editions, English, French, German, etc., it sold millions of copies, and was more popular than even Hendrik van Loon's *Story of Mankind* or the collected poems of the late Ella Wheeler Wilcox. That this popularity proves Wells's imaginative experience to have been closely related to the realities of history is doubtful, and I would not have expected such a verdict from Professor Toynbee. Moreover a candidate for a Ph.D. in history might do well to collect the criticisms that historical specialists

have made on Wells's *Outline,* and to add up the inaccuracies that have been discovered in all the "tiny allotments";
they might total up to something far from "insignificant."

A more topical thesis would be a similar treatment of
Professor Toynbee's *A Study of History.* I have confined
myself to three writers of repute, Professor Peter Geyl,
Professor Herbert J. Muller of Purdue University, and Professor Pitirim Sorokin of Harvard. From the first I have already quoted. I quote further:

"There is hardly an incident or a phenomenon quoted
by Toynbee to illustrate a particular thesis that does not
give rise to qualifications in the reader's mind—*if the
reader is conversant with the matter.* Most of the time
our author is writing about Greek or Arabic or Hittite or
Japanese history where one—where I at least—find it,
more difficult to check him" (*The Pattern of the Past,*
1949, p. 21). And where Professor Geyl happens to be
"conversant with the matter" he observes: "We come to
Vol. IV, which deals with the breakdowns of civilizations. On looking closely we soon discover that the author does some violence to the facts to make them fit
[his] thesis" (ibid., pp. 36 f.). "My most essential criticism, the criticism which embraces all others, is connected
with [his] claim that the entire argument is based on
empirical methods, in which it seems to me that the
author is deceiving himself. . . . On looking closely,
after rubbing his dazzled eyes,[1] the reader will see that
Toynbee does not after all serve up more than a tiny
spoonful out of the great cauldron . . . *he selects the
instances which will support his thesis, or he presents
them in a way that suits him*" (*Debates with Historians,*
p. 97).

[1] I am touched to find that so distinguished a scholar should have gone
through the same disillusioning experience as a simple layman like myself.

From Professor Sorokin, writing likewise in *The Pattern of the Past*, I quote a single passage here, but will return to him later:

> ". . . in spite of his astonishing erudition the author displays either an ignorance or a deliberate neglect of many important sociological works . . ." (p. 107).

It appears, then, that I am not alone in my complaint that Professor Toynbee is guilty of a purposive and tendentious choice of his material, of doing violence to facts, of ignorance or deliberate neglect. But while we cannot find out whether his suppression of the last two thousand years of Jewish history is purposive (consciously or unconsciously), we are going to see in the closing part of this commentary (Chapter xiv) that he is also capable of ignoring extremely important contemporaneous facts *which he himself helped to report*. In other words, he is not content with choosing his material to fit his theses out of the debatable past; he does the same with contemporaneous events with which he has shown a fuller acquaintance elsewhere.

From Professor Muller's wise and humane *The Uses of the Past* (1952) I quote a few passages. Professor Muller objects to Professor Toynbee's "killing off the Eastern Roman Empire" by the year 602 and starting a new Byzantine Empire, whereas "almost all other historians stress the essential continuity of the Eastern Roman-Byzantine Empire throughout all its ups and downs" (p. 14 n.).

He objects to Professor Toynbee's statement that the "Orthodox Christian piety" of Byzantium preserved the heritage of Greek culture. "Actually," says Professor Muller, "this piety was inimical to Greek humanism, and at times openly hostile" (p. 19).

He objects to Professor Toynbee's enumeration of civilizations, the list being twice as long as Spengler's, and objects likewise to the *"necessity* of cycles" (p. 67).

He objects to Professor Toynbee's description of "the triumph of Christianity as a triumph of the 'way of gentleness' " (p. 186). (I should think so!)

He objects to Professor Toynbee's acclamation of Pope Gregory the Great "for having laid the most solid kind of foundation for the civilization to come" (p. 197).

He objects that Professor Toynbee "oversimplifies both the success and the failure of the [Roman] empire when he treats it merely as a phase of the 'Hellenic society' " (p. 206).

He objects to Professor Toynbee's dismissal of modern democracy, science, and technology as "an almost meaningless repetition of somethings that the Greeks and Romans did before us and did supremely well" because "in fact, they are strictly, profoundly unique" (pp. 226 f.).

He objects to Professor Toynbee's analysis of the breakdown of Russian society, and adds: "One need not admire this history, however, to suspect that what breaks down here is Toynbee's diagrammatic schema" (p. 289 n.).

Speaking of China as the oldest living civilization, Professor Muller writes: "Toynbee splits it into two distinct civilizations . . . but this again looks like an arbitrary division for appearance's sake. Other historians agree with the Chinese themselves on the essential continuity of Cathay" (p. 338 n.).

I do not suggest that where these writers disagree with Professor Toynbee he is necessarily in the wrong. But it is a curious circumstance that their admiration of his work is generally confined to the sections they are incompetent to challenge.

We must assume that the inaccuracies discovered by the specialists in H. G. Wells's *Outline of History* are, in Professor Toynbee's opinion, unimportant in principle—here

and there a date or a people misplaced, a minor contribu-
tion to civilization ignored. What are these in comparison
with the *sweep* of the vision? An obscure people, still living,
might feel itself slighted. What of it? We listen to their
protests, if they ever reach our ears, with a smile. No of-
fense intended—and one mustn't be so serious about one's
little self in a big, big world.

But suppose the people is, even in the opinion of the
ecumenical historian, so far from obscure that he devotes
to it a relatively large proportion of his work? Suppose also
that the attitude of the Western World toward this people
is itself part of the history of the Western World, as well
as a clue to its present state of mind? Suppose the "inac-
curacy" represents a fateful folk bias that has played quite
a role in the spiritual development of the Western World?
Is the correction altogether parochial or pedantic then?

There is a charming Jewish story that bears on this question. It belongs to the days when parts of the Chassidic
movement were declining from their original purity, and
Chassidic rabbis were becoming wonder-workers and
wealthy rulers of dynastic "kingdoms" that counted their
subjects by the thousands. One such rabbi held his court
in a townlet three days distant from Warsaw, and to him
was brought one day a skeptical Lithuanian Jew, a "Litvak,"
one of those Talmudically trained intellectualist representatives of orthodoxy whom the Chassidim, with sublime im-
pertinence, had already labeled Misnagdim, or schismatics,
when Chassidism was still in its infancy. The ardent Chassid who persuaded the Litvak to attend the court promised
him revelations that would melt his stony Misnagdic heart
into submission. At the customary public meal, the Litvak
sat among the Chassidim and watched with contempt the
competition for scraps from the rabbi's dish. He was re-
pelled by the superstitious obsequiousness of the rabbi's

followers, he was moved to disdain by the occasional "learned" comments on the Torah which fell from the rabbi's lips. "Wait," his Chassidic friend enjoined him with expectant exultation. "The moment is yet to come."

The moment came. Toward the end of the meal the rabbi closed his eyes and seemed to be passing into a trance. The murmur at the long table died into a deathly silence. Then from the rabbi's lips came these words: "Warsaw is burning!" A shudder passed through the assembly. So powerful was the general effect that the Litvak started in terror. The rabbi did not come out of his trance, and the Chassidim remained rooted to their places. Several minutes passed and the rabbi spoke again: "The Emperor of China has been assassinated!" Once more a shudder of awe followed by silence. Finally a third revelation: "The lost ten tribes have been found in Peru!"

The Litvak fled as soon as he could, and to satisfy a lingering skepticism traveled at once to Warsaw. A week later he was back in the rabbi's village, and, encountering his Chassidic friend, said hotly: "What is all this? I have no means of finding out what happened in China or Peru; but I went specially to Warsaw, and there was not even a single fire there last week."

"Pedantic Litvak!" the Chassid answered with icy contempt. "What does it matter whether the rabbi was right or wrong about Warsaw? Have you no reverence for the *sweep* of his vision?"

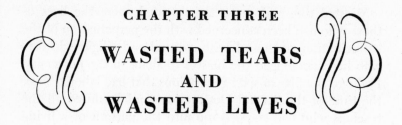

CHAPTER THREE

WASTED TEARS
AND
WASTED LIVES

I RETURN to my first reading of A *Study of History*, on the trans-Atlantic crossing in 1939, and to the conclusions to which its views on the Jewish people pointed.

Half the burden of sorrow should have been lifted from our hearts. It was proper, it was commendable, to be concerned with the sufferings of our fellow Jews, even though the fellowship was of such an ambiguous nature. But if Professor Toynbee was right, our lamentations for the spiritual losses we had sustained and those we were facing were based on pure hallucination. There had been, there were, no spiritual values to lose. Our protests against the suppression of Judaism in Russia had been a howling injustice to the Communists. Neither had we had the right to press, at the Treaty of Versailles, for cultural minority rights for the Jews of Poland. Fossils have no cultural rights; their constituent atoms have no living spiritual community. No corporate folk-soul had been done to death in Russia, and none was threatened now in the impending destruction of Polish Jewry. And those of us who saw in the Zionist movement and in the nascent Jewish homeland the continuity of a living spiritual heritage were perhaps the sorriest dupes of the illusion. Our hopes were chimeras, our tears wasted.

Wasted too, and worse than wasted, were the lives of those who had been concerned with the perpetuation of the hallucination, of those Jewish cultural and religious leaders who had encouraged the masses to share in the perversity. I saluted the fifty or sixty generations that had labored since the time of the Second Destruction, and I saluted all the teachers who had trapped me into the pattern of a living death. "All of you," I said (or was supposed to say), "have wronged me. We have long outstayed our significance on this planet, and it is more than twenty centuries since we were part of its reality. We have been nothing but an arteriosclerotic discomfort to ourselves and an irritation to others. Our identity, if it can be called such, is not worth having. We would confer a favor on the world, and on ourselves, by relinquishing it." And, having hypothetically uttered this reproachful salutation, I had to consider what was to be done next.

Unfortunately I was and still am in the grip of the great hallucination, and I was like a man who is using his complexes in an effort at self-analysis. I simply cannot get rid of the feeling that I am Jewish through and through. I was and am under the ineradicable impression that it was my people who had brought me back from the stale horrors of modern secularism to glimpses of the God it had revealed. I do not say that it could not have happened otherwise; I only say that it happened—or seems to me to have happened—thus and thus only.

For I must emphasize that side by side with my formal teachers of the past, from the Bible to the Baal Shem, and of the present, from Chaim Weizmann and Chaim Nachman Bialik and Shmarya Levin to a host of others (*mikol melamdai hiskalti*—all men have been my teachers), there was always at work in me the Jewish environment of my childhood. I saw it otherwise until recently. I was long un-

der the impression that my "return" after a period of alienation was owing entirely to an effort of my maturing will. I
did not realize, until recollection of the early years began to
reassert itself toward the rounding-off, that I had been
guided by certain childhood experiences that the time of
alienation had not expunged from my soul. I believed that
I had rediscovered the living qualities of Judaism solely
from the books and men and experiences of my adult years,
and that I had begun with a *tabula rasa*. Actually a large
body of knowledge and experience had lain covered up in
me since childhood, and had co-operated invisibly with my
teachers.

My memories start up against two backdrops, one behind
the other. The nearer one, on which are painted certain
streets and alleys of Manchester, England, is semi-trans-
parent; but it turns opaque when the light of conscious
recall shines on it from this side. Most of the time I can
see only my beginnings in England. Occasionally, and of
late with increasing frequency, a light shines between the
two backdrops, to bring out another and competing scene
composed of the lanes and houses of the Romanian village
of Maçin. This interior backdrop corresponds to the first
five and one-half years of my life.

When the backdrops blend I cannot always be sure on
which of them certain memories are at play; some memories,
auditory as well as visual, are common to both. Such is, for
instance, the sound of the rebbi's voice leading us in the
consecrated chant of the Hebrew alphabet and the first syl-
lables: it might be Maçin, it might be Manchester. Such
too are the sounds of my father's voice and the picture of
the family seated about the lamp on the table as he reads
forth in Yiddish from the silly romances of Shomer or the
enchanting stories of Sholom Aleichem. For during our
first years in England we continued to use the kerosene

lamp, out of habit, or from nostalgia, or under the impression that it was necessarily cheaper than so remarkable a thing as a gas-bracket with an incandescent mantle. Particularly strong is the pictorial recollection of the faces grouped in a shining cave hollowed out from the surrounding darkness, and with it the mingled emotions at the pit of my stomach, the delight at being permitted to listen, and the terror of being remarked and sent peremptorily to bed.

Distinctly Romanian, however, is the cry of the muezzin from the minaret of the near-by mosque, blending with the murmur of my father's morning prayers and the beat of his footsteps (in those days my father was more observant than in his English period). As distinctly Mancunian is the rattle of the tramcar as it passes outside the window of the *cheder* on Waterloo Road, drowning out the singsong of some thirty young voices (audible study being a commandment in the *Ethics of the Fathers*) and enabling us to exchange hasty and disrespectful opinions of our long-suffering rebbi.

Common to both, again, is a certain feeling of otherness from the rest of the world; this attaches itself, however, to distinctly separated scenes. Gavreel, the son of the gentile barber Todoracu in Maçin, was permitted to laze away the whole day in the summer, to run down to the bank of the Danube, there to cut himself a reed, and play on it to his heart's content. But not I. "A Jewish boy doesn't do those things. A Jewish boy learns." Just so, in Manchester, when regular school hours were over at half past four, and the non-Jewish children were free, *we* had to go to *cheder* for two or three hours (except on Fridays in the winter, when the Sabbath fell early) and also on Sunday mornings and afternoons. I cannot remember a feeling of special rebellion; there was only the general dislike of the young for any kind of disciplined effort. We were no more resentful of the *cheder* than of the school. Rebellion came later, and on other grounds. It was as natural to be Jewish as to be human.

We could not have defined what being Jewish was, any more than we could have defined the meaning of being human. We knew some of the characteristics, but a list of characteristics does not add up to an identity. It was Jewish for parents to insist on the all-importance of "learning," not as an aid to one's career (that was the remarkable thing among these poor people), but as the way to be a *mensch*, a proper person. It was Jewish to get new clothes for the Passover, and to eat only unleavened bread for its eight days, and to participate in the wonderful home ritual of the seder; Jewish also to derive from the place-names Jerusalem, and Hebron, and Carmel, and Jordan, a mysterious, intimate, and somewhat frightening hint of responsibility. It was Jewish, again, to approach with terror the Ninth Day of Ab and its introductory, tearful evening, when the elders sat with stockinged feet on the floor and by candlelight read from Jeremiah's Book of Lamentations in a doleful chant. But even in childhood we assumed that some equivalent set of ceremonial associations existed for non-Jews, for we knew of Christmas trees, and carols, and churches, and Sunday services; so that being "peculiar"—and we were that—did not reside in definable differences.

The home of my parents was not orthodox, nor was there in any of the homes of relatives and friends of ours, in Maçin or Manchester, as far as I remember, a strictly orthodox regimen. Nevertheless the atmosphere was thoroughly Jewish. The common language was Yiddish throughout until the children, and the parents after them, had acquired English in their different degrees. My mother did not keep two sets of dishes, for milk and meat, as the orthodox do; but she did not mix milk and meat on the table, and would not serve us milk immediately after meat. She lit and blessed the candles on the Sabbath eve, and the meal that followed was always the best of the week. It was festive in other ways too; unlike the weekday evening meals, it never failed to bring together all the members of the family. The house had just been cleaned; the white tablecloth was fresh, with its neat folds still visible; the candles isolated the table in their aura, and my father hallowed the occasion by refraining from smoking—no little sacrifice for him.

And yet all these things, if not exactly outward, were not the essence of the inwardness either; they belonged to being Jewish, but were not the Jewishness.

One was Jewish; one belonged to a people who had no land of their own, but had to subsist in groups in the midst of other people, usually hostile, sometimes murderous. That one should voluntarily cease to subsist would have been the most unnatural thing in the world. To ask my parents to become Christians would have been like asking them to turn into giraffes; they simply would not have understood the suggestion. One was Jewish; and that meant, in addition to discomfort from the pressures of the gentile world, and in addition to a way of life and rituals and beliefs, a great warmth, and a great nostalgia, and a great hope, all emanating from a supreme plan apprehended in a dim way even by the children, and perhaps not too clearly by the parents. There, in the plan, lay the meaning of everything. It had begun with Abraham the father, and had continued ever since, and would continue forever. It had been passed on to Isaac and Jacob, it had been associated with Egypt and Pharaoh. It had poured itself into Moses and Sinai and the Torah; and it had woven itself about those persons and places which had that mysterious quality not to be found in any others: King David, and King Solomon, Elijah the Prophet, Jerusalem and Hebron and Hermon, and Reb Meir, the Master of the Miracle, and the Baal Shem, the

Master of the Good Name. The order of these persons in history and the locations of the places on the map were confused in my mother's mind. She knew that we had once lived in the glory of Palestine, that we had been expelled thence for our sins, that two thousand years had passed, and that at the proper time, probably with the coming of the Messiah, we should be restored. Till then we should suffer; but our suffering was made bearable by the glow of the supreme plan and by our loving attachment to the memories of the men and women and places, the Matriarchs and the Patriarchs and the Prophets and the Kings, the pious men and the learned men, the cities and hills, which were the plan in evolution.

My mother believed in the Messianic restoration, but not so rigidly that she could not thrill to the news of the mundane efforts to restore the Jewish Homeland. It strikes me as quite extraordinary that simple people—none of those I knew in childhood were learned—should be living in a continuous awareness of history. More extraordinary was the nature of that awareness; for it came into their everyday behavior. I do not wish to imply that there was anything saintly about them. Their spiritual standards were, I think, higher than those of the Romanian peasantry they had left behind, and of the surrounding Manchester slum dwellers. Still, much that was sordid and mean would be found among them; snobbery was not wanting, nor envy, nor spite. What touched them with the extraordinary, as I see it now, was the ever-present admonition—and I know of nothing like it among the plain, simple folk of other peoples I have lived with—of a larger outlook, an acknowledgment of the essential sanctity of history. Here, I would say, was the core of the identity, the naturalness, which fused the words "Jewish" and "human" and yet constituted the "peculiarity." They would not have put it that way; they would not have said that what separated them from the gentile was the absence in him of a sense of the sanctity of human history; but that is approximately what it amounted to.

The rituals and disciplines that surrounded my childhood sensitized my spirit, made it permanently susceptible to the messages behind them; the names of the Patriarchs and the Kings and holy places were permanently lodged in me, and at a later period in my life reverberated again with those overtones which accompany and distinguish the essential nature of tradition. I know that it has been otherwise with many Jews who have had a Jewish upbringing; they have either "repressed" their early responses or repudiated them by an effort of will—though not always, in either case, with complete success. But thus it was with me and with many others; and thus it has been since the Destruction. I think of the persistence of the message, and I am awed by the procession of the generations of simple folk—let us leave the scholars and the self-consciously dedicated to one side— who have been its carriers. The mosque in the village of Maçin symbolizes for me the variety of worlds through which the message has been carried—European and Asiatic, Christian and Moslem, Roman and Byzantine. And all of it in order that I might be I, and not someone else.

But here was Professor Toynbee, leading me to the conclusion that I should not be I, and my parents should not have been my parents; that the whole vast process that is continuing in my children, and that they plan to continue in theirs, is not a process but a paralysis. We are here, it seems, and we have been here these two thousand years, not because we know how to live, but because we do not know how to die; or rather because, dead without knowing it, we cannot perform the act of self-burial. What a ghastly mistake it has all been! The expulsions, the autos-da-fé, the wanderings, the laborious reconstructions in new and strange lands, the pious cultivation of books, the obstinate transmission of the foolish hope—all, all as senseless as the wash of the waves which accompanied my first reading of this illumination of our destiny. Now I did not know whom to pity more, the lifeless living or the deluded dead.

CHAPTER FOUR

THE
FOSSIL CREATES
A LANGUAGE

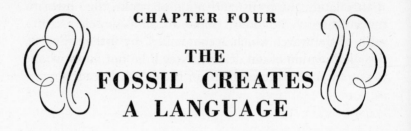

PROFESSOR TOYNBEE is not alone in his impression that Yiddish is nothing more than a "dialect of German"; it is shared by millions who are ignorant of the language, among them many Jews. But while it is natural for everyone to have impressions, it is not permissible for scholars to present them in a learned work as informed opinions. My purpose in devoting a chapter to the subject is twofold. I wish to describe a Jewish cultural phenomenon of first-rate importance; and I wish to place in evidence part of the continuous spiritual creativity of the Jewish people.

Yiddish is a dialect of German in the same sense as French and the other Romance languages are "dialects of Latin," which is the way the older scholars often referred to them. In its raw material—that is, its basic, literal vocabulary--it is closer to German than French is to Latin; in its spirit—which, after all, identifies a language—it is much farther away. It is true that nearly nine tenths of the Yiddish vocabulary derives from medieval High German; but the common etymology and the syllabic similarity only bring into starker contrast the spiritual incommensurability of the two languages.

Yiddish began to evolve in the Rhine Valley about one thousand years ago in answer to the specific need of the

Jews who had gone there from France and Italy under external pressures. Traces of the Romance languages that they brought with them are still embedded in modern Yiddish. From the Rhine Valley Yiddish spread, in the course of the centuries, southward and eastward, carried by refugees and settlers. It took firm hold in some areas; it faded out in others. By the seventeenth century it was the dominant language of the Jews of eastern and central Europe. It crossed the Atlantic in the eighteenth century and more particularly in the nineteenth and twentieth centuries; by the beginning of the twentieth century it was solidly established in North and South America, as well as in South Africa and Australasia. It had therefore become a world language, and according to Lestchinsky, the foremost Jewish demographer, it was spoken in the middle of the third decade of the twentieth century by more than ten million of the more than sixteen and one-half million Jews who then constituted the Jewish people. It was also the language that held together in a single linguistic grouping the largest number of Jews so united at any time in Jewish history. Its status as a world language was recognized by the *Encyclopædia Britannica*, which in 1953 included it in its multiple dictionary of five world languages, though the number of its users had by then been reduced to perhaps one third by the Hitler massacres and the forcible assimilation of Russian Jewry.

What specific inner needs led to the creation of the Yiddish language and imparted its special character to it? Or, to rephrase the question, why were the Jewish immigrants of the Rhine Valley one thousand years ago, and their descendants, and the Jews who were added to them, and those among whom they spread later—why were all these not content with a local dialect, and why did they have to create a distinctive language that in important re-

spects is not European at all in spite of its predominantly
Germanic base? A contemporary of theirs could not have
answered the question, because when the process began, its
development was not foreseen. Who, watching these hand-
fuls of refugees streaming in, would have dared to foretell
that they would found, against the continuous pressure of
an alien and hostile environment, a form of life that would
embrace millions of their kin a thousand years later? Who
then could have foreseen that they would take a German
dialect and transform it into a semi-Oriental and wholly
Jewish instrument of expression, unintelligible to the German and not wholly translatable into English or French or
Italian? (I speak only of the languages in which I have read
translations from the Yiddish.) Could even Maimonides
(1105–1204), who lived when the process had begun, and
who knew the needs of the Jewish people—could he, even if
he had assumed the transference of great masses of Jews
from the Arabic to the European world, have foreseen that
hundreds of years after his death the Talmud and his codi-
fication of it would be studied with oral translation into a
language developed out of a dialect of the northern barbarians? Or that in the new and as yet unformed language
Judaism would be expressed in new forms and remain faithful to the contents of the old?

The specific inner need that led to the creation of Yiddish and imparted its special character to it arose from a
compulsion to perpetuate a sacred history, a cosmic ethical
concept entrusted to the Jewish people. For they thought of
themselves as the thread of intelligibility running through
the tapestry of human events; and therefore, in so far as
was possible, they had to Judaize whatever elements of the
outside world they lived with internally.

Did simple, unliterary people think of themselves as "the
thread of intelligibility running . . ."? Of course not. Such

high-flown descriptions were foreign to the minds of my parents and relatives and their circle. Nevertheless, they lived, as I have said, in a continuous awareness of a planned history. They knew that the Jewish people, older by far than any about it, had a pattern to conform to; the pattern came from God; being Jewish was "everything" because it was history and religion and morality and everyday life. Not that all folk-Jews everywhere remained faithful to the pattern. We shall see how far from the truth is the popular notion that the Jews have survived monolithically from the Destruction until recent times. I speak, however, of the Jews who did remain faithful; and the evolution among them of the Yiddish language, their creation of a remarkable instrument of expression, is perhaps the outstanding illustration of what they did "with whatever elements of the outside world they lived with internally."

As long as their number was small, all of them had to know the language of the surrounding people; also because their number was small, no internal language could long survive in daily use. Again, for the same reason, their modifications of the new language were random and individual, not "purposive" or mass-directed. Thus the earliest traces of Yiddish carry the strongest evidences of the sub-dialects of Middle High German. As their numbers grew, they exerted an increasingly concerted pressure on the language as they spoke it among themselves, so that it began to assume a new and unifying character. Later, when the center of gravity of Jewish life shifted eastward into Slavic-speaking countries, communal life was strong enough to make Yiddish sufficient for a considerable proportion of the Jewish community. In the eighteenth, nineteenth, and even twentieth centuries many Jews living in Russia, Romania, and Poland had a foreigner's imperfect knowledge of Russian, Romanian, or Polish; the majority of them could not read or write in any of these languages. Very few of them, however, were illiterate in Yiddish.

Hebrew was the language of prayer and the medium for scholarly works and communication among scholars. But that did not prevent an infiltration of Hebrew words—to the final extent of about ten per cent—into Yiddish; and this infiltration was symbolic of the "purpose" for which Yiddish was developed.

Part of that purpose, in fact, was the maintenance in popular, living usage of some part of the Hebrew language. It must not be thought that ritualistic Hebrew was as far from the Yiddish-speaking masses as ritualistic Latin of the Middle Ages was from the European peasant masses. We hear of medieval non-Jewish scholars who learned Yiddish for the sake of the Hebrew elements in it. Thus if the Jews, in contradistinction to the Irish, have been able to "revive" a "dead" language, it is because the language was never really dead. Nor is this to be interpreted as meaning that it was the mechanical infusion of Hebrew words into the Yiddish language that kept Hebrew in a state of suspended animation, susceptible—though with an effort—to revitalization. Far more was at play, as we must at once perceive when we consider that the revitalization of Hebrew was in part connected with the re-creation of the Jewish Homeland in Palestine.

The spirit of Yiddish should be analyzed along two coordinates: the will to remain Jewish and the handicaps of the exile.

Let us begin with the second, as being the easier to dispose of. The abnormal seclusion of the Jews from a life on the soil is reflected in the poverty of nature terms in Yiddish. Similarly the guilds, armies, and navies, government and its pageantry, fair and tournament, were not for the Jews; so that the terminology of these activities, too, remained cor-

respondingly undeveloped in Yiddish. The gaiety, earthi-
ness, and gallantry of the non-Jewish world have their established phraseology in English, French, and German (and
no doubt in all the other European languages), but not in
Yiddish. The concept of courage differed fundamentally in
the two worlds. Among gentiles it was combative, among
Jews passive. The idea of dying merely for the sake of
showing that one was not afraid to die, and the code compulsion to accept a challenge only to demonstrate one's
courage, can of course be explained in Yiddish, but the self-
understood technical terms of this complex do not exist in
it. But to die at the stake or on the gallows for *kiddush
ha-Shem* (Sanctification of the Name—that is, choosing
to remain Jewish in the face of death) is as current, as
folkish a phrase in Yiddish as *mort sur le champ d'honneur*
is in French. While the latter, however, is surrounded by an
aura of physical exaltation, the former is associated with
torture and outer ignominy. The glorification of physical
prowess is a dull and difficult business in Yiddish, which
lacks the more picturesque terminology of combat; one
would have to describe first a mace, a falchion, a halberd,
a quarterstaff, and provide words for them, and by that
time, of course, all the lyrical aspects of bloodshed would
be lost.

As against these deficiencies the affirmations of Yiddish
are considerable. It is a language of peculiar intimacy, re-
flecting an unusual, perhaps unique, national experience.
On the one hand there was the consciousness of not being
wanted by the other peoples or nations, on the other the
certainty of being wanted by God even in rejection—the
rejection being in fact the sign of an offended but enduring
love. The hostility of the world pushed the Jews together;
its ignorance of their ways sharpened an intramural
"knowingness." In addition to the exclusions already noted,

there was the Church, from which the Jews excluded themselves, and from which all the other exclusions flowed. Yiddish began to evolve at a time when the Christian world was
religiously deeper and more uniform than today, and when
the Church provided a much larger proportion of the means
of self-expression. The area of common ground for Jewish
and Christian contact was therefore the smaller, and the
isolation of the Jews correspondingly greater. "The world is
not for us as long as the exile lasts," said the Jews. To compensate, they intensified the response to memory and the
intellect, giving them great range and effectiveness. The
emotional and allusive side of Yiddish is of unusual power,
but to reproduce it in English (let us say) is as difficult as
to reproduce the chivalresque tonality of *Idylls of the King*
or of the *Roman de la Rose* in Yiddish. In attempts to
translate some of the Yiddish classics into English I run
up repeatedly against the absence of equivalent or analogous
areas of experience, and therefore of terms, in the non-Jewish world, so that I must interpolate explanatory phrases or
remain completely unintelligible (and, as it is, I remain
partly so). While this must happen in translations between
languages belonging to the same world, the points of intelligibility do not there, of themselves, build up into anything like the same divisive barrier.

A simple instance is the word *golus* (*galut* in the Se-
phardic or Israel pronunciation), which I have just translated as "exile." To one conversant with Yiddish the translation is painfully empty. To capitalize it into Exile, as some
do, is only to hint at inadequacy without doing anything to
compensate for it. In English "exile" is not loaded with
particular associations; in Yiddish it is a summary of history, an identification, a badge, almost the equivalent of the
word "Jew." "A Jew is in exile," or "The Jew is in exile,"
runs the Yiddish phrase, which comes up apropos of any

kind of misfortune. It actually means: "To be Jewish is to be in exile," "To be Jewish one has to endure." And "exile" is heavy with wanderings, discriminations, blood-libel legends, pogroms, and interminable humiliations.

One would imagine that a word like "Sabbath," common to the Jewish and Christian vocabularies, would mean substantially the same thing in both. That is not the case. Professor Toynbee writes: "For example, the social function of the Jewish Sabbath—and of the Sabbatarian Sunday of Scotland, England, and the Transmarine English-speaking countries of our modern Western World—is to insure that, for one whole day out of every seven, a creature who has been specializing for six successive days in the week in sordid business for private gain shall remember his Creator and shall live, for a recurrent twenty-four hours, the life of an integral human soul instead of quite uninterruptedly performing the vain repetitions of a money-making machine" (IV, 241). Such is certainly part of the meaning, to the Jews, of that seventh day which they hallowed of old—to the amusement and contempt of the classical world—and passed on as a heritage to Christianity without themselves relinquishing possession of it; and as an achievement the creation of such a concept, from whatever original tabu materials, which elsewhere produced only the nefast days, ranks with the Jewish relationship to monotheism, being, in fact, part of that concept and inseparable from it. The Jewish account of the creation of the world is climaxed by the divine example of the Sabbath. Nothing less than God's own participation in its sanctities could, for the Jews, convey its exalted function.

In one of the numerous *chochmos*, or flights of philosophic fancy, which enliven his pages, Professor Toynbee writes thus of the account given in the first chapter of Genesis:

"According to the Syriac [1] legend of the creation of the Physical Universe, when 'God saw everything that He had made, and, behold, it was very good; and the evening and the morning were the sixth day . . . and on the seventh day God ended His work which He had made; and He rested on the seventh day from all the work which He had made; and God blessed the seventh day and sanctified it, because that in it He had rested from all His work which God had created and made'—the immediate result was a static paradise, and it needed the Serpent's undesignedly beneficent intervention to liberate God's energies for performing a fresh act of creation in spite of Himself" (IV, 257 f.).

Professor Toynbee is writing here in quite another connection, of course; he is "explaining" through myth and legend the nature of the impulses that start off civilizations. Yet I think he could not have pulled in this particular illustration from the "Syriac" document if he had been, I will not say a participant in, but cognizant of the Jewish relationship to the Sabbath and aware of the difference between the Sabbath of the Christians and the Jewish *Shabbos*. To the Jews of Biblical and immediately post-Biblical times the Sabbath was made peculiar by the uncomprehending derision of the pagan world; among those of later post-Biblical times—when the Sabbath had indeed been taken over by non-Jews, and shifted one day—it accumulated values to which the others were alien because they had no need of them.

To the Jew the Sabbath became far more than the recurrent extrication of the soul from the degradations of workaday worldliness. It was also a release from the degradations

[1] See observations below on this use of the word "Syriac" (pp. 68, 69, etc.).

he suffered at the hands of the outside world. For him the world faded away with the lighting of the candles on Friday evening, and he was confirmed in both his relationship to God and in his hope of that time when all days would be, Sabbaths. It could be said of the Jew that he lived the first three days of the week in the memory of the past Sabbath, and the last three days in anticipation of the next. He understood as no one else the frequency with which the desecration of the Sabbath is denounced by the Prophets as part of the falling away of the people from God's purposes; the Sabbath is stressed more insistently than any other sacred institution, and it occupies the central place among the rituals that are bound up with Jewish morality. A saying of Achad Ha-am's has become a Jewish folk-word: "More than the Jewish people has done to keep the Sabbath alive, the Sabbath has done to keep it alive."

The Sabbath also stands apart in that it has the power to repress all fasts in the Jewish calendar save the Day of Atonement. The Black Fast of the Ninth of Ab for the Destructions may not be observed or remembered on the Sabbath. The private mourner, too, must forget his loss on that day; for it is a day of serenity and wholeness. A vast literature of legend and commentary has sprung up about its origin and efficacy. It was created before the physical universe; the stormy river Sambattyon rests on that day; the sinners in hell obtain a twenty-four-hour reprieve; and on that day the poorest Jew is elevated to the rank of a king, his wife to that of a queen.

The oncoming of the Sabbath is attended by an uplifting of the heart, its departure by a gnawing melancholy. Farewell to the glimpse of paradise! Its hours are treasured for prayer, for sacred study, for purity of conversation and thought, for the complete deletion, of course, of worldly calculations (it is even forbidden to have money in one's pocket on the Sabbath!), for rest, for gratitude, and for the impotence of the outside world to inflict suffering. Thus it was; the exile itself was forgotten on the Sabbath.

This and more is the word *Shabbos* in Yiddish. How is it to be "translated"?

In the superb nine-hundred-page *Thesaurus* of the Yiddish language compiled by Nahum Shtuchkoff and published by the Yiddish Scientific Institute (YIVO) one may study with delight and profit the peculiarities of the idiom. There one observes how intimately and particularly Jewish are those turns of thought and phrase which draw on Hebrew and on religious sources. How much more "correct" it is to say that a man being praised is being given, not a *"kompliment"* (the Yiddish-Germanic word), but a *"mi-sheberach"*—the phrase that opens the ritualistic blessing bestowed publicly, in the synagogue, upon a member of the community. (But *"mi-sheberach"* can also be used sarcastically for a violent dressing-down.) How much more of the folk (cf. Anglo-Saxon words in English) it is to say, instead of *"rekomendatzia,"* *"haskomeh"*; instead of *"ibbertreibung"* (German *Übertreibung*), *"guzmah"*; instead of *"mihe"* (German *Mühe*), *"terchah."* How gracefully the saying runs: "A *shikseh bei a rov ken oich paskenen a shaileh.*" I invite Professor Toynbee, with his command of German, to understand that. Literally it means: "The peasant servant girl in the rabbi's house can also solve ritualistic problems." But the difficulty in understanding or translating does not lie merely in the use of the Hebrew words. A whole cultural complex is involved here. The saying refers ironically to ignoramuses who, frequenting the company of scholars, have learned to quote glibly so as to impress other ignoramuses. But it is, I fear, useless to multiply instances that would appeal only to those familiar with Yiddish, and

perhaps leave others unimpressed. It is more or less for the
record that I mention them here.

The incidence of God in Yiddish usage also sets the language apart. In it God appears in the double and not contradictory role of the Infinite and the Homebody. One may
speak of Him as "He that lives forever," and also address
Him as "Dear little God, dear little Father" (*Gottenyu,
Tattenyu*) without incongruity. The intimacy with which
the Chassidic Jew in particular treats the Everlasting at
times would shock outsiders; it verges now on argumenta-
tive impudence, now on a maudlin assumption of kinship;
and it passes from these without difficulty to resignation,
humility, and awe. One might almost say that the Jew per-
mits himself to tease the Creator of the universe. This peculiar perfection of relationship is mirrored with supreme
skill in Sholom Aleichem's *Tevye the Dairyman*; it runs
through the work of the classical writers, through the Chassidic stories of Peretz, and through the cruel satires of Mendele. It depends for its effect on the spirit of Yiddish, which
is to say on the spirit of the people who created Yiddish.
It is practically unintelligible in English terms, or French,
or—almost of all—German.

The immanence of God in Yiddish meant also the immanence of the sacred places with which His Self-revelation
to the Jewish people is associated. Most of the religious festivals are attached to the landscape of ancient Palestine or
to Egypt and Sinai. Yiddish folk literature is rich in these
associations. When my mother was a girl in Yasse, she
knew in person the famous Abraham Goldfaden, that play-
wright-composer-actor-manager-entrepreneur whose operas
on Biblical and historical themes have penetrated into
every corner of Yiddish-speaking Jewry. She knew and loved
many songs from *Shulamis* and *Bar Kochba*: some of them,
like "Raisins and Almonds" and "The Shepherd of Canaan"

have acquired an almost religious standing. But here again
I may be confusing some readers, for it is impossible, in the
Yiddish experience, to draw a hard and fast line between the
religious and the secular. I think, for instance, of a charming
folk song that tells of a smith, a tailor, and a carpenter each
giving his happy impressions of the visiting cantor who led
the services on the previous Sabbath, each in turn expressing
his delight in the terms of his craft, as though the cantor
were a fellow craftsman—as indeed he was. It is a merry
song, made for laughter. I should like to stress the "secular-
ness" of all songs of that type; they are not hymns, they are
not self-conscious tributes to "the higher things." They are
natural, heartfelt outbreaks of "life" in the native medium
of this people. They are effective because they rest in the
deepest of this people's memories—the religious memory.
I should also like to point out that they are not the products
of the scholars and thinkers and teachers in Israel, about
whom I shall say little because *their* function is so obvious.

Abraham Goldfaden was not among the great lights of
Yiddish literature, but he was marvelously alive, and his
works have played their role in the expression of the continuous Jewish awareness of history. Pride in the past, sorrow for our present condition, hope for the future ring
through his musical dramas. Melodies and words come
back to me more vividly these years, in my mother's voice
and that of an Uncle Moishe (on my father's side) of
Piçiniagu, who used to visit us in Maçin with his son
Shmeel (Samuel), who was twelve years older than I. (I
have a special reason for mentioning these relatives, which
will be revealed in the closing section of this book.) Often,
when I am alone, I find myself humming the Pilgrim's
Chorus from *Shulamis*:

> Each man bowed beneath his gift,
> Each one with his staff in hand,

> We go marching forward swift
> To our far-off Holy Land . . .

or the plaint of the bereaved daughter of Zion mourning
among the ashes of the Temple:

> Look, O God, upon our tears,
> See, O God, our want and pain;
> We shall sorrow through the years
> Till Thy help will come again;

and they both evoke backdrops, Maçin and Manchester,
with the suggestion of a third, antenatal—vistas of lands and
cities and roads, and of pilgrims laden not with gifts, but
with the remnants of their household goods, with a Torah
scroll in the lead, and not marching toward the Holy Land,
but fleeing, men and women and children, from the pyre,
the scaffold, and the knout.

It is not my intention, however, to write here of Yiddish
literature. I wish only to convey some of the warmth and
the ingratiating appeal of the Yiddish language, which has
arisen out of a type of consciousness and a set of circumstances that imparted to it an altogether special character
and an inimitable functional grace. And I must not omit
mention of the stamp that has been set upon it by the
Chassidic movement. In its beginnings Chassidism was entirely Yiddish in its field of action and means of expression.
Its founder (Israel of Medziboz, 1700–59) was no scholar;
neither he nor his immediate disciples, religious geniuses
of a high order, went to the learned and the high-placed.
They worked among the poorest, among the most humble.
Later the movement degenerated in many places into thau-
maturgy, gross superstition, and exploitation, with ugly dynastic rivalries. But from the beginning it infused into Yiddish a renewal of that deeply religious mode of self-expres-

sion which is one of the folk needs of Jewry. Without pressing the analogy too far, we may compare its role in Yiddish with that of the King James Bible in English.

Neither the language nor the literature of Yiddish can be said to stand in the first rank, let us say with English or French; but to ignore them completely is to commit a far greater error in the opposite direction. Nor am I pleading for lenience—"considering that, etc. . . ." On its merits Yiddish is an instrument of great beauty and force. It is remarkable, too, for the ingenuity with which it has woven from its constituent elements the proper garb, fitting like a glove, for the spirit of a living people.

There is an interesting passage in the first volume of A *Study of History* (pp. 152 f.) from which I select a few sentences without, I think, marring the intention of the whole:

> When we Westerners call people 'natives' we implicitly take the cultural colour out of our perceptions of them. We see them . . . not as men of like passions with ourselves; and, seeing them thus as something infra-human, we feel entitled to treat them as though they did not possess ordinary human rights. . . . Evidently the word is not a scientific term but an instrument of action: an *a priori* justification for a plan of campaign.

This is finely said. Let us substitute "Professor Toynbee" for "we Westerners," and "fossils" for "natives." The passage now reads:

> When Professor Toynbee calls people 'fossils' he implicitly takes the cultural colour out of his perceptions of them. He sees them . . . not as men of like passions with ourselves; and seeing them thus as something infra-human, he feels entitled to treat them as though they did

not possess ordinary human rights. . . . Evidently the word is not a scientific term but an instrument of action: an *a priori* justification for a plan of campaign.

A new light is shed on the treatment of the Jews in *A Study of History*.

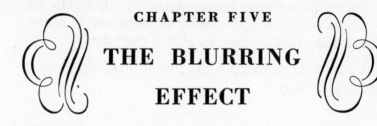

CHAPTER FIVE

THE BLURRING
EFFECT

I

I INTEND in this chapter to employ chiefly the first of the
three types of criticism enumerated in Chapter ii above:
namely, the one directed at the intelligibility of sections of
A *Study of History*. I spoke there of a "peculiar method"
which it employs, whereby it achieves "complete self-obfuscation." To this method I give the name of the Blurring Effect, and I will note again that for its detection no knowledge of history is required. It is, however, necessary to warn
the reader that he must on no account let himself be di-
verted from the following analysis of Professor Toynbee's
text by his disagreement with any "facts" as presented by
Professor Toynbee; once the reader starts arguing about
particular "facts" he will lose sight of *the* fact: namely, that
the text as such makes nonsense. Thus he will have fallen
into a trap, which is exactly what has happened to those
scholarly critics of A *Study of History* whom I have consulted; he will be debating only the debatable instead of
directing some of his attention to the undebatable.

II

To appreciate the character of the Blurring Effect we
must first acquaint ourselves with Professor Toynbee's over-
all purpose. That, he tells us, is the search "for some objec-

tive 'intelligible field of historical study' " (I, 17); "for fields
of historical study which would be intelligible in themselves within their own limits in Space and Time, without
reference to extraneous historical events" (VII, 1).

The minimum unit within which he finds such intelligibility is the Society, or Civilization, twenty-odd specimens
of which, dead and living, he exhibits as making up the sum
total of mankind's historical development. While some
civilizations cannot (yet), however, be linked with preceding civilizations, there are many in which he perceives such
a relationship; and to this extent, therefore, even a civilization is not strictly intelligible in itself. We have, thus, the
two sets of relationships to observe: those of societies or
civilizations to each other, and those of the constituent
parts or members (peoples, nations) of a society or civilization to each other and the whole. We assume that the more
organic the relationship established in any field, the greater
the degree of intelligibility attained. I propose now to examine Professor Toynbee's treatment of the rise of the
"Syriac" society within which he places the Jews, and of
the place of the Jews within that society; *my* purpose is to
determine what interdependence he establishes, and how
much intelligibility is thus created.

He apparently wants to regard the Syriac and Hellenic
civilizations as being "affiliated" to the preceding Minoan
civilization in the Ægean. On the origins of the Syriac civilization he writes:

The final convulsion of the post-Minoan Völkerwanderung, which the Egyptian records enable us to date about
1200/1190 B.C., was not a raid in quest of plunder but a
migration in search of new homes; and the migrants seem
to have been a mixed multitude of Achaeans and Minoans, driven pell-mell by the impetus of a new human

avalanche from the European hinterland of the Aegean: the 'Dorians' . . . [I, 100 ff.]. On the north-eastern corner of 'the New Empire' of Egypt (an empire which survived, dead-alive) the intruders settled in a district which, as Philistia (Palestine), became part of the original home of the Syriac Society. Along the border between the coastlands and the interior, between the lowlands and the highlands, the Philistine refugees from the Minoan World encountered the Hebrew nomads who had been drifting into the Syrian dependencies of 'the New Empire' of Egypt out of a no-man's-land in Arabia. Farther north, the mountain range of Lebanon set a limit to the simultaneous infiltration of the Aramaean nomads and gave shelter to the Phoenicians of the coast, who had managed to survive the passage of the Philistines. . . . Out of these elements a new society . . . which we have decided to call 'Syriac'—emerged slowly as the convulsion subsided.

As far as the Syriac Society was related at all to any older member of the species, it was related to the Minoan, and this in the degree in which the Hellenic Society was related to the Minoan—neither more nor less. One heritage of the Syriac Society from the Minoan may have been the Alphabet; another may have been the taste for long-distance sea-faring which declared itself in the exploration of the Red Sea and the Mediterranean and in the discovery of the Atlantic. That the Syriac Society, too, should stand in this relation to the Minoan is somewhat surprising. One would rather expect to discover that the universal state in the background of Syriac history was not the 'thalassocracy of Minos' but 'the New Empire' of Egypt, and that the Monotheism of the Jews was a resurrection of the monotheism of Ikhnaton. The evidence, however, as far as it goes, does not warrant the hypothe-

sis of such an 'affiliation.' Nor is there any evidence that
the Syriac Society was either 'affiliated' or related in any
lesser degree to the society represented by the Empire of
Khatti. . . . Finally, there is no evidence of any 'affiliation' of the Syriac Society to . . . the Empire of Sumer
and Akkad. . . . The culture of the society of which this
empire was the universal state made a deep impress upon
all the countries and peoples which it embraced; and for
seven centuries after Hammurabi's death the Akkadian
language, conveyed in the cuneiform script, continued to
be the *lingua franca* of commerce and diplomacy throughout all South-Western Asia. The impress of this culture
was as deep in Syria as in any other country outside the
actual homeland of the culture in 'Irāq. It is stamped
upon the manners and customs of the Syrian people as
we see them, from the sixteenth century b.c. to the thirteenth, through Egyptian eyes. . . . When the darkness
which descends upon the history of Syria after the migration of 1200/1190 begins to lift, the old impress has disappeared. The cuneiform script has been superseded by
the Alphabet without leaving a trace of its former currency in Syria. *The Minoan influence has prevailed.*
[I, 102 f.]

I call additional attention to the words I have italicized.
They establish, in fairly strong terms, an unmistakable re-
lationship. But reverting to the subject in the next volume,
Professor Toynbee writes:

The Syriac Civilization has three great feats to its credit.
It invented an alphabetic system of writing; it discovered
the Atlantic Ocean; and it arrived at a particular conception of God which is common to Judaism, Zoroastrianism, Christianity, and Islam, but alien alike from the
Egyptiac, Sumeric, Indic, and Hellenic veins of religious

thought and feeling. Which were the Syriac communities by whom these achievements were severally contributed? The Philistines may prove to have been the
transmitters, if not the inventors, of the elements of the
Alphabet, if the conjectured derivation of the Alphabet
from some Minoan script is substantiated in the future
investigations of our Western archaeologists. Pending
further archaeological research, the credit for the invention of the Alphabet must at present be left unallocated.
When we come, however, to the other two Syriac achievements, the history of which is a matter of common
knowledge, *we find that the Philistines have no part or
lot in them* [II, 50 f.].

Now the Philistines are the only Minoan refugees mentioned by Professor Toynbee as the transmitters of Minoan
influence to the Syriac Society. But they had, we have just
read, nothing to do with two of the three great achievements of the Syriac Society, and their connection with the
third is highly conjectural. We also learn from the footnote
to the foregoing passage that the conjecture has been further
weakened by the discovery at Sinai of an archaic alphabet
long preceding the Minoan; in fact, Professor Toynbee himself has to leave the credit for the invention of the alphabet
"unallocated."

He also goes into a detailed denial of the role of the Philistines as the creators or initiators of Syriac seamanship.

Who were those Syriac seafarers who ventured to sail the
whole length of the Mediterranean to the Pillars of Her-
cules and out beyond? Not the Philistines, whose Minoan
ancestors had been the pioneers of long-distance seamanship in the Mediterranean. In the Philistine communities
of the maritime plain, the ancestral seafaring tradition
was buried, with the sowing-corn, in the furrows of the

broad ploughlands; and so, when the Philistines came to
feel the need to expand, they took the same wrong turning
as the Argives took in the Peloponnese. Turning their
backs on the sea, the Philistines took up arms to conquer
the arid lowlands of Beersheba and the well-watered val-
leys of Esdraelon and Jezreel. . . . The discovery of the
Atlantic was achieved not by the Philistine Lords of the
Shephelah, but by the Phoenician tenants of the rugged
middle section of the Syrian coast [II, 51].

In the birth of "Syriac" monotheism, too, the absence of
Minoan influence is exposed in detail.

For the greatest creative achievement of the Syriac Society was neither its discovery of the Atlantic nor its discovery of the Alphabet but its discovery of God; and the
particular conception of God at which the Syriac Society
arrived—a conception which is common to Judaism and
Zoroastrianism and Christianity and Islam—is alien (as
we have seen) not only from Babylonic religious thought
and Egyptiac religious thought (apart from the flash of
illumination in the single soul of Ikhnaton) but also from
Hellenic religion and from Minoan (as far as the êthos of
Minoan religion is known to us) [II, 387].

Wherein then, in heaven's name, has the Minoan influence manifested itself in the slightest degree, let alone "prevailed"? Is this a slip of the pen? Or did a compositor omit
the word "not" and a careless proofreader pass over the
omission? Either explanation would be plausible if Professor Toynbee did not, to our utter discouragement, reassert
his theory of the Minoan influence in the continuation of
the very passage, just quoted, in which he demonstrates its
absence:

The Syriac Civilization, arising in an interstice between
the Egyptiac Society and the Babylonic, was neither be-

holden to, nor impeded by, either of them; and so far as it was related to any antecedent civilization at all, its affinity was not with a society whose roots were in the soil of Egypt or Shinar but with the relatively distant Minoan Civilization of the Aegean. In virtue of this affinity, the Syriac Civilization was not only the contemporary of the Hellenic Civilization, but its sister; *and it revealed its common descent from the Minoan Civilization* in a common taste for long-distance deep-sea navigation [II, 386].

And elsewhere we read:

And what of the environment which gave birth to the Syriac Civilization? The non-human environment here was provided by the climate and topography of the Syrian coast-lands, *the human environment by the Minoan Civilization,—inasmuch as the Syriac Civilization emerged among Minoan refugees who secured a footing on the coast of Syria during the post-Minoan interregnum, and there encountered the Hebrew and Aramaean barbarians who were drifting into Syria out of its North-Arabian hinterland* [I, 267].

And finally, in connection with this general subject, and in particular with the last implication (that the "encounter" between the Minoan refugees and the "Hebrew and Aramaean barbarians" explains in some degree the emergence of the Syriac civilization), I quote a passage that stresses equally the grandeur of the religious achievement of the "Syriac Civilization" and the isolation of the people to which that achievement is credited:

Thus the maritime achievement of the Syriac Civilization was contributed not by the Philistines but by the Phoenicians. The physical discovery of the Atlantic, how-

ever, is surpassed, as a feat of human prowess,[1] by the
spiritual discovery of Monotheism; and this achievement
was contributed by a Syriac community that had been
stranded by the Völkerwanderung in a physical environment that was still less inviting than the Phoenician
coast . . . it was populated by the adventurous vanguard
of the Hebrew Nomads who had drifted into the fringes
of Syria out of the North Arabian Steppe. . . . In such
a country, and under such conditions, the Israelites continued to live in obscurity until the Syriac Civilization
had passed its zenith. As late as the fifth century before
Christ, at a date when all the great prophets of Israel had
already said their say, the name of Israel was still unknown to the great Greek historian Herodotus, and the
Land of Israel was still masked by the Land of the Philistines in the Herodotean panorama of the Syriac
World. . . . Yet in these barren, land-locked highlands,
which were not of sufficient worldly importance to acquire even a recognized name of their own, there was
immanent (to paraphrase Plato's language) a divine inspiration which made this uninviting country a means of
grace to those who came to settle there [II, 52 f.].

Nothing remains now but a blur. Within that blur, however, looms a vague impression that somewhere, somehow,
Professor Toynbee has said something that establishes an

---

[1] I have had great difficulty in determining Professor Toynbee's religious
views, although (or because, perhaps) he is at such frequent pains to
express them. The comparison between the Phœnician discovery of the
Atlantic and the Jewish discovery of God puzzles me. One might as rele-
vantly compare the Emperor Domitian's addiction to and skill at fly-catching
(Suetonius, *Lives of the Cæsars, Domitian*, III) with the Emperor Marcus
Aurelius' devotion to the Stoic philosophy. On the whole Professor Toynbee's religious declarations put one in mind of George Gissing's description
of a certain type of Englishman: "His religion, strictly speaking, is an
ineradicable belief in his own religiousness" (*The Ryecroft Papers*). For
further observations on Professor Toynbee's religious views, see below, p. 95 f.

"Apparentation-and-Affiliation" relationship between the Minoan and the Syriac civilizations. Somewhat less forthright than the man

> Who rose and answered hotly:
> "Certainly, certainotly!"

Professor Toynbee has the habit of passing from: "It is not too fantastic to suggest" to: "We have already seen that," and then to their opposites—or rather, of passing back and forth between these positions without embarrassment. For the exercise of this habit, as well as for its concealment, volume is essential, thousands of pages, hundreds of cross-references and quotations. It is only by collation of the passages on a given subject scattered throughout the vast embedding material that we become aware of the Blurring or Dizzying Effect, which leaves the reader under the impression that a point has been made when it has actually been avoided in a welter of words.

We may well ask how much intelligibility has been added to our picture of the origins of the Syriac society and its relationship to other societies. We shall be confronted with a similarly baffling situation when we turn to the internal relationships of the constituent sections of the Syriac society as illuminated by Professor Toynbee.

III

At the beginning of his work Professor Toynbee cites an example of the absurdity of trying to understand the history of any small people (and for that matter a large one) except in terms of the history of the entire society of which that people is a part.

It would be impossible to write intelligible histories of **Slovakia** or **Croatia** in which those territories, or their peoples, were given the role of protagonists, even in their own small corners of the broad Western stage. It would be impossible, in their case, to distinguish from their external relations an internal history which was something specifically their own. It would be found that *every* experience which they underwent and every activity into which they entered had been shared by them with other communities whose share had been greater than theirs, and in attempting to make their history intelligible we should find ourselves extending our field of vision to include one after another of these other peoples. Possibly we should have to extend it until we had included the whole of our Western Society. In any case, the intelligible field, when we found it, would certainly prove to be some field of which Slovakia or Croatia itself was a small and comparatively unimportant fraction [I, 13].

Accepting the level on which this statement is made, we can agree with it in a general way. We take it that Professor Toynbee does not mean that the Slovaks or Croatians should, in deference to the bigness of the Western World and the interdependence of historic destinies, suppress their own languages, their customs, their ancestral memories, and their special pieties (how *did* they come to possess such things?). And when he says that Slovakia or Croatia is a comparatively unimportant fraction of the intelligible historical field, he does not mean that the right of the Slovaks or Croatians to their cultural and spiritual forms of self-expression is an unimportant principle. We know that the history of an individual is even more unintelligible than that of a people unless conceived in the setting of his relationships; but that *every* experience which an individual undergoes has been shared by masses of people whose shares have, in the aggregate, been much larger than his, would be a doubtful proposition. There is in every individual a vastly important residue of particularity which we should be at pains to understand and safeguard, if not to encourage. It may even be said that the history of this or that individual is meaningless unless it leads up to this particularity; also that while the history of Slovakia or Croatia (for that history does exist, as the history of any hamlet exists) is unintelligible except as a small part of the whole, it is also unintelligible as nothing but a part of the whole.

The danger of the big historical sweep is, of course, that it overencourages a statistical frame of mind and lends itself to intellectual bullying. We know that an actuarial computation yields substantially the same results if one or two small contributory figures are removed. The annual percentage of suicides, for instance, is not affected by the rescue of an individual here and there; actually such rescues are already comprised in the statistics. Yet, while the over-all study is of immense importance for the contrivance of general remedial measures, it does not absolve me from the duty of paying attention to my neighbor's particular form of melancholia. I may, indeed, be of help to him in impressing upon him the fact that his personal condition must be viewed in the framework of society as a whole; but I must also pay attention to the particularity of his case. Similarly we must be careful not to approach the problems of small peoples in the spirit of historical elephantiasis.

Against this danger Professor Toynbee guards himself at one point when he treats of the individuality of each component part of a society.

A society, we should say, is confronted in the course of its life by a succession of problems, which every member has to solve for himself as best he may. The presentation of each problem is a challenge to undergo an ordeal, and through this series of ordeals the members of the society progressively differentiate themselves from one another. On each occasion some fail, while others succeed in finding a solution; and, again, some of the solutions found are imperfect or commonplace or inimical to success in solving subsequent problems, while others are exact or original or fertile in possibilities of further progress. As ordeal follows ordeal, some members of the society at some point fail altogether to adjust themselves, and fall by the way; others struggle on, strained or warped or stunted; others grow in wisdom and stature, and in making their own way discover new avenues for a general advance of the society to which they belong. Throughout, it is impossible to grasp the significance of a particular member's behaviour under a particular ordeal without taking some account of the similar or dissimilar behaviour of his fellows and without viewing the successive ordeals as a series of events in the life of the whole society [I, 22 f.].

For the purpose of my inquiry the key sentence in this passage is the last, and I venture to repeat it: "Throughout, it is impossible to grasp the significance of a particular member's behaviour under a particular ordeal without taking some account of the similar or dissimilar behaviour of his fellows and without viewing the successive ordeals as a series of events in the life of the whole society."

Now let us turn to the immediate subject-matter. We have been told that the Philistine, the Phœnician, and the Israelite members of the Syriac society took three different paths in answer to the challenge of their environments: the Philistines turned their backs on the sea and entered the same blind alley as the Argives of the Hellenic society; the Phœnicians became deep-sea mariners and discovered the Atlantic; the Israelites went up into the hill country and discovered God. Now in what way were these three responses related to each other, in what way interdependent? How did they effect each other? What, as far as Professor Toynbee's account of them goes, have these responses in common beyond the geographic contiguity of the peoples who made them? And wherein does he help us, on the basis of some demonstrated relationship, "to grasp the significance of a particular member's behaviour"?

IV

Of the Jewish achievement we read:

It was, indeed, a mighty feat of spiritual intuition to perceive in the lineaments of a primitive volcano-demon of the Arabian Wilderness the epiphany of a God who was omnipresent and omnipotent. What the Israelites had come to see in their hereditary tribal divinity Yahweh was never apprehended in Chemosh by the Moabites or in Rimmon by the Damascenes or in Melkart by the Tyrians or in Dagon by the Philistines. In this chapter of their history the Children of Israel had been gifted with an unparalleled spiritual insight [IV, 262].

This, then, was the specific manner in which the Jewish "member" differentiated itself from the others, and Professor Toynbee cites no evidence that this act of differentiation owed anything at all to the other members. And yet from dozens of allusions and innuendoes scattered throughout all the volumes one gathers that the Jewish concept of God was Syriac not just by geographic location, but also by organic spiritual interconnection with the whole Syriac civilization. Thus: "The greatest achievement of the *Syriac* Society was . . . its discovery of God; and the particular conception of God at which the Syriac Society arrived . . ."

(see above, 61). But the Syriac society as such never arrived at this conception of God, as Professor Toynbee has just recognized. As far as he knows, or says, it was a spontaneous eruption in the soul of the Israelites alone. He cannot trace it to the Egyptians or the Babylonians or the Khatti (Hittites) or the Minoans or anyone else. As far as he knows, or says, the strange spiritual eruption would have occurred among the Israelites if the Phœnicians had never turned to deep-seafaring and the Philistines had never forgotten their ancestral maritime traditions. What we do know is that the Syriac society was forever seeking to seduce the Jews from their particular conception of the Godhead, and that if anything at all was characteristic of the Syriac society as such in the religious field, it was the Dagons and Melkarts and Rimmons and the rest.

I continue to quote: ". . . if we remind ourselves of the origins of Judaism and Zoroastrianism, we shall remember that, while they are indeed, both of them, religions with a *Syriac* inspiration . . ." (V, 369); "The Old Testament . . . this old-fashioned *Syriac* oracle . . ." (I, 211); and: ". . . we perceive that the germ of creative power in Islam was not alien from, but native to, the *Syriac* Society. The founder, Muhammad, drew his inspiration primarily from Judaism, which was a purely *Syriac* religion . . ." (I, 83); and: "The genesis of this 'higher religion' of Judaism among the submerged *Syriac* elements in the Babylonic internal proletariat . . ." (V, 120); and: ". . . it may be recalled that Judaism is a fossil of the extinct *Syriac* Civilization . . ." (II, 402); and: "The great creative period of *Syriac* history—the age of the Prophets of Israel . . ." (III, 140).

Similarly, while Professor Toynbee acknowledges that Christianity was born within the Jewish people (whatever the later contributions of other peoples), he blurs the impression by references of the following kind: "In Christianity, for example, we are aware of Hellenic elements . . . which the original *Syriac* germ assimilated . . ." (I, 83); and: "Christianity was begotten in *Syriac* territories that had been incorporated into the Hellenic universal state, and it was introduced into the Hellenic World by *Syriac* 'Natives' who had been forcibly enrolled in the internal proletariat of the Hellenic Society" (I, 90); and: ". . . the germ of creative activity, derived from the *Syriac* Society, out of which the internal proletariat of the Hellenic Society generated the Catholic Church . . ." (I, 154); and: ". . . The germ of creative power from which the Christian Church has sprung was derived by the internal proletariat of the Hellenic Society from *Syriac* 'Natives' who were forcibly enrolled in its ranks" (I, 165), etc., etc. (The Syriac natives in these references were of course all Jews.)

To say that the Jews had been gifted with "an unparalleled spiritual insight," and that they came to see in their God that which their Syriac neighbors had never apprehended in *their* gods, and then to refer (as he does again and again) to this Jewish creation as "a Syriac religion" is like saying: "The British alone had the moral resources to stand up to Hitler when the rest of western Europe collapsed before him," and then to repeat, in a variety of forms: "Hitler found the spirit of western Europe unconquerable." It is, if one likes, not wholly inaccurate; but it is none the less wholly misleading. Professor Toynbee fails to shed any light on the cultural interrelationship between the rise of monotheism among the Jews and the religious life of the neighboring peoples; he has given us no clue to the special circumstances that would account, at least in part, for the strange differences of abilities and destinies of the Jewish people, any more than he has helped us to account for the maritime skill of the Phœnicians or the emergence of the alphabet in Syria.

The Blurring Effect, having first created the erroneous impression of an established "Apparentation-and-Affiliation" relationship between the Minoan and Syriac societies, next proceeds to make it seem that there was a significant and instructive community of circumstance (not the purely geographic among the achievements of the various members of the Syriac society, and that therefore something has been added to the intelligibility of the whole and its parts; in other words, we are left with the hazy feeling that the writer has here vindicated his thesis: "Throughout it is impossible to grasp the significance of a particular member's behaviour without taking some account of the similar or dissimilar behaviour of his fellows, etc.", when in fact he has left the thesis untouched.

Of Professor Toynbee's theory of civilizations Professor Sorokin writes: ". . . like so-called 'functional anthropologists' he assumes that his 'civilizations' are a real system and not merely congeries of various cultural (or civilizational) phenomena and objects adjacent in space or time but devoid of any causal or meaningful ties (see the analysis of sociocultural systems and congeries in my *Social and Cultural Dynamics*, Vol. I, Chap. i; an unfolded theory of sociocultural systems is given in Vol. IV of the *Dynamics*" (*The Pattern of the Past*, p. 111).

Professor Sorokin makes it appear that it is necessary to have read his formidable *Social and Cultural Dynamics* in order to see that Professor Toynbee is all wrong. This is a mistake. Professor Sorokin merely has a theory that Professor Toynbee is wrong. The irrefutable proof that Professor Toynbee is wrong is supplied by Professor Toynbee himself, who invalidates his own thesis without the assistance of other historians. At best one may quote here Professor Geyl's observation in another but similar connection: "It is one instance out of the innumerable fallacious arguments and spurious demonstrations *of which the whole book is made up"* (*Debates with Historians,* p. 154). But in order to be fair, I must point out that Professor Geyl goes on to say: "I want nevertheless to make it clear that there is much in Toynbee's book that I warmly admire." I think it is also fair to add that historians are rather astonishing people.

In closing this chapter I should like to observe that I do not challenge the principle of cultural interrelationships and interdependences. As regards the Hebrew achievement we are all familiar by now with the parallels between the Biblical story of the Flood and the Gilgamesh cycle, between some of the Mosaic legislation and the Hammurabi Code, between Egyptian and Hebrew Wisdom Literature, etc., etc. Professor Toynbee does not dwell on these parallels; he does not commit the error that equates the raw material with the inspiration that transfigures it—as if someone were to account for the greatness of Shakespeare's historical dramas by saying complacently: "He got it all from Holinshed or Plutarch." Professor Toynbee does worse; in the matter of the birth and significance of Judaism he distributes the credits and fuses the sources without producing any parallels at all; and he does so in a baffling, tangential, insinuative manner that leads us, once we have caught on to it, to suspect a prejudice that he cannot bring himself to perceive rather than a conviction at which he has consciously arrived.

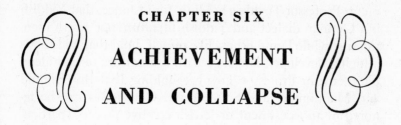

CHAPTER SIX

ACHIEVEMENT

AND COLLAPSE

I

When we collate the numerous and often repetitious passages on the Jews in *A Study of History* we discover, behind the arabesques of erudition, three familiar and rather shopworn ideas:

1. That there has been only one episode of value in Jewish history, the Prophetic;
2. That the spiritually fatal mistake of the Jews was their rejection of Christianity;
3. That it was by this rejection that they condemned themselves to everlasting sterility.

These ideas have been discussed so frequently that there would seem to be no point in re-examining them; but it may be of interest to find out whether Professor Toynbee has presented them with unusual cogency. Moreover, the issue here is not merely Professor Toynbee's personal views. It is also what I have called (above, p. 29) an "attitude of the Western World toward this people . . . a fateful folk bias that has played quite a role in the spiritual development of the Western World."

I shall not attempt a Jungian analysis of Professor Toynbee's views; but I believe that an examination of the manner in which he presents them will help us to understand more than an individual case. And, once again, it is not merely a question of straightforward agreement or disagreement, Professor Toynbee holding, for instance, that Yiddish is a German dialect and Yiddish literature not worth mentioning, while I, and others like myself, hold that Yiddish is a highly developed language with a literature of considerable merit; or Professor Toynbee holding that the Talmud and Maimonides and Spinoza and Chassidism can be ignored in an assessment of Jewish creative powers (particularly in the religious field), while I, and others better qualified than I, and in great numbers, consider them quite extraordinary spiritual phenomena. There is little to be learned, too, from a mere denial that the Jewish people is a fossilized remnant of a perished civilization. There is, however, much particular and general instruction to be derived from the "internal evidence" in Professor Toynbee's work.

We observe first, side by side with the Blurring Effect, what seems to be a kind of uneasiness or ambivalence, which in a less distinguished person might be described as "double-talk." Professor Toynbee is enormously impressed by the sheer survival, even in fossil form, of the Jewish people. He calls it "the most extreme example of Challenge-and-Response in the human realm that can well be imagined" (II, 274). And again:

. . . the Jews live on—*the same peculiar people*—today, long after the Phoenicians and the Philistines have lost their identity like all the nations. The ancient Syriac neighbors of Israel have fallen into the melting-pot and have been re-minted, in the fullness of time, with new images and superscriptions, while Israel has proved impervious to this alchemy—performed by History in the crucibles of universal states and universal churches and wanderings of the nations—to which we Gentiles all in turn succumb [II, 55].

What here looks like an awed tribute to the vitality of the Jewish people must, however, be reconciled, if possible, with Professor Toynbee's general view. I therefore place this passage among the appropriate reflections that the compulsive writer must record when gazing on an insect embedded in amber, or on an ancient sequoia: "While nations have risen and fallen, this insect, this tree, etc."—something like Sir Thomas Browne's reflection on the bones discovered in Roman urns, which have "outlived the living bones of Methuselah . . . and quietly rested under the drums and tramplings of three conquests."

But it is not so easy to reduce to consistency with the larger context a passage like the following: "The secret of this latter-day Jewry's survival power lies in its persistent cultivation of the êthos which Johanan ben Zakkai has bequeathed to it" (V, 75). One can easily imagine a fossil proving impervious to the alchemy of history, but to say that it does so by the persistent cultivation of an ethos is to put an unfair strain on the normal imagination. We are, it is true, given some assistance by the following:

Let us glance at the various 'fossils' of the Syriac Society which have been deposited, in successive social strata, during the much-interrupted and long-drawn-out course of Syriac history. In the oldest stratum there are the Jews and the Parsees, who are relics of the Syriac Society as it was in its universal state, under the Achaemenian régime, before the Hellenic intrusion. . . . The medium in which all these Syriac 'fossils' have been preserved is a religious medium; their religious idiosyncracies, which have safeguarded their identities and perpetuated their existence in their fossil state, have also exposed them to religious discrimination . . . [II, 234 f.].

A religious idiosyncrasy is, after all, not a true religion; in a fossil we find petrified rituals, spiritless postures of seeming worship, and these may be termed a religious idiosyncrasy. Unfortunately Professor Toynbee speaks, as we have just seen, of the persistent cultivation of an ethos, that bequeathed to the Jews by Johanan ben Zakkai. We must somehow conclude, then, that the ethos of Johanan ben Zakkai is itself an idiosyncrasy, a spiritless posture. But no, Professor Toynbee ranks the ethos of Johanan ben Zakkai with that of Jesus himself, as we shall see when we come to another part of the argument (below, p. 86). We are really at a loss to get a clear view of what Professor Toynbee thinks of the Jews and Judaism in this respect. (I shall leave the Parsees to look after themselves.)

II

Let us now proceed to discover at approximately what date Professor Toynbee *really* thinks the Jews lost their creative power. This is not an idle exercise in the exposure of a writer's perhaps irrelevant inconsistencies. The view that the Jewish people, somewhere along the historical line, rose to a single climax of value, and thereafter collapsed into a spiritual worthlessness from which it has never emerged, and that its refusal to accept Christianity is overwhelming evidence of its inertness and even perversity—this view is not, as I have mentioned, original with Professor Toynbee. But his restatement of it is, in some ways; and its effect on the public is, for the time being, quite marked. It is therefore important, for those who have such matters at heart, to subject the restatement to close, honest scrutiny.

I have already quoted the passage in which Professor Toynbee identifies "the great creative period of Syriac history" as "the age of the Prophets of Israel," by which he means the century and a half or so from Amos to Jeremiah and Ezekiel—that is to say, from the eighth century before the Christian era to the middle of the sixth. But this statement is blurred by another:

> In a period of their history which began in the infancy of the Syriac Civilization [i.e., about 1200 B.C.] and which *culminated* in the Age of the Prophets of Israel, the people of Israel and Judah raised themselves head and shoulders above the Syriac peoples round about in responding to the challenge of a 'Time of Troubles' by rising to a higher conception of Religion [IV, 262].

The Prophets are, then, a culmination, not an innovation, and we have here a process covering—up to this point—a stretch of some six hundred years. That the Jews had been developing high insights from the beginning seems to be clear, again, from the following:

> In the Syriac World in its 'Time of Troubles,' when it was being battered by an Assyrian flail, we see the Prophets of Israel and Judah offering themselves as martyrs in protest against the truancy of a paganizing faction who were seeking an escape from intolerable miseries *in a deliberate repudiation of the Chosen People's priceless peculiar heritage,* with the base intention of purchasing some relief from pressure at the cost of re-merging the potter's half-shaped vessel into the still shapeless common clay of the unregenerate Gentiles [V, 410 f.].

We must take this to mean that by the time of the Prophets of the eighth century the peculiar Jewish vision of God, unglimpsed by the surrounding peoples, had already become a national heritage. We now return to the preceding passage, which continues:

Keenly conscious, and rightly proud, of the spiritual treasure which they had thus wrested from an ordeal that had
broken the spirit of their Aramaean and Phoenician and
Philistine neighbours, the Jews allowed themselves to be
'betrayed, by what' was 'false within,' into an idolization
of this notable, yet *transitory*, phase of their own spiritual
growth. . . . In this chapter of their history the Children of Israel had been gifted with an unparalleled spiritual insight. And then, after having divined a truth which
was absolute and eternal, they allowed themselves to be
captivated by a temporary and relative half-truth. They
persuaded themselves that Israel's discovery of the One
True God had revealed Israel itself to be God's Chosen
People; and this half-truth inveigled them into the fatal
error of looking upon a *momentary* spiritual eminence,
which they had attained by labour and travail, as a privi-
lege conferred upon them by God in a covenant which
was everlasting. In this delusion—which was a moral as
well as an intellectual fault—the Jews 'rested on their
oars' when they were called upon to respond to a new
challenge which was presented to the Syriac Society *post
Alexandrum* by the impact of Hellenism, and, through
persisting in this posture, they 'put themselves out of the
running' for serving once more in the next advance of the
Syriac spirit.[1] Brooding over a talent which they had per-
versely sterilized by hiding it in the earth, they rejected
the stilll greater treasure which God was now offering
them [i.e., the Christ] [IV, 262 f.].

Now when, in the centuries between the Major Prophets
and the coming of Jesus, did the Jews sterilize their own
talent? We cannot find *in Professor Toynbee's account* a
period of Jewish sterility! There is, according to him, no fall

[1] What Syriac spirit?

from grace! Let the reader make his way through the following statement, which tells of the period immediately following the Major Prophets:

> While the later incorporation of the Syriac Society into
> the Hellenic internal proletariat was to bear fruit at the
> beginning of the Christian Era in the birth of Christian-
> ity out of Judaism, the earlier incorporation of the same
> Syriac Society into the Babylonic internal proletariat bore
> fruit in and after the eighth century B.C. in the birth of
> Judaism itself out of the primitive religion of one of the
> parochial communities into which the Syriac Society had
> come to be articulated. . . .[2] Moreover, Gentleness even-
> tually prevailed over Violence in this case likewise; for
> the 'Time of Troubles,' as it reached and passed its cli-
> max, delivered a series of hammer-stroke lessons which
> taught even the 'Die-Hards' in the tribe of Judah the fu-
> tility of attempting to repay Violence in its own kind.
> The new 'higher religion' which was born in eighth-
> century Syria, in Syriac [3] communities which were then
> still being pounded on their native threshing-floor by an
> Assyrian flail, *was brought to maturity in sixth-century
> and fifth-century Babylonia among the uprooted and de-
> ported descendants of one of these battered Syriac peo-
> ples.*

Like the Oriental slave-deportees in Roman Italy, the
Jewish exiles in Nebuchadnezzar's Babylon were proof
against the facile adaptability of the Russian slave-deportees in Ottoman Rumelia. These uprooted Syriac [3]
members of the Babylonic internal proletariat were no
chameleons.

[2] The religion of the Jews is now "primitive" down to the coming of
the Great Prophets in the eighth century.
[3] For "Syriac" read "Jewish."

'If I forget thee, O Jerusalem, may my right hand forget
her cunning.
If I do not remember thee, let my tongue cleave to the
roof of my mouth.' [4]

Yet the memory of their home which these exiles cherished in a strange land was not just a negative imprint:
it was a positive act of imaginative creation. In the un-
earthly light of this vision seen through a mist of tears
the fallen fastness became transfigured into a holy city
built upon a rock against which the gates of Hell should
not prevail. And the captives who refused to indulge their
captors' whim by singing them one of the songs of Sion,
and stubbornly hanged up their harps on the willows by
Euphrates' stream, were at that very moment composing
an inaudible new melody on the invisible instrument of
their hearts.

'By the waters of Babylon we sat down and wept when
we remembered thee, O Sion';
*and, in that weeping, the enlightenment of Jewry was ac-
complished* [V, 119–21].

And now, if I may be colloquial, let's get this thing
straight. According to one part of the account we are studying, the Jews are allowed a "momentary spiritual eminence"
that coincided with, or was constituted by, the age of the
Prophets. According to another part, the Prophets were
conserving a "peculiar heritage" already in existence by their
time, and threatened with desertion by a faction. Nevertheless this peculiar heritage, the higher religion, "was born in
the eighth century B.C." and actually it was "brought to ma-
turity in sixth-century and fifth-century Babylonia among
the uprooted and deported descendants" of the Jewish com-

[4] The Jews who repeated these words in the centuries after the Second
Destruction were of course not chameleons either; they were fossils.

munity. We are therefore dealing with a "momentary spiritual eminence" which has been manifesting itself—always according to Professor Toynbee's account—for some seven centuries. And, still according to the same account—or parts of it—we are not through with it yet, for Professor Toynbee now defers the perverse burial of the peculiar Jewish talent for another three centuries.

Writing of "Futurism" and of the Way of Gentleness (spiritual) versus the Way of Violence (mundane), Professor Toynbee says:

> For example in the Syriac Society—both in its Iranian and in its Syrian wing—the Messianic form of Futurism made its first appearance as a positive attempt to follow the way of Gentleness. Instead of persisting in a disastrous attempt to maintain his political independence here and now against the assaults of Assyrian militarism, the Israelite, like the Mede, bowed his head to a present political yoke and reconciled himself to this painful act of resignation by transferring all his political treasure to the hope of a savior-king who was to arise and restore the fallen national kingdom at some hidden future date. *When we trace out the history of this Messianic Hope in the Jewish Community, we find that it worked in favour of Gentleness for more than four hundred years—from 586 B.C., when the Jews were carried away into Babylonish captivity by Nebuchadnezzar, until 168 B.C., when they were subjected to a Hellenizing persecution by Antiochus Epiphanes* [V, 387].

We are now justified in concluding that, always in Professor Toynbee's view, or at least one intermittent aspect of it, the spiritual grace of Judaism, exemplified by the Prophets, and matured in Babylonia, endured in the subject Second Jewish State until the time of the Maccabees; and if

we take seriously his statement that before the Prophets the
Jews had already raised themselves head and shoulders above
their pagan neighbors, we have a total span of more than
one thousand years. "Momentary" and "transitory" are
hardly the right words.

But now, it would appear, a term is at last put to Jewish
spirituality, and we are entering on the era of fossilization,
also called Self-Idolization, or Idolization of an Ephemeral
Self. The last quoted passage continues:

> The first Jewish martyrs who gave their lives for Judaism
> in its three-hundred-years-long struggle with Hellenism
> all suffered and died without offering any physical resist-
> ence. Yet the discord between a confidently expected
> mundane future and an excruciatingly experienced mun-
> dane present resolved itself in Violence in the end. The
> martyrdom of Eleazar and the Seven Brothers was fol-
> lowed, within two years, by the armed insurrection of Ju-
> das Maccabaeus; and the Maccabees inaugurated that
> long line of ever more fanatically militant Jewish zealots—
> the innumerable Theudases and Judases of Galilee—
> whose violence reached its appalling climax in the Satanic
> Jewish *émeutes* of A.D. 66–70 and 115–17 and 132–5 [V,
> 387].

Professor Toynbee seems to think that the Maccabees,
like the Pharisees, began well but ended ignobly; their fall,
however, was much more rapid and not from so high an
eminence.

> For example, when the Maccabees changed, before the
> close of the second century B.C., from being militant
> champions of the Jewish religion against a forcible Hel-
> lenization into being the founders and rulers of one of the
> 'successor-states' of a Seleucid Empire whose cultural pol-
> icy they had succeeded in frustrating by force of arms

within their own parochial radius, these violent-handed opponents of a persecuting Power immediately became persecutors in their turn. They turned the swords that had first been drawn in self-defence, in order to save the Jewish religion from extinction, to the new and sinister use of imposing this self-same Judaism upon the neighboring non-Jewish populations . . . [V, 657].

Professor Toynbee then observes that the Pharisees opposed this shift of purpose, and therein they represented the true Jewish spirit.

The gentle response is as genuine an expression of the Proletariat's will to secede as the violent response is; for the gentle martyrs who are commemorated in the Second Book of Maccabees are the spiritual progenitors of the Pharisees, and the Pharisees are 'they who separate themselves'—a self-conferred title which would translate itself into 'secessionists' or 'schismatics' in the official language of an Antiochus or a Titus—or indeed of a Jannaeus and a Herod [V, 73 f.].

But ultimately, it would seem, the Pharisees too went the way of violence:

. . . in the history of the internal proletariat of a disintegrating Hellenic World, the rank-and-file of Jewry had been betrayed and deserted, by the time of Christ, by their own former leaders the Scribes and Pharisees. These Jewish 'separatists' lived to deserve their self-imposed name in a sense which was the opposite of their meaning at the time when they originally assumed it. The original Pharisees were Jewish puritans who separated themselves from the Hellenizing Jews when these renegades were joining the camp of an alien dominant minority. On the other hand the distinguishing mark of the Pharisees of the time of Christ was their separation of themselves from the rank-and-file of the loyal and devout members of the Jewish community, to whom they still hypocritically professed to be setting a good example [V, 542 f.].

Here Professor Toynbee quotes Eduard Meyer on the Pharisees:

'The learned in the Scriptures, as well as the worldlings, belong to the upper strata of Society; and their attitude is one of condescension mingled with contempt as they look down upon the masses of the working population whom it is their intention to instruct and lead. In [the souls of] these masses, however, the religious life pulsates with a far fiercer intensity . . .' [V, 543].

Professor Toynbee adds: "This is the historical background of the scathing denunciation of the Pharisees which echoes through the pages of the Gospels," and then quotes from Matthew the famous passage beginning: "The Scribes and Pharisees sit in Moses' seat. . . ." And a final note of condemnation:

Nor was this assimilation of the *ci-devant* spiritual leaders of Jewry to both the two main types of their former Hellenic adversaries just a curiosity of history without practical consequences. In the tragedy of the Passion of Christ we see the Scribes and Pharisees not merely inclining in the privacy of their hearts to the spirit and behaviour of a dominant minority, but also actively ranging themselves at the side of the Roman authorities in the public light of the forum in order to compass the death of one of their very own race who had been putting them to shame by doing the very works of which these 'whited sepulchres' made no more than a hollow pretense [V, 544].

Here it is at last. We have come to the collapse of the Jewish spirit, *il gran rifiuto*. (It is a little spoiled by Eduard Meyer's reference to the fierce intensity of the religious feelings of the masses, but we let that pass.) Henceforth the sterility is such that the word "fossil" can be applied with propriety. But can it? Unfortunately for the argument Professor Toynbee says something like the opposite, for he opens a new era in the spiritual development of Jewry through Johanan ben Zakkai.

Johanan ben Zakkai is the great Jewish teacher who at the time of the Vespasian siege and destruction of Jerusalem escaped from the city by having himself lowered from the walls in a coffin, and obtained from the besieging Romans permission to establish his Academy at Jabneh. To this Academy Jews customarily point as the symbol and instrument of their survival. Professor Toynbee writes:

Before the net of Roman circumvallation finally closed in upon the devoted Holy City, Rabbi Johanan ben Zakkai *independently* took the momentous decision *to break* with the tradition of militancy which Judas Maccabaeus had inaugurated. Eluding the vigilance of the Jewish Zealots, he slipped across no-man's-land and prevailed upon the Roman High Command to let him through in order that he might quietly continue his teaching out of earshot of the battle; and, when the tidings of the inevitable catastrophe eventually reached him in the Hellenized Philistine township of Jabneh, where he had reassembled his school, and the disciple who brought the bad news exclaimed in anguish: 'Woe to us, because the place is destroyed where they make propitiation for the sins of Israel,' the master answered: 'My son, let it not grieve thee; we have yet one propitiation equal to it, and what is that but the bestowal of kindnesses?—even as it is writ-

ten: "I desire kindness and not sacrifice." ' In act and
word Johanan ben Zakkai was proclaiming his *conversion*
from the way of Violence to the way of Gentleness; and
through this *conversion* he became the founder of the
new Jewry which survived—albeit only as a fossil. . . .
The secret of this latter-day Jewry's extraordinary survival power lies in its persistent cultivation of the êthos
which Johanan ben Zakkai has bequeathed to it . . . [V,
75, already quoted in part, above, p. 75].

Professor Toynbee assigns a very high place in the scale
of spiritual values to this ethos of Johanan ben Zakkai. Writing of non-violence as a principle, and of its degradation to
a form of political strategy, he says:

> While Mr. Gandhi practices Non-Violence because he
> considers this to be the most efficacious means of pursu-
> ing an aim that is mundane, the Non-Violence of Jesus
> and Johanan ben Zakkai as a reflexion, on the mundane
> plane, of a transference of the field of action from that
> mundane plane to another [V, 589].

Professor Toynbee thus brackets the names of Johanan ben
Zakkai and Jesus for their moral significance, and it was, as
we have seen, by its persistent cultivation of the ethos which
Johanan ben Zakkai bequeathed to it that Jewry in exile
achieved the longevity that so impresses him.

We may observe here that to speak of Johanan ben Zakkai's "conversion" to the way of non-violence is an ingenious piece of nonsense. There is not a shred of evidence
that Johanan ben Zakkai had to be converted. He and his
school had always represented the traditional, the fundamental order of Jewish ideas. He did not "break with" the
militancy inaugurated by Judas Maccabæus. The Pharisees
had always been at loggerheads with the Hasmonean (Mac-

cabean) conquistadors and with the worldlings who came after them; and far from being a lone figure, ben Zakkai had about him a great galaxy of teachers and a mighty following. Actually ben Zakkai, besides being a historical figure, is also a historical mnemonic for a process that occupied several centuries. From the time of Ezra and Nehemiah onwards the synagogue and school were slowly taking over the survivalist function for the Jewish people; the spiritual predominance in Jewry was with the Pharisee teachers, not the Sadducee Temple functionaries. Alexander Jannæus, who had insolently united in his own person the offices of King and High Priest, earned the hatred of the Pharisees, and when a throng of worshippers objected to his desecration of the ritual, and pelted him with citrons, he turned his troops loose on them and slaughtered some thousands. It is with the conduct of this King that Professor Toynbee reproaches the Jewish people, citing him and his line as evidence of the Jewish spiritual decline. He might as justly have cited against it the wicked kings of the time of the Major Prophets, which he does not do, having decided that the time of the Major Prophets was the high point of Israel's spiritual trajectory.

Of course the struggle between the Temple cultists and the ethicists in Jewry was an old one, and went back to the time of the Prophets. The belief that the survival of Judaism depended more on the spirit than on animal sacrifices, on submitting to God's will, walking humbly with Him, and doing kindnesses, than on tending His altars, is reiterated in magnificent language in the prophetic books. And the Pharisees were the heirs of the Prophets. What an extraordinary perversion to make Johanan ben Zakkai, the great Pharisee, a "convert," a man who had just had his eyes opened!

One of the climactic confusions of A *Study of History*

is a curious passage to which I shall have to refer again later
in other connections:

> It is the supreme irony of Jewish history that the new
> ground captured for Judaism by the spear of Alexander
> Jannaeus (*regnabat* 102–76 B.C.) did bring to birth,
> within a hundred years, a Galilean Jewish prophet whose
> message to his fellow men was the consummation of all
> previous Jewish religious experience, and that this in-
> spired Jewish scion of forcibly converted Galilean Gen-
> tiles *was then rejected and done to death by the Judaean
> leaders of the Jewry of his age.* In thus deliberately refus-
> ing the opportunity that was offered it of realizing its
> manifest destiny of flowering into Christianity by open-
> ing its heart to the gospel of its Galilean step-child, Juda-
> ism not only stultified its spiritual past but forfeited its
> material future into the bargain. In declining to recognize
> its expected Messiah in Jesus, Judaism was renouncing its
> birthright in two great enterprises which eventually made
> the respective fortunes of two different daughters of Ju-
> daism by whom these enterprises were duly carried out in
> the fulness of time. In the first place Judaism was aban-
> doning the fallow and fertile mission-field of the Hellenic
> universal state [5] to a Christian Church that was to be
> driven into independence by its eviction from the Jewish
> fold; and in the second place Judaism was leaving to an
> Islam whose founder was to be rebuffed by the Jewish
> Diasporà in his native Hijāz the subsequent political task
> of reuniting a Syriac World which had been divided
> against itself as one consequence of the forcible intrusion
> of Hellenism upon Syriac ground. Instead of embracing
> either of these alternative opportunities for a great career
> when it had the refusal of both of them, Judaism pre-

---

[5] See footnote, p. 91 below.

ferred to fling itself into the forlorn hope of Zealotism—
in order to be retrieved as a mere fossil, by the *tardy* wisdom of Johanan ben Zakkai, from the wantonly incurred
cataclysm of A.D. 70 [V, 658 f.].

When we try to hold simultaneously before our minds
these various statements on the time of the collapse of the
Jewish spirit, we achieve a strange result: we know more or
less what view Professor Toynbee wants to hold and wants
us to hold, but we do not know how to arrive at it from the
variety of views which he actually expresses himself as holding. We are in the very thick of the Blurring Effect, and are
reminded of the poet satirized by Pope:

> who now to sense now nonsense leaning
> Means not but blunders round about a meaning.

III

In spite of the general canceling out of views which Professor Toynbee has here managed to achieve, we must pay
special attention to some sentences quoted above: "In thus
deliberately refusing the opportunity of realizing its manifest destiny of flowering into Christianity by opening its
heart to its Galilean step-child, Judaism not only stultified
its spiritual past but forfeited its material future into the
bargain. In declining to recognize its expected Messiah in
Jesus, Judaism was renouncing its birthright in two great
enterprises which eventually made the respective fortunes
of two different daughters of Judaism by whom these enterprises were duly carried out in the fulness of time."

It is difficult to see how accepting Jesus as the Messiah
would have given Judaism a share in the fortunes of Mohammedanism. It is even more difficult to see with what forfeited *material* profits Professor Toynbee is here twitting

Judaism. Are we to assume that if the Jews had accepted Jesus as their Messiah they would have never lost their homeland? Does Professor Toynbee mean that Rome would have been more sparing of a Christian than of a Jewish Palestine? Or does he mean that Jews, still identifiable in Judaism, would today be recognized as "charter-members" of the Christian Church? Or that Jerusalem would today be occupying in Catholicism the position occupied by Rome? One can understand him when he says that Jews should have become Christians (or at least, hang it all! Mohammedans), but *what* does he mean when he speaks of Judaism having lost its birthright in the "two great enterprises which ultimately made the fortunes" of Christianity and Mohammedanism? He mentions—rather coarsely, considering the lofty plane on which he is operating—the "material future," but if he really means spiritual achievement, it is arguable from his own text that Jewry, throughout the past nineteen centuries, has been as near to the ethos of Johanan ben Zakkai as Christians have been to that of Jesus. Or does Professor Toynbee, in his preoccupation with big things, and in his identification of size with spiritual significance, simply mean that a little group cannot, in the nature of things, sustain a true spiritual birthright of its own?

But let us for the moment leave on one side the question of whether Judaism, in rejecting Christianity, made the worst of both worlds, and once more turn our attention to the spiritual condition of the Jewish leadership in the time of Jesus' ministry. In quoting Eduard Meyer on the Pharisees, and then following this up with quotations from the Gospels, Professor Toynbee seems to be drawing on two independent sources, the first of which he describes as the "historical background" to the second. But as Eduard Meyer himself uses the Gospel texts as his source, the apparent reinforcement is merely a stage trick. More important, however, is the contradiction between Professor Toynbee's interpretations of the Gospel texts on the one hand and of the Old Testament texts on the other.

It is necessary to repeat at some length the Gospel passages quoted or mentioned and others like them:

> The Scribes and the Pharisees sit in Moses' seat: all, therefore, that they bid you observe, that observe and do; but do not ye after their works; for they say and do not. For they bind heavy burdens and grievous to be borne, and lay them on men's shoulders; but they themselves will not move them with one of their fingers. . . . They . . . love the uppermost rooms at feasts and the chief seats in the synagogues and greetings in the markets, and to be called of men Rabbi, Rabbi . . . [Matthew xxiii, 2–7].
>
> Beware the Scribes, which love to go in long clothing, and love salutations in the market-places, and the chief seats in the synagogues, and the uppermost rooms at feasts [Mark xii, 38 f.].
>
> Beware of the Scribes, which desire to walk in long robes, and love greetings in the markets, and the highest seats in the synagogues, and the chief rooms at feasts; which devour widows' houses, and for a show make long prayers . . . [Luke xx, 46 f.].
>
> O generation of vipers . . . [Matthew iii, 7; xii, 34; Luke iii, 7].
>
> Ye serpents, ye generation of vipers, how can ye escape the damnation of hell? [Matthew xxiii, 33].[6]

---

[6] To this may be added, for an additional purpose: "Woe unto you, scribes and Pharisees, hypocrites—for ye compass sea and land to make one proselyte, and when he is made, ye make him twofold more the child of hell than yourselves" (Matthew xxiii, 15). The verse testifies, though in an adverse spirit, to the great proselytizing activities of the Jews about the time of Jesus. Far from "abandoning the fertile and fallow field of the Hellenic universal state," the Jews were greatly concerned to win souls, there and elsewhere. It is universally recognized that the "God-fearers"—

These quotations may be compared for totality of denunciation with many prophetic verses relating to the condition of the Jewish people in the eighth and seventh and sixth centuries before the Christian era. It is the *entire* Jewish people which is indicted by Isaiah:

> Ah, sinful nation, a people laden with iniquity, a seed of evildoers, children that are corrupters; they have forsaken the Lord, they have provoked the Holy One of Israel unto anger, they are gone away backward . . . the whole head is sick, and the whole heart faint. From the sole of the foot even unto the head there is no soundness in it; but wounds and bruises and putrifying sores . . . (I, 4–6).

Similarly:

> Now therefore go to, speak to the men of Judah, and to the inhabitants of Jerusalem saying: Thus saith the Lord: Behold, I frame evil against you, and devise a device against you: return ye now every one from his evil way, and make your ways and your doings good. And they said: there is no hope, but we will walk after our own devices, and we will every one do the imagination of his evil heart . . . (Jeremiah xviii, 11–12).

Nevertheless Professor Toynbee writes: ". . . we see the Prophets of Israel and Judah offering themselves as martyrs in protest against the truancy of a paganizing faction . . ." (V, 410, quoted above, p. 77). Would it not seem from these Prophetic passages that the Judaizers are the faction— if they exist at all? Why does Professor Toynbee take the denunciations of the Gospels literally, and those of the Proph-

---

non-Jews who had been won over to a partial acceptance of Judaism—not only were very numerous in the Roman Empire, but were of great help in obtaining for Christianity its first foothold. As to whether the Jews abandoned the field to Christianity, or were outmaneuvered when Christianity attached itself to the Greco-Roman myths, see below, 96 ff.

ets metaphorically? Why does he thus write of the Jews
of the Prophetic era that they had raised themselves to
heights of unparalleled spiritual insight, while he pictures
the Pharisees, in their totality, as the betrayers of the Jewish
people? He supplies us with "historical background" from
Meyer to the effect that "the learned in the Scriptures as
well as the worldlings, belong to the upper strata of Society." Certainly there were wealthy and arrogant Pharisees;
but what has become of Hillel, the sweet and patient one,
and Rabbi Ilai the carpenter, and Rabbi Johanan the shoe-
maker, and Rabbi Joshua ben Hananya the needle-maker?
What has become of Rabbi Haninah ben Dosa, of whom it
is written: "The world is sustained for the sake of My son
Haninah ben Dosa, and My son Haninah ben Dosa is sustained by a measure of carob each day"? What has become
of Rabbi Akiba? Not that poverty and pacifism always went
hand in hand, for Akiba stood with Bar Kochba and even
believed him to be the Messiah; but among the Ten who
suffered martyrdom in the Hadrianic persecutions the majority were spirits as gentle as those martyrs of the Antio-
chan persecutions for whom Professor Toynbee has only
admiration. It is true, again, that not all of the humble
Pharisees mentioned above were the contemporaries of
Jesus, but there is no warrant for the suspicion that Pharisaism underwent any change of essence from the first century to the second.

While on the subject of the Prophetic denunciations, we
may note that if many of them are to be taken literally the
Jewish people of *all* the Biblical generations were corrupt
through and through. The unnamed prophets in the reign
of the abominable Manasseh had this to say:

Therefore thus saith the Lord God of Israel, behold, I
will bring such evil upon Jerusalem, that whosoever hear-

eth of it both his ears shall tingle . . . Because they have
done that which was evil in My sight, and have provoked
Me to anger, since the day their fathers came forth out of
Egypt, even to this day [II Kings xxi, 12–15].

And again:

For I earnestly protested to your fathers in the day that I
brought them up out of the land of Egypt, even to this
day, rising early and protesting, saying, Obey My voice.
Yet they obeyed not, nor inclined their ear, but walked
every man in the imagination of their evil heart . . .
(Jeremiah xi, 7 f.).

If these, and many other, Prophetic utterances were to be
treated as Professor Toynbee treats those of the Gospels
against the Pharisees, it is utterly impossible to understand
how the Jewish people survived at all even in its Syrian environment, just as it is impossible to understand from the
picture he draws of Jewish leadership in the time of Jesus
how Johanan ben Zakkai single-handedly equipped the Jewish people with the means to survive the nineteen centuries
of the Diaspora even as a fossil.

IV

The central reason for the Jewish rejection of Jesus is put
by Professor Toynbee in the following sardonic terms:

'A son of man the Son of God? Was a generation in Jewry
that was heir to the whole of God's revelation to Abraham and Moses and the Prophets now called upon to betray this magnificent Jewish spiritual heritage by accepting one of those childishly shocking Hellenic *contes* of
the amours of Zeus which the wisdom of the Greeks
themselves had long since rejected as being neither intel-

lectually nor morally credible of the Godhead?' The question had only to be framed in order to answer itself in the negative in the mind of an orthodox Jew of the generation of Jesus. And so it came to pass that the Gospel of a Jewish Messiah who was God Himself incarnate was preached by Galileans and taken to heart by Gentiles [IV, 263].

Professor Toynbee seems to have forgotten that Justin Martyr, one of the greatest of the Church Fathers, appealed to the reading Roman world on the very basis of those "childishly shocking Hellenic *contes*."

When, indeed, we assert that the Word, our Teacher, Jesus Christ, who is the first-begotten son of God the Father, was not born as the result of sexual relations, and that he was crucified, died, arose from the dead, and ascended into heaven, we propose nothing new or different from that which you say about the so-called sons of Jupiter. You know exactly the number of sons ascribed to Jupiter by your respected writers . . . [*The First Apology*, Ch. 21, translated by Thomas B. Falls, 1948].

One would imagine from his tone of indignant irony that Professor Toynbee is himself a fundamentalist believer after the manner of the ancient Galileans whom he commends. Such, certainly, is the impression of Professor Geyl, who writes: "God become man in Christ is to him the veritable sense of history" (*Debates with Historians*, p. 96). But Professor Toynbee is a fundamentalist only when it suits a particular argument. Most of the time he is a religious relativist. As one of his correspondents complains:

Your description of Christianity is philosophical rather that historico-theological. . . . The Christian reader misses, in your account of Christianity, this insistence

upon its springing from a unique and particular historical event which is charged with eschatological significance. . . . The apparent under-estimation of the exclu-
siveness and universality of Christianity (the Christian
critic might continue) throws your comparison of Christianity with the other Higher Religions out of focus [Mar-
tin Wight, in Appendix to VII, 737–9].

In other words, Professor Toynbee makes the general impression of regarding Christianity as *a* religion, not *the* religion, which he could not if he believed that Jesus was God
Himself incarnate. Thus in one place he expresses himself
with ironical contempt for the Jews because they would not
believe what he himself rejects in other places. And thus,
unlike the Jews, he makes the best of both worlds or, as the
popular saying goes, works both sides of the street.

It is hardly correct to speak of the Christian Church as
having suffered "eviction from the Jewish fold" (see above,
p. 88). By the time there was a recognizable Christian
Church its dogmas were so utterly at variance with the beliefs of the Jewish people that it was obviously the Christian
Church that had "evicted" Judaism; unless, that is, one
wants to describe the Jews as "evicting" Christianity in not
accepting it. On the other hand it is undeniable that many
Jews who accepted Christ even as God's son were later
alarmed by the continuing infiltration into Christianity of
Greco-Roman Mystery rituals and Mystery meanings, and,
expressing their alarm, it was they who were evicted—from
the Christian Church. Rightly or wrongly they shrank from
the blood-and-flesh ritual—and one wonders whether Professor Toynbee is himself a believer in Transubstantiation,
or whether he actually agrees, at any rate occasionally, with
those dissident Jews of ancient times. The drinking of
blood, even in symbolic form—and Transubstantiation will

not permit the symbolizing away of the wine and the wa-
fer—was particularly abhorrent to the Jews. It is repeatedly
forbidden, in the most express terms, in the Jewish Bible;
and until this day the abhorrence is expressed in the preparation of meat for the orthodox Jewish kitchen. Professor
Toynbee is of course fully aware of the extent to which early
Christianity continued to take on Hellenic content and
form after its separation from Judaism. He observes, in fact,
that in its original form, with the Judaic element still strong
in it, Christianity was an alien intrusion into the Western
World.

Concerning the evolution of Christianity he writes: ". . .
the germ of creative activity, derived from the Syriac Society, out of which the internal proletariat of the Hellenic
Society generated the Catholic Church . . ." (above,
p. 70). Or, putting it conversely: "In Christianity, for example, we are aware of Hellenic elements . . . which the
original Syriac germ assimilated . . ." (above, p. 69 f.). The
less "alien" the "intruder" became—that is, the more the intruder Hellenized—the more alarmed many of the Chris-
tianizing Jews became. They had taken the first step, but
they could not take the second, or third, or fourth. Does
Professor Toynbee include *these* Jews in his ironical reference to Jewish intellectual-religious snobbery? Does he forget how many of these steps have, in fact, been retraced by
various branches of Protestantism, which have repudiated
them as concessions to idolatry? However that may be, the
mass of Jewry would not take even the first step, feeling,
perhaps, instinctively that a second, a third, and a fourth
would be demanded. And it is this refusal that so many
Christians throughout the ages have found unforgivable.

It is an ancient grudge. We may measure the rapidity of
its growth by comparing the Epistle of Clement of Rome,
third bishop of that city, in which the Eucharist is never

mentioned, and the guilt of the Jews in the Crucifixion never implied, with the Apologies of Justin Martyr, written more than fifty years later, in the middle of the second century, when the Gospels had assumed their final form and attained their permanent authority. That grudge represents the first great failure of Christianity, its lapse into anti-Jewishness and anti-Semitism; and it is none the less a failure if one retorts that it was from Judaism that Christianity acquired its intolerance. What was its special virtue if it could do no better? Christian thinkers, especially of late, have done their best to moderate the ancient resentment; it is disheartening to find the bitterness of the early Christians echoing, nearly eighteen centuries later, in the erudition of an Oxford don.

The hostility of Professor Toynbee is clearly revealed in another instance of "double-talk." Let us set side by side two quotations already made above:

1. "It is the supreme irony of Jewish history that the new ground captured for Judaism by the spear of Alexander Jannaeus . . . did bring to birth, within a hundred years, a Galilean Jewish prophet whose message to his fellow men was the consummation of all previous Jewish religious experience, and that this inspired Jewish scion of forcibly converted Galilean Gentiles was then rejected and done to death by the Judaean leaders of the Jewry of his age" (above, p. 88).

2. "In the tragedy of the passion of Christ we see the Scribes and Pharisees . . . actively ranging themselves at the side of the Roman authorities in the public light of the forum in order to compass the death of one of their very own race" (above, p. 84).

What are we to make of this curious injection of the racial factor into the question of Jesus' origins "according to the flesh"? And what are we to make of the shift of empha-

sis? When it is a question of Jesus' ministry, and his message, and his inspiration, he is entered in the register as the
scion of "forcibly converted Galilean Gentiles." When he is
"done to death" with the approval or assistance of the
Scribes and Pharisees he is "one of their very own race."

V

Deeper than this goes Professor Toynbee's treatment of
the meaning of the Crucifixion. I am not concerned here
with the historicity of the incident, for that is irrelevant to
Professor Toynbee's point. Let us concede that everything
happened more or less as the Gospels report, fusing the separate accounts into an acceptable unity. What do we have
then? That the Jews, or their leaders, had "done to death" a
great prophet, perhaps the greatest they had ever produced?
Not at all. That would not serve the point of view which
Professor Toynbee is projecting here as his own. For all peoples are, alas, in the habit of killing their prophets and
teachers. The English martyred their Protestant teachers
(having failed to martyr Wycliffe, they desecrated his
corpse); the French martyred Joan of Arc. The Bohemian
princes betrayed John Hus. If these do not rank among the
world's greatest, Socrates, put to death by the Athenians,
does. The death of Jesus, thus seen, would be such a tragedy, even if the most famous. But if Jesus was indeed, as
Professor Toynbee presents him here, God Himself incarnate, the problem takes on another aspect, which has often
been discussed, but nowhere, to my knowledge, more lumi-
nously than by the late Hayim Greenberg in his remarkable book *The Inner Eye.* (Would that he were alive and
writing in my place!)

As God Himself incarnate, Jesus differs from the Prophets
in that He came to earth for the express purpose of saving

mankind by being crucified. *He was not to be stopped from this fulfillment by any consideration.* He knew and foretold the manner of His death—the betrayal and the agony; and He rebuked any attempt to interfere with it. What we have here, therefore, is a unique incident of unique meaning, not to be confused with any other that resembles it, however closely, to the outward eye. I quote from Greenberg's "Letter to a Christian Clergyman":

> It is thus almost impossible to escape the conclusion that according to the authors of the New Testament there occurred in Jerusalem the enactment of a drama of providential fulfilment. Without this drama, without a crucified Jesus, there could have been no salvation nor that new covenant spoken of by Saul: "This is my body which is given for you. . . . This cup is the new testament in my blood. . . ." The guilt of the Jews who shared in the crucifixion must, according to the word and spirit of the New Testament, be considered as a *tragic guilt*; . . . on Golgotha there occurred not a historical event but a cosmic one, a divine comedy of fulfilment. To blame the Jews for the crucifixion is an indication that one is not, according to his mental make-up, a Christian, and has no conception of the mystery of death which became the foundation of a universal religion. One who does have that concept (a concept which must remain irrational) will, upon reading the New Testament, feel more sympathy for the two thieves who were crucified together with Jesus, two embittered and probably cynical human beings, than for the mortal incarnation of the deity and the suffering that He chose to undergo. A monotheistic religion may command that its followers *love* God, an emotion that cannot be compared with love of man, but it cannot preach *pity* for God. Only a primitive religion

could insert in its decalogue the commandment: "Thou shalt not kill thy God."

I have already indicated that for the most part Professor Toynbee takes the position of a religious relativist; or so it seems to his correspondent and me. Perhaps we are wrong. But if he does indeed accept Jesus as God incarnate, representing Him as God Self-sacrificed for the salvation of mankind, and then proceeds to denounce the Jews for His death, he degrades Him to the level of an *agent provocateur*.

VI

I have thought it proper to review with detailed comment the views expressed by Professor Toynbee on the Jewish relationship to Christianity, the Crucifixion, and certain other matters in the first six volumes of A *Study of History* even when in the last four volumes, published fifteen years later, he changes his ground on these matters and writes in a somewhat different tone. My reason for thinking it proper is that he does not retract and does not recognize that he has shifted ground; he does not admit that he has performed a public disservice by setting down as his own, and with whatever persuasiveness he commands, the immemorial prejudices that have been so costly to Jewish lives and to Christian morality. There is a bewildering unselfconsciousness in the total performance which is, perhaps, a necessary concomitant of the Blurring Effect; so that when he says something not in agreement with what he has said before, he does not seem to make a retraction, or even a modification, much less a confession of error. It is rather as if he would like to profess—not merely state—various points of view after the manner of someone building up a balanced portfolio of investments in stocks and bonds.

But it must be understood that retraction or self-correction is difficult when the original group of statements is itself vaporized by the Blurring Effect. When the larger blur emerges from the subsequent statement there is almost nothing the mind can fasten on as points of departure and arrival for the purpose of correction or retraction. In Volume VIII Professor Toynbee has this to say in explaining Christian mistreatment of Jews throughout the ages:

> One reason was that in the New Testament the Gospel of Love was accompanied by a polemical attack on the Pharisees [7] and was consummated by the story of the Passion of Christ; for these two particular ingredients in Christianity's holy writ could be taken by a latter-day Christian, who had the perverse will so to believe, as evidence that he was warranted by the New Testament itself in refusing to give the Jews the benefit of a Christian's general obligation to love and cherish his fellow human beings. In persuading the Roman authorities to put the founder of the Christian Church to death, the Jews in Christian eyes had committed a capital offence which was also an unspeakable impiety on the assumption that the Jews were grievously mistaken in rejecting the Christians' claim that the crucified Jesus was an incarnation of the Godhead. Thus, by a tragically ironical *peripeteia*, a Passion which, according to the Christian Church's theology, was a supreme act of self-sacrifice, willed, out of love for Mankind, by a God incarnate in a man who was a Jew, could be taken by professing Christians as a justification for persecuting latter-day kinsmen of Jesus' murderers, who were consequently kinsmen of Jesus himself; and the animus shown by the Evangelists in recording a contro-

[7] Alas for the Gospel of Love which is accompanied by a polemical attack! I prefer to believe that the polemical attack was attached later to the original gospel of love.

versy between Jesus and the Pharisees which was a family quarrel within the bosom of Jewry, and indeed *within the bosom of Pharisaism itself,* could incite Jesus' latter-day Gentile adherents to condemn their professed Master's own religion and community, root and branch [VIII, 283].

There is no meaning in the word "animus" if it does not apply to the quoted passages from Professor Toynbee's version of the story of the Crucifixion; there is no meaning in the word "polemical" if it does not apply to his repetition, with every mark of approval, of the New Testament denunciations of the Pharisees. And of retraction there is not the faintest hint.

CHAPTER SEVEN
THE NATURE OF JEWISH MONOTHEISM

I

Take away the flourishes, the bravuras of erudition, and what is left of Professor Toynbee's main presentation of the Crucifixion as it stands in the midst of his picture of the Jewish condition? Essentially, the old bogeyman story of the people accursed (fossilized) and doomed to live on under the curse (fossilization) for its inexpiable crime—a story no less miserable in its effects on Jewish-Christian relations than on the purity of Christian thought. For the charge of God-murder is one of the foundations of that anti-Semitism which, as a demonology, has afflicted the mind of the Christian West for many centuries, and by its supra-pathological nature stands apart from "normally" pathological hatreds of minorities.

Linked with this presentation is Professor Toynbee's espousal (intermittently contradicted, as usual, but frequent enough to leave its effect) of the view that Judaism had and has little value save as a prelude to Christianity, which is, says Professor Toynbee, "the consummation of all previous Jewish religious experience." According to this view the Prophetic inspiration which came from Israel, the vision of the One God, had as its sole purpose the ushering in of the Christian faith. But neither the ancient (or later) history of the Jewish people nor the content of the Jewish Bible—commonly called the Old Testament—is intelligible to the modern mind on those assumptions, which began to be untenable when Christian scholars admitted that in the famous sentence "Behold, a virgin shall conceive" (Isaiah vii, 14) a mistranslation had substituted "a virgin" for "the young woman." But on more general grounds a study of the Jewish Bible and of the total Jewish experience leads to an appreciation of the intrinsic significance of Judaism through an understanding of the nature of Jewish monotheism.

The Jewish Bible does not, contrary to the popular impression, shared by many Jews, state or imply that the first acknowledgment of the One God was Abraham's peculiar achievement or that He was unknown to others than Abraham's descendants. God spoke to Adam and Eve before the Fall, and received the offering of Abel after it; He also carried on a colloquy with Cain; and His identity was known to all four. For that matter, He addresses Himself, directly or in dreams, or through messengers, to unbelievers like Lot and Laban and the Abimelechs and Pharaoh. Noah and his sons too, long before Abraham, were addressed by God and knew Him. We are also told in the fourth chapter of Genesis that as far back as the second generation after Adam "men began to call upon the name of the Lord." Before the Flood, "Enoch walked with God, and he was not, for God took him." In the time of the Flood, Noah stood in an intimate relationship to God. In the time of Moses there was Balaam, a prophet of God belonging to another people than the Israelites. The Jewish Tradition exalts Enoch (Jewish boys, too, are still named after him), and places Balaam in the highest human rank imaginable to it, making him the equal of Moses, and adding that he was given to the non-Jewish peoples in order that they might not complain of discrimination.

Outside of the Bible there are instances of the recogni-

tion of God in ancient times, the most famous, perhaps, being that of Ikhnaton, mentioned by Professor Toynbee. Certain of the Stoics—Cleanthes, Epictetus, Marcus Aurelius,
and others—might be included. But the argument as to who
first conceived the notion of the One Universal God is as
pointless as the arguments that once went on as to who
first discovered and located the planet Neptune, the Englishman Adams or the Frenchman Leverrier, or who first
worked out the differential calculus, Newton or Leibnitz.
Not in the "discovery" of God lies the meaning of the Jews,
but in what they did with that discovery. For whereas many
individuals in moments of brilliant insight made the discovery before and after them, the Jews alone as a people sweated
out (the Yiddish word *oisgekrenkt* is better than "sweated
out") their monotheism over the millennia; they alone
made it their obsession as a people and somehow or other
hung on to it with unbelievable doggedness from its first
emergence four thousand years ago until this day; and the
record of the first half of this multimillennial torment is
that collection of books known as the Jewish Bible. One
may properly say that Judaism is meaningless without the
Jewish Bible, not because it tells of the discovery of God,
but because it mirrors the struggle of recalcitrant man with
the consequences of his discovery.

Thus we are dealing not with a discovery, but with a process. The Biblical record is a continuing drama. It is fragmen-
tary, a sacred anthology of excerpts in which there is frequent reference to other records, now lost. And yet, with
all its incompleteness, it is magnificently consistent and instructive. The theme is struggle: inspiration, defection, return, near-obliteration, re-emergence against all probability,
the picture of a people possessed by a divine destiny reluctantly assumed, everlastingly repudiated, everlastingly re-
claimed.

Professor Toynbee does not understand, does not seem to be willing to understand, that this is the peculiar drama of the peculiar people. He repeatedly gives ancient Judaism the aspect of a feature common to the "Syriac Civilization." Thus, as we have seen, he writes of "the Syriac legend of the creation of the Physical Universe when 'God saw everything that He had made' "! This attribution of the Genesis account of the Creation to the Syriac civilization utterly confounds the significance of the Jewish Bible at its outset. The late Solomon Goldman opens his vast, uncompleted study of the Jewish Bible with these striking words: "The Book of Genesis is the great clearing which the fashioners of the Jewish saga made in the jungle of primitive folklore." This is correctly and powerfully put. But the Book of Genesis is more than that. It is the repudiation by the Jews, the deliberate, willed, daring, single-handed repudiation of the Syriac and all the other ancient civilizations in the matter of their wild God-ideas. It is the *shofar*-blast before which the towers and temples and groves, with their images of demons and dragons and phallic and theophagous gods, collapse. The ruins of the buildings and their inhabiting monstrosities are scattered throughout the Jewish Bible, to the confusion of the literal-minded and the gratification of the cynical.

It is the proper task of the archæologist of ideas to try to identify the fragments: Was the *t'hom* ("the deep") originally *Tiamat*, the Babylonian dragon? It is worth thinking about, though not worth losing sleep on. Whence the story of the sons of God mating with the daughters of man to produce a race of giants? To what particular or general source may we trace the serpent? And so on, through not merely Genesis, but many of the Biblical books. Here is, indeed, a fruitful field for the study of cultural interrelationships. But these very fragments bring into bolder relief the unique nature of the effort which, beginning with the trumpet peal of the first sentence, gives the Book of Books its perdurable position among human utterances. In the ancient world that effort, so far as we know, is unique; as Professor Toynbee himself says, neither the "Syriac," nor the Egyptic, nor the Babylonic, nor the Minoan civilizations participated in it; and that effort, bound up with the everlasting struggle against inertia, relapse, and apostasy, expressed itself in the record that constitutes the Bible.

So much has been written, and by the most gifted writers, of the magnificence of the exordium to the Bible, that it would be absurd of me to seek to emulate them. I am concerned only with the definition of the Jewish drama as a peculiar and, thus far, humanly inexplicable experience. I am concerned with it here because an understanding of it destroys the theory of the one-time or non-recurrent inspiration as the basis of Judaism.

The drama of the Jewish people seems to proceed in a series of life-and-death crises, like one of the continuous movies of forty years ago. There is hardly a century in which the outside observer would give Judaism a dog's chance of surviving. At the very outset, during that theophany at Sinai which is remembered forever after as the binding agreement, the Israelites make themselves a molten calf; and the infuriated Deity bids Moses stand aside, "and My wrath shall wax hot against them, and I will make an end of them, and I will make of thee a great nation" (Exodus xxxii, 10). What an inauspicious start! Who, thereafter, would have counted on a future for this people? But this was not the only occasion on which immediate and total destruction threatened it from the very Source of Life even before it had set foot in the Promised Land. When the Israelites let themselves be frightened out of their wits by the reports the spies brought back from the still unconquered land, God said to Moses: "How long will this people despise Me? And how long will they not believe in Me, in spite of all the signs which I have wrought among them? I will strike them with the pestilence and disinherit them, and I will make of you a nation greater and mightier than they" [Numbers xiv, 11 f.].

On both these occasions God inspired Moses to dissuade Him from His fierce purpose, but the Israelites did not escape severe punishment. On the first occasion they were decimated, on the second they were sentenced to perish in the wilderness—only their children, a generation hence, should inherit the Promised Land. The Israelites, reacting blasphemously against the punishment for blasphemy, made their own forbidden attempt at immediate conquest and were disastrously repulsed. They proved their unworthiness again at Baal-Peor, where they yielded to the attractions of the temple prostitutes of the local idol and thousands of them died in the disciplinary action that followed (Numbers xxv). But is it necessary to dwell on the defections of the desert generation? Has it not become a byword among the nations?

One would have expected that the generation born in the desert, and the generations that followed, those which were in fact privileged to enter and conquer, would show a steadfastness lacking in the slave forebears whom Moses had led out of Egypt. They were no better. For we read, immediately after Joshua's death:

And the children of Israel did evil again in the sight of the Lord, and served the Baalim; and they forsook the Lord, the God of their fathers. . . . They went after other gods, of the gods of the people round about them, and worshipped them. . . . And the people of Israel did that which was evil in the sight of the Lord, and served the Baalim and the Asheroth. Therefore the anger of the Lord was kindled against Israel, and He gave them over into the hands of Cushan-Rishathayim, King of Aram-Narayim. . . . But when the children of Israel cried out unto the Lord, the Lord raised up a deliverer for the people of Israel . . . Othniel the son of Kenaz . . . and the people of Israel again did that which was evil in the sight of the Lord; and the Lord strengthened Eglon the King of Moab against Israel. . . . But when the people of Israel cried out unto the Lord, the Lord raised up a deliverer for them, Ehud the son of Gera. . . . And the people of Israel again did that which was evil in the sight of the Lord . . . and the Lord sold them into the hand of Jabin King of Canaan. . . .

Then it was Deborah the Prophetess who was sent to their rescue; and after forty years of tranquillity the monotonous chant is resumed:

The people of Israel did that which was evil in the sight of the Lord, and the Lord gave them into the hand of Midian seven years. . . . When the people of Israel cried unto the Lord on account of the Midianites, the Lord sent a prophet unto the people of Israel . . .

and the prophet chose Gideon to deliver the Israelites.

But the people of Israel again did that which was evil, and served the Baalim and the Asheroth, the gods of Syria, the gods of Sidon, the gods of Moab, the gods of the Ammonites, and the gods of the Philistines, and they forsook the Lord and did not serve Him . . . [Judges, passim].

One is tempted to say that the Israelites and God could neither get along together nor let go of each other. The period of Judges ends when the Israelites in one of their ever-recurrent assimilationist moods demand a king of Samuel.

All the elders of Israel gathered themselves together and came unto Samuel at Ramah. And they said unto him: "Behold, thou art old, and thy sons walk not in thy ways; now make us a king to judge us, like all the nations." But the thing displeased Samuel, and Samuel prayed unto the Lord. And the Lord said unto Samuel: "Hearken unto the voice of the people in all that they say unto thee; for they have not rejected thee, but they have rejected Me, that I should not be king over them. According to all the works which they have done since the day when I brought them up out of Egypt even unto this day, in that they have forsaken Me, and served other gods, so do they also unto thee" [I Samuel viii, 4–8].

If the reader objects, saying: "All this is legend. It was set down many centuries after the purported time," I answer that the consistency of the story with the later behavior of the Jewish people bespeaks more than legend. I also ask: "What purpose was there in the creation of such a discouraging legend by those who were obviously trying to influence the people to greater faithfulness? Far more intelligible would have been the usual romanticizing of the past into an example of purity and fidelity." To this, indeed, the Prophets did resort now and again, as when Jeremiah exclaims: "I remember thee, the kindness of thy youth, the love of thine espousals, when thou wentest after Me in the wilderness, in a land that was not sown" (Jeremiah ii, 2). And: "When Israel was a child, then I loved him, and out of Egypt I called My son" (Hosea xi, 1). But these praises of the dead past are few, while innumerable and crushing are the condemnations of Israel's ever-recurrent defections.

The pattern is maintained until the destruction of the Jewish Kingdoms. A brief and not wholly satisfying interlude is afforded by the reigns of David and Solomon: al-

ready Solomon, for all his wisdom, and for all God's favor,
failed in his later years:

> For it came to pass when Solomon was old, that his wives
> turned away his heart after other gods. . . . For Solo-
> mon went after Ashtoreth the goddess of the Zidoni-
> ans. . . . And Solomon did that which was evil in the
> sight of the Lord . . . [I Kings, xi, 4–6].

And after Solomon the Kingdom is split into Israel and
Judah.

If there are two periods of particular discouragement in
the story, they center on Elijah in Israel and Jeremiah in
Judah. We abandon all hope for Israel in the days of Elijah, when Jezebel, with the people collaborating, had liquidated all the Prophets of Jehovah; and Elijah, a broken-
hearted refugee in the wilderness, pours out his plaint to
God, and asks for death:

> It is enough; now, O Lord, take away my life. . . . I
> have been very jealous for the Lord, the God of hosts; for
> the children of Israel have forsaken Thy covenant, and
> slain Thy prophets with the sword; and I, even I only, am
> left; and they seek my life, to take it away [I Kings xix, 4,
> 14].

The last spiritual convulsions of the doomed Northern
Kingdom are portrayed with terrifying vividness in Ezekiel.
Samaria

> played the harlot when she was Mine: and she doted on
> her lovers, on the Assyrians, warriors, clothed in blue, gov-
> ernors and rulers, handsome young men all of them,
> horsemen riding upon horses: and she bestowed her har-
> lotries upon them, the choicest men of Assyria, all of
> them; and on whomsoever she doted, with all their idols
> she defiled herself . . . [Ezekiel xxiii, 5–7].

And so the Northern Kingdom of Israel was destroyed, and the ten tribes were scattered, never to be reassembled. The Southern Kingdom of Judah saved itself, or was saved —how and why we do not know if we take the narrative literally; for her behavior was apparently no better than that of the Northern Kingdom; if anything it was, according to the Prophet last quoted, worse. Jerusalem's lust for the worldly, the flashy, the vulgar, the successful, the militarily triumphant, the self-destructive, surpassed that of Samaria:

> She was more corrupt in her doting, and in her harlotries more than her sister in her harlotries. She doted upon the Assyrians, governors and rulers, warriors clothed most gorgeously, horsemen riding upon horses, all of them handsome young men. And I saw that she was defiled; they both took one way. And she increased her harlotries, for she saw men portrayed upon the wall, the images of the Chaldeans, portrayed with vermilion, girdled with girdles upon their loins, with pendant turbans upon their heads, all of them captains to look upon, the likeness of the sons of Babylon . . . [Ezekiel xxiii, 11–15].

But survive the Kingdom of Judah did—for a time; and the drama of the people and its God is now focused on that remnant of territory. Now surely the end must come, not only of the Kingdom, but of the people that inhabits it. For now that God has shown that He can destroy five sixths of His people, what hope for the remaining unrepentant sixth? Who can read the closing chapters of the Second Book of Kings, and the life of Jeremiah as it unfolds in his Book, without being tempted to exclaim: "Surely the remnant of this people disappeared from the face of the earth long ago, and these are its last utterances, miraculously preserved for a far-off future and—fortunately—deciphered by the labors of ingenious scholars. Or perhaps this people never existed, the record is such an improbable one. Perhaps it is all a fable, not quite intelligible to our modern mind. Perhaps it is a fabrication—perhaps—perhaps . . ."

To such reflections we would be tempted if the improbable record were not topped by the even more improbable survival of the people into our own day, and its vigorous protests against premature burial.

I will not rehearse here the stages of the fall of Judah; but I must point to the *completeness* of the demoralization as portrayed by Jeremiah at the time of the First Destruction. Even the remnant that might guarantee a future is defiled. When the Babylonian conqueror, unwilling to "create a desert and call it peace," leaves a portion of the people in Judah to carry on a minimum of economic activity, and appoints a Jewish Governor, Gedaliah, who pleads for submission and peace, the war party assassinates him; and to this day orthodox Jews observe an annual fast for Gedaliah. The handful flees the country into Egypt, dragging with it the protesting Jeremiah. There he still exhorts them, an old man, shattered in body, unshattered in spirit, pleading with his people till the end. His admonitions are greeted with mockery:

> Then all the men who knew that their wives offered unto other gods and all the women that stood by, a great assembly, even all the [Jewish] people that dwelt in the land of Egypt, in Pathros, answered Jeremiah, saying: As for the word that thou hast spoken unto us in the name of the Lord, we will not hearken unto thee. But we will certainly perform every word that has gone forth out of our mouths, to offer unto the Queen of Heaven, and to pour out drink-offering unto her, as we have done, we and our fathers, in the cities of Judah, and in the streets of Jerusalem . . . [Jeremiah xliv, 15–17].

The Tradition adds that Jeremiah was finally stoned to death by the Jews in Egypt.

And now let us note again that this is commonly regarded as the period of Israel's or Jewry's unchallengeable spiritual greatness. Where is that greatness? In the single soul of Jeremiah? Or shall we add his contemporary Ezekiel? Is this the greatness of a people? We shall have to return to this strange question: it is fundamental to our discussion.

Meanwhile, we move with the centuries. After an interval of two generations, a number of Jews returned from Babylonia to Judah, encouraged and assisted by the Emperor Cyrus. You will read of their condition and of the "promise" they held out, in the books of Nehemiah and Ezra and the last Prophets, Haggai and Zechariah and Malachi. It is the old story! For they failed again. It was to rescue them from the spiritual abyss into which they had fallen that Ezra and Nehemiah came to them from the Persian Empire with a new group of zealots (and how did *these* happen to arise?). We read the words of Nehemiah the son of Hachalia:

> Now it came to pass in the month of Chislev, in the twentieth year, as I was in Shushan the castle, that Hanani, one of my brethren, came out of Judah, he and certain men; and I asked them concerning the Jews that had escaped, that were left of the captivity, and concerning Jerusalem. And they said unto me: "The remnant that are left of the captivity there in the province are in great affliction and reproach. . . ." And it came to pass when I heard these words, that I sat down and wept . . . [Nehemiah 1, 1–4].

And now three hundred years pass, between the days of Ezra-Nehemiah and the days of the Maccabees, and for these three hundred years nothing is known of the history of the Jews in Judah. A few names have come down to us; an institution, The Great Synagogue, is mentioned; it is assumed that the Jews lived submissively under the alternating overlordships of the Egyptian Ptolemies and the Syrian Seleucids, the heirs of Alexander. And when the record resumes, we find, to our stupefaction, that a people has been reconstituted, a people so powerful that it can take up with undiminished vigor the everlasting drama! Powerful enough, that is, to go on struggling internally, to split, to be faithful, and to continue a relationship with God.

Of all the miracles of Jewish history I find none more baffling than this one. How did the handful of demoralized Jews—they cannot have numbered more than one hundred thousand—who in Ezra-Nehemiah's time were without Sabbaths and without festivals, who were dissolving out by intermarriage with idolatrous wives, how did this shapeless mass of Judeans, who, it would seem, were hardly better than the slaves who came out of Egypt, become the people that yielded a renegade half to the Asiatic Greeks and with the other half rescued itself for the far-off future? Ezra has been given the name of "the second Moses." If he was indeed responsible, by the laws and customs he instituted, for the re-establishment of the people, he merits the title. But we do not glimpse in him the magnificence of the first lawgiver; and we cannot understand, in the terms of this personality, how the mounting process continued for those three hundred years. We only know that in those blacked-out centuries the Books, with all their denunciations and tales of horror, but with all their incomparable visions of the One God, were edited, and perhaps some of them written; the Oral Tradition became a mighty thing; the Jewish Bible took on about the form in which we have it today; the foundations of the Mishnah were laid; the Pharisees emerged to leadership; the focus of vitality passed from the

Temple to the synagogue, from sacrifice to study, from the building to the Book.

The stories of the Jewish people's survival of the Seleucid and Roman attempts to destroy it are not less improbable than the earlier stories. To the north and south of Maccabee Judah were the Seleucids and the Ptolemies. Edom, Moab, Ammon, Philistia were vanishing—Judah should have vanished too. It did vanish under the Roman assault, but not before it had succeeded, while fighting off the Seleucid assault, in consolidating the new fortress, that of the spirit ("the ethos of Johanan ben Zakkai"), which was to withstand the battering of eighteen centuries. It perfected, beyond the power of time to destroy, that instrumentality of beliefs, rituals, traditions, and attachments which was to ensure the resumption, in the same place, of the same Jewish effort to come to terms with God.

II

To see the Jewish Bible as a static document rather than as the dynamic record of a long, painful, ever-unresolved struggle, is to miss its meaning. How completely Professor Toynbee has missed it we gather from his suggestions for its abridgment. He writes:

When the first translation of the Bible into a Teutonic language was made by Ulfilas, the apostle of the Goths, in the fourth century of our era, the translator wisely omitted the Books of Samuel and Kings, on the ground that war and bloodshed were too much in the minds of the Goths as it was, without their proclivity in this direction being consecrated and confirmed by the authority of the sacred book of their new religion. It is a pity that Luther and the English translators did not follow Ulfilas' example—or, indeed, improve on it by omitting Joshua and Judges as well! [I, 212 n.]

What Professor Toynbee would omit is the very heart of the portrayal of the process by which a people, sinful and obdurate, but somehow God-possessed, lived out the basic human drama. We should lose the clue to the organic meaning of the Prophets; we should be left with imperishable but enigmatic books from which the living background would have been removed. Nor can I refrain from pointing out that now these offending portions of the Bible have in fact been translated, and have achieved a certain currency, Professor Toynbee himself is not above making literary use of them, for he too is under the domination of their vivid reality. When he blames the Catholic Church and its oppressive attitude toward its sister churches for the spiritual debacle of modern Christianity, the simile that springs to his mind is the secession of Israel from Judah under the oppressive policy of King Jeroboam. When he seeks a simile for the totalitarian governments, he again brings up Jeroboam and his golden calves (IV, 581). When he wishes to illustrate one of the peaks of man's spiritual achievement, he must quote the vision of Solomon. Yet he would have the Western World ignorant not only of Solomon, but also of the characters of Gideon, Samson, Samuel, David, and of course of Ahab, Jezebel, and many others. He would omit Nathan's immortal and shattering rebuke to David for the murder of Uriah the Hittite, and the no less shattering rebuke of Elijah to Ahab for the judicial murder of Naboth. We should be lacking in the English language certain phrases which, though now overworked, are an organic part of it: "The still, small voice," "tell it not in Gath," "passing the love of women," "let my soul perish with the Philistines," and so on. Though, to be sure, we should have in their place Professor Toynbee's ten-volume work in its un-diminished plenitude.

But to return to the character of the Jewish Bible: Professor Toynbee cites, as I have mentioned, the vision of Solomon as one of the loftiest moments in human experience. He writes:

A Syriac [1] fable tells how this divinity once tested a king of Israel with the most searching test that a God can apply to a mortal. 'The Lord appeared to Solomon in a dream by night; and God said: "Ask what I shall give thee." And Solomon said: ". . . Give . . . thy servant an understanding heart." . . . And the speech pleased the Lord, that Solomon had asked this thing. And God said unto him: "Because thou hast asked this thing, and hast not asked for thyself long life; neither hast asked riches for thyself, nor hast asked the life of thine enemies; but hast asked for thyself understanding to discern judgment; behold, I have done according to thy words: lo, I have given thee a wise and an understanding heart, so that there was none like thee before thee, neither after thee shall arise any like unto thee. And I have also given thee that which thou hast not asked, both riches and honour, so that there shall not be any among the kings like unto thee all thy days." '

This fable of Solomon's Choice is a parable of the his-

[1] Cf. André Gide's *Journals*, Justin O'Brien's translation (IV, 297): "I pick out this gem from *Les Lettres françaises* of 28 April 1949: 'An ancient legend relates that two women had come before a very wise judge; they were disputing over the possession of a certain infant. The woman who wanted to pass herself off as the mother answered the judge: "Cut the child in two." She spoke thus because the child was not hers. . . .' (Ilya Ehrenburg: *Speech at the Congress of Peace*.)" Poor Ehrenburg, not wanting to give any credit to the Bible (or perhaps not wanting to betray any knowledge of it though finding the anecdote irresistible) was not quick-witted enough to make a learned noise and refer to a "Syriac" fable.

tory of the Chosen People. In the power of their spiritual understanding, the Israelites surpassed the military prowess of the Philistines and the maritime prowess of the Phoenicians. They had not sought after those things which the Gentiles seek, but had sought first the kingdom of God; and therefore all those things were added unto them. As for the life of their enemies, the mighty men of the Philistines were delivered into Israel's hands to be smitten with the edge of the sword. As for riches, Jewry entered into the inheritance of Tyre and Carthage to conduct transactions on a scale beyond Phoenician dreams in continents beyond Phoenician knowledge [II, 55].

Not bad, by the way, for a people that had "forfeited its material future." But this "Syriac" fable, which for some incomprehensible reason is a parable of the history of the Chosen People, and not of the Syriac society, has been misread by Professor Toynbee. The "fable" has a wider meaning in its wider context; and if it is a parable of the Jewish people and its Bible, it is so by virtue of those imperfections in Solomon's character which struggled with his wisdom. The point of the whole fable is that the wisest man in the world was able to make a fool of himself. Even so the most God-haunted man, David, was able to commit murder. The most commanding figure in Jewish history, Moses —and he praised for his meekness, too—was subject to disastrous fits of choler and forfeited his right to enter the Promised Land by losing his temper with a rock. The Patriarchs, too, were not without blemish: Abraham and Isaac disowned their wives in moments of cowardice; Jacob discriminated almost fatally among his sons. The Jewish Tradition, which, since the completion of the Bible, provides an ever-renewing commentary on the Text, shows no inclination to gloss over these imperfections, let alone excise them from the record; for the Jewish Tradition understands the purpose of the Bible.

One can sympathize with Ulfilas, who, as Professor Toynbee puts it, was afraid that the Goths, studying the Jewish Bible, would find their bloodthirstiness "consecrated and confirmed." And Professor Toynbee himself traces to Old Testament influence the bloodthirstiness of the Protestant peoples toward "Natives" and alien races generally:

> . . . our modern Western race-feeling—inspired, as we have seen it to be, by the spirit imbibed from the Old Testament by Protestantism . . . [I, 223].

One could have added much in the way of edification to the Old Tesament—and also reduced it to inanity—by omitting the nasty parts; and it would be interesting to see what Professor Toynbee would produce by playing Parson Weems to it. Perhaps what we should learn from the Old Testament as it stands is the danger of public confession; and I have observed elsewhere that the penitent sinner makes a poor teacher because his pupils always want to go to the same school.

It may surprise the reader to learn that Professor Toynbee, the believing Christian, does not credit the New Testament with such improvement as has now taken place in this regard among modern Christians.

> Of course the fanaticism and ferocity of the race-feeling which the Old Testament once instilled into Protestant souls have both considerably abated as Protestantism itself has evolved through Rationalism toward Agnosticism [I, 214].

If the Old Testament instills race hatred and the New Testament does not drain it away, what does Professor Toynbee want either of them for? But of this question of the Old Testament attitude on race and on strangers, more below.

When the sins of the Jews are cited against them on the authority of the Prophets, it is easily forgotten that the Prophets themselves are products of the Jewish people. The record of their ministrations from Moses to Malachi shows that a continuous force was at work in the people, and its survival as a Jewish people is connected with the persistence of that force. One cannot tell where the force resided, or in what proportion of the people. Clearly the denunciations of the Prophets are hyperbolic: a people as rotten as they represent the Jews to have been could not have survived for a single century.[2] We see an instance of this exaggeration in Elijah's case. He complains to God: "The children of Israel have forsaken Thy covenant, and slain Thy prophets with the sword; and I, even I only, am left." And God answers: "Yet will I leave seven thousand in Israel, all the knees which have not bowed to Baal, and every mouth which hath not kissed him." And in fact by the time Elijah was carried to heaven in the fiery chariot, a considerable school of prophets had already been established by Elisha (II Kings ii).

"Whatever lives," says Goethe, "deserves to die." This is as true of the Jewish people as of every other. But the Jewish people does not die. Its refusal to do so is bound up with an obstinate principle of search which keeps on triumphing over successive failures. Somewhere in the folk, even when the largest part of it has fallen away, the principle reasserts itself and maintains the line. It is as though

[2] Cf. Samuel Dill's observations on Juvenal's extravagant denunciations of Roman society, which "suggest a doubt whether the cancer of luxury had struck so deep as satirists thought into the vitals of a society which remained for so many centuries erect and strong" (*Roman Society from Nero to Marcus Aurelius*, 1920, p. 67).

the folk-soul were saying to itself: "I am not going to die until I have found out what this is all about." The principle which runs through the Bible and gives a special meaning to its monotheism, making it infinitely more than a single flash of intellectual insight, runs also through the later history of Jewry; the story continues with a consistency that reflects a convincing verisimilitude back on the Bible narrative, and we shall see that while the Bible has given that principle classical expression, it has not exhausted its operation.

CHAPTER EIGHT

THE BAD
EXAMPLE

I

THERE are still one or two matters to be dealt with in the values of ancient Jewry, Biblical and post-Biblical, as portrayed in A *Study of History* before we proceed to medieval and modern times.

Professor Toynbee writes:

> The race-feeling engendered by the English Protestant version of our Western culture became the determining factor in the development of race-feeling in our Western Society as a whole.
>
> This has been a misfortune for Mankind, for the Protestant temper and attitude and conduct in regard to Race, as in many other vital issues, is inspired largely by the Old Testament; and in matters of Race the promptings of this old-fashioned Syriac oracle are *very clear and very savage* [I, 211].

We shall find in Professor Toynbee's remarks on this subject some rather fine examples of the Blurring Effect at its best. A little farther on we read: "Our modern Western race-feeling, inspired, as we have seen it to be, by the spirit imbibed from Old Testament Protestantism . . ." (quoted above, p. 121). We have, of course, not seen it to be anything of the sort; we have only seen Professor Toynbee's statement that he sees it to be so. But I shall shortly quote still another passage, occurring only twenty-three pages far-

ther on, in which it appears that Professor Toynbee does
not think the Old Testament promptings in matters of race
"very clear and very savage." Before I do that, we may as
well consider the facts.

As anyone with a moderate knowledge of the Old Testament knows, its attitude on *race* is very clear, but the reverse
of savage. "Can an Ethiopian change his skin?" (Jeremiah
xiii, 23) affirms the immutability of physical racial characteristics; but that the physical characteristics of a race are
not linked with damnation or salvation is clear in: "Are ye
not as the children of the Ethiopians unto Me?" (Amos ix,
7); for the meaning is: "If the Ethiopian is precious to Me,
are not you, Israel, at least as precious?" But the matter is
placed beyond all doubt by the incomparable prayer occurring in Solomon's dedication of the Temple:

> Moreover concerning the stranger that is not of Thy peo-
> ple Israel, when he shall come out of a far country for
> Thy name's sake—for they shall hear of Thy great name,
> and of Thy mighty hand, and of Thine outstretched arm
> —when he shall come and pray toward this house; hear
> Thou in heaven Thy dwelling-place and do according to
> all that the stranger calleth to Thee for [I Kings viii,
> 41-3].

This passage would be unknown if all we had was Professor
Toynbee's expurgated translation of the Bible.

Further, it is recorded that Moses in his latter years married an Ethiopian (Numbers xii, 1)—to the resentment of
his family; but it is not stated that their resentment was directed at her race. Ebed-melech the Ethiopian is one of the
fine characters in the Book of Jeremiah (xxxviii f.). Naaman
the Syrian had but to bathe in the Jordan at Elisha's suggestion, and, being cured of his leprosy, became a believer

(II Kings v—another of Professor Toynbee's "suppressed" books).

The attitude of the Old Testament on *nations* which were to be conquered is sometimes very savage indeed, but we shall learn from additional quotations that the racial factor had nothing to do with that. We shall see that the admonitions to treat with the utmost solicitude the man of alien *race* dwelling among the Jews build up a moving ethic of, I will not say tolerance, but interracial brotherhood.

I ought to remark that in a dim way Professor Toynbee seems to suspect at the outset that somewhere or other he is going to change his mind, for he adds in a footnote:

> The Old Testament, of course, *is only representative of the Syriac religious genius in its young and callow phase;* and even in this phase, toward its latter end, there was an outburst of spiritual experience and spiritual creation—recorded in the Books of the Prophets—which points forward to the New Testament [I, 211 n.].

This mumbled correction of the error contains an additional error which is perhaps graver than the first; for the powerful admonitions on the subject of the stranger and foreigner (that is, the man of different race dwelling among the Israelites) occur with great frequency in those strata of the Bible which are accepted as preceding the later Prophets; they were not, therefore, first uttered during what Professor Toynbee here calls the later "outburst of spiritual experience."

Apart from this, we have already seen (above, p. 121) that Professor Toynbee ascribes the credit for the abatement of race feeling among modern Protestants not to the "ripened" phase of the Syriac religion—that is (according to him), the New Testament and Christianity—but to the spread of Rationalism and Agnosticism. It is also well to

compare the above "damn-with-faint-praise" reference to
the old heritage defended by the Prophets with the passages
("mighty feat of spiritual intuition," "unparalleled spiritual
insight," etc.) that speak of it with apparently boundless
admiration.

The savageries committed by the Israelites in their conquest of the Promised Land were revolting. There are
open admonitions to the indiscriminate slaughter of men,
women, and children. But as regards the race feeling behind
these admonitions, as regards the extent to which the Jews
were convinced that they alone had the kind of blood which
ensures to a people salvation and survival, Professor Toynbee expresses himself thus:

> The Jews have been intensely conscious of being not as
> other men are. In their view of the World, there is a great
> gulf fixed between them and the Gentiles; and they are as
> sincerely convinced as the English or the Americans of
> their own immeasurable superiority to 'the lesser breeds
> without the Law.' . . . Yet, in their heart of hearts, the
> Jews—unlike the English-speaking Protestants who claim
> to be their spiritual heirs—have ever been aware that Yah-
> weh's choice is neither irrevocable like the Laws of the
> Medes and Persians, nor immutable like 'the Laws of Na-
> ture'; and their self-complacency was not impervious to
> John the Baptist's mortal thrust: 'Think not to say within
> yourselves: "We have Abraham to our father"; for I say
> unto you that God is able of these stones to raise up chil-
> dren unto Abraham.' This text is a profound criticism of
> the fallacy of Race—a fallacy to which the Jews, to their
> credit, have never succumbed completely [I, 246 f.].

This is surely an astonishing exhibition of self-contradic-
tion; but it is capped by the following:

The Jewish and Christian doctors have never fallen into
the error of accepting Race as an explanation of the actual differences in human performance and achievement,
whether between communities or between individuals;
and they have satisfied their intellectual demand for an
adequate cause by postulating an act of God. This postu-
late, which Syriac and Western theologians have made in
all good faith, has been commended by a Hellenic philosopher [Plato] as a pious fraud which is required by social expediency and is justified by *raison d'état* [I, 247].

And now in a contradiction within a contradiction which
reminds one of an exhausting spy-counter-spy story, Professor Toynbee has the following:

> The Protestant background of a Modern Western race-
> feeling has been examined in II. i. 211–27. In this context
> it has been pointed out that, though this moral and in-
> tellectual aberration was inspired by an interpretation of
> the Pentateuch (bic., pp. 211–12), this latter-day Protes-
> tant Western Christian reading of the Hebrew Scriptures
> *had no warrant in the traditional attitude of the Jews*,
> whose consciousness of being distinct from, and superior
> to, the rest of Mankind was founded on a belief that they
> were a 'Chosen People' in virtue of an historic covenant
> made with Abraham by the One True God, and not on a
> belief that they were scions of an aboriginally and inde-
> feasibly superior physical race. . . . the Jews themselves
> never fell into their Protestant Western Christian paro-
> dists' error of ascribing a rigidly racial significance to the
> historic distinction between 'the seed of Abraham' and
> 'the Goyyim' till the Zionists caught this psychic infec-
> tion from their Nazi persecutors [VIII, 576, n. 2].

John the Baptist's "mortal thrust" is not the first repudiation of race pride among the Jews. Ezekiel, six centuries be-

fore him, flung these words at the Jews: "Your mother was a Hittite and your father was an Amorite" [xvi, 45]. Marriage with women of alien race was not forbidden to the ancient (as it is not to the modern) Jews, as we know from the ritual prescribed for the taking to wife of a woman of alien race captured in war [Deuteronomy xxi, 10 ff.]. Moses had as his first wife a woman of the Midianites, and in his old age, as we have seen (I mean *really* seen), an Ethiopian —that is, a Negress. Ruth the Moabitess, who married into the faith, is accepted as the progenitress of the Messiah. It was the sapping of the faith by idolatrous wives, not the deterioration of the stock through an admixture of foreign blood, that had to be prevented; and the instances of Solomon in his old age, seduced to the gods of the surrounding peoples by his numerous wives, and of Ahab, married to the slayer of Prophets, Jezebel, daughter of Ethbaal, King of Zidon, are sufficient to point the moral.

Thus the merciless directives given the early Israelites against the people they were conquering reflect their proneness to idolatrous infection and do not rest upon a racial principle. In the wilderness, shortly before their entry into Canaan, the Israelites were led into apostasy by the women of Midian and Moab at Baal-Peor. In the ensuing war against the Midianites, the Israelites were victorious and took the women captive. Then we read:

And Moses was wroth with the officers of the host . . . when they came from the service of the war. And Moses said: Have ye saved all the women alive? Behold, these caused the children of Israel, through the counsel of Balaam, to revolt so as to break faith with the Lord in the matter of Peor [Numbers xxxi, 14–16].

The problem of survival for the Israelites was spiritual, not ethnic, and this overriding ideological factor, recurring con-

tinuously in the conquests of the Israelites, removes from
them—as Professor Toynbee himself is compelled to agree
(with calm disregard of his indictment to the contrary)—
the charge of racism.

But when we come to the laws and exhortations having
to do with the treatment of children of alien race dwelling
among the Israelites, we of the modern world are—or should
be—rebuked by the understanding and compassion there displayed. The same note dominates from—again—Moses to
Malachi. The stranger, the homeless one, the alien, are
classed with the widowed and the fatherless in their special
claim to just and gentle treatment; and the Jews are sternly
reminded that they must *understand* the stranger, they must
see into his heart.

> For the Lord your God He is a God of gods, the great
> God, the mighty, and the awful, who regardeth not per-
> sons, nor taketh reward. He doth execute justice for the
> fatherless and the widows, and loveth the stranger. Love
> ye therefore the stranger, *for ye were strangers in the land
> of Egypt* [Deuteronomy x, 17 f.].
> Cursed be he that perverteth the justice due to the stran-
> ger, the fatherless and the widow [Deuteronomy xxvii,
> 19].
> And a stranger shalt thou not oppress, *for ye know the
> heart of a stranger, seeing ye were strangers in the land of
> Egypt*. . . . Thou shalt not glean thy vineyard, thou
> shalt not wholly reap the corner of thy field, neither shalt
> thou gather the gleaning of thy harvest . . . neither
> shalt thou glean the fallen fruit of thy vineyard; thou
> shalt leave them for the poor and the stranger: I am the
> Lord your God [Exodus xxiii, 9; Leviticus xix, 9 f.].
> The stranger that sojourneth with you shall be unto you
> as the home-born among you, and thou shalt love him as

thyself; *for ye were strangers in the land of Egypt:* I am
the Lord your God [Leviticus xix, 34].
One law and one ordinance shall be both for you, and for
the stranger that sojourneth with you [Numbers xv, 16].

So much for the earliest Mosaic laws and admonitions
preceding the spiritual "outburst" referred to by Professor
Toynbee. For disobeying these laws and admonitions the
Israelites were furiously upbraided by the Prophets.

If ye thoroughly amend your ways and your doings; if ye
thoroughly execute justice between a man and his neighbor; if ye oppress not the stranger, the fatherless and the
widow . . . then I will cause you to dwell in this place
[Jeremiah vii, 5 f.].
Do no wrong, do no violence, to the stranger, the fatherless, nor the widow [Jeremiah xxii, 3].
The princes of Israel . . . in the midst of thee have dealt
by oppression with the stranger [Ezekiel xxii, 6 f.].
The people of the land have used oppression, and exercised robbery, and have wronged the poor and the needy,
and have oppressed the stranger unlawfully [Ezekiel
xxii, 29].
Oppress not the widow, nor the fatherless, nor the stranger, nor the poor [Zechariah vii, 10].
I will be a swift witness . . . against those that oppress
the hireling in his wages, the widow and the fatherless,
and that turn aside the stranger from his right, and fear
not Me [Malachi iii, 5].

It is important to remember that the problem of race feeling relates not only to external contacts between peoples,
but to internal contacts with individuals and minorities. If
race feeling is present in the quotations here given, it is in
the admirable sense of a generous sympathy, a gentle ap-

proach to the unlike. Let it also be noticed that the Jews could and did recognize the inalienable right of neighboring peoples to the possession of their territories. Concerning the Edomites we read:

> Ye are to pass through the border of your brethren the children of Esau, that dwell in Seir; and they will be afraid of you; take ye good heed unto yourselves, therefore; contend not with them; for I will not give you of their land, no, not so much as for the sole of the foot to tread on; because I have given Mount Seir unto Esau for a possession. Ye shall purchase food of them for money, that ye may eat; and ye shall also buy water of them for money, that ye may drink [Deuteronomy ii, 4 f.].

And concerning the Ammonites:

> When thou comest nigh over against the children of Ammon, harass them not, nor contend with them; for I will not give thee of the land of the children of Ammon for a possession; because I have given it unto the children of Lot [Deuteronomy ii, 19].

Why do Christian racists and anti-racists alike point to the Biblical Jews as the classic, or indeed the first, protagonists of race hatred, upon whose descendants has properly been visited the curse they spread among mankind? And why does A Study of History intermittently give the accusers aid and comfort? The deliberate misrepresentation of a clear text to support the opposite point of view, so that, in this case, insult is added to boundless injury, is surely something to which Philosophers of History should not lend themselves.

Moreover, if one takes the ancient Jewish record as a whole, it is seen as a struggle between good and evil at a time and in a setting that give that struggle poignant significance. No record resembling it has come down from any other people; and no other people has admitted its guilt and accepted its punishment in the astonishing terms that the Jews have made their sanctity. Why, then, does a "Christian" writer focus on sins that have been atoned for, and add to them sins never committed? And could not Bible-readers who are so inclined find the sin of adulterous murder "consecrated and confirmed" in the case of David and Bathsheba? But these are rhetorical questions that invite reflection and do not require an answer. They are relevant here only to the extent that *A Study of History* is symptomatic of this problem.

II

We have just reviewed, all too hastily, the ideal attitude toward the alien set forth in that Old Testament, which is, after all, as Professor Toynbee reminds us, "only representative of the Syriac religion in its young and callow phase." Of course the behavior of the Jews was often very far from ideal. Not that Christianity has, in Professor Toynbee's view, done any better:

> The ideal of our modern Western Democracy has been to apply in practical politics the Christian intuition of the fraternity of all Mankind; but the practical politics which this new democratic ideal found in operation in the Western World were not oecumenical and humanitarian [after eighteen hundred years of Christianity] but were tribal and militant. The modern Western democratic ideal is thus an attempt to reconcile two spirits and to resolve two forces which are in almost diametrical opposition. [I, 9].

And again:

> In the history of Man's attempt at Civilization hitherto
> there has never been any society whose progress in Civ-
> ilization has gone so far that, in times of revolution or
> war, its members could be relied upon not to commit
> atrocities. To confine ourselves to the history of our own
> society in our own generation, we can cite the behaviour
> of the German Army in Belgium in 1914 and the British
> 'Black-and-Tans' in Ireland in 1920 and the French Army
> in Syria in 1925–6 and the German Nationalist-Socialist
> 'Storm Troops' at home in 1933 [this was written before
> the Second World War] and the Italian Blackshirts at
> Addis Ababa in February 1937 . . . [IV, 128 f.].

We are, incidentally, the more disappointed in the "Black-
and-Tans" because, according to Professor Toynbee, they
had already had the benefit of that humanizing movement
through "Rationalism toward Agnosticism" which applies
to the Old Testament the moral corrective lacking in the
New.

His strictures against the Jews for not accepting Christianity are repeated in another form, and with equal severity, when he speaks of the allied sin of their mundaneness
and their proneness to rebellion against oppression before
and after the coming of Christ. He sets up for this people *as
a whole* a wildly unrealistic standard of behavior, and is not
content that a significant part of it clings to the ideal. He
lumps together as equally reprehensible Zerubbabel's deter-
mination to reconstruct the Jewish State after the Babylonian captivity, the conquest of Galilee by the Hasmonean
Alexander Jannæus, and the revolts of 66–70, 115–17, and
132–5. He writes:

Bar Kōkabā in A.D. 132–5 was pursuing the same end by the same means as Zerubbabel about the year 522 B.C. [VI, 123].

Now, this Second State, founded by Zerubbabel, did, in Professor Toynbee's view, follow the Way of Gentleness for three hundred years (above, pp. 81 f.). It did more, as we have seen. It kept Judaism alive. The Babylonian community that first established and then reinvigorated the Second Jewish State disappears from history for several hundred years. No word has reached us of its condition between the time of Ezra-Nehemiah and the first centuries of the Christian era except what can be doubtfully gleaned from the Book of Esther. Hillel had come from Babylon to Jerusalem, some two generations before the Christian era, to receive his education. Nearly three centuries later Rab "Arika," the most important figure in the history of Babylonian Jewry, also came, together with his uncle Hiya, to study in Palestine under the great Judah the First. Rab, unlike Hillel, returned to Babylon to become the molder of its Jewish life. And this, let us remember, was two centuries after the Romans had done their best to stamp out Judaism altogether with the Second State. In that State, so unworthily created by mundane means ("every one with one of his hands wrought in the work and with the other hand held a weapon": Nehemiah, iv, 17), the Bible was preserved, edited, and put into that permanent form which was to be the heritage of Jews and Christians for millennia to come. It is idle to plead that all this could have been done elsewhere and otherwise. This is how it happened.

I am not seeking here to justify the means by the end. I am only drawing attention to the tangle of good and evil in history. It is Professor Toynbee who beclouds the ends-and-means issue. For if the Jews set a bad example in re-creating their state by mundane means after the Babylonian exile, they did not set a good one when they founded it originally by conquest. But in regard to that first episode Professor Toynbee strikes a quite different note, in spite of his dislike of the means.

In their Exodus from Egypt, the Children of Israel—though they hanker in the wilderness after the fleshpots of the house of bondage—give birth to a generation which helps to lay the foundations of the Syriac Civilization in taking possession of the Promised Land [II, 73].

The readiness of Professor Toynbee to see in the earlier "evil" a creative act casts a shadow of partisanship (to put it mildly) on his condemnation of the identical later "evil." If he were to argue: "Better if the Israelites had never conquered Canaan, and had never established the First Kingdom! Better if they had never been than that they should have fought with material weapons for their existence! Better, in fact, if all history had not been!" one might understand him as a total pessimist. As it is, he leaves us with the strong presumption that if the Jews had accepted Christianity he would not have been so hard on Zerubbabel, on Judas Maccabæus, and perhaps even on Alexander Jannæus. At any rate, he does not seem to hold it against the Italians, who are Christians, that *their* ancestors had something to do with the Crucifixion.

But as usual we shall find a bewildering fuzziness of view even in this condemnation in the use of Violence. Concerning the Maccabees he writes, as we have seen, that they originally drew their swords in self-defense "in order to save the Jewish religion from extinction" [above, p. 82]. He does not seem to condemn that. Why then, once more, does he condemn the establishment of the Second Jewish State, which certainly as much as the Maccabean revolt saved the Jewish religion from extinction? He condemns, of course, the Hasmonean conquest of Galilee and the forcible Judaization of the Galileans. It is proper to note once more that the Hasmonean rulers were deviants from the Jewish tradition; and until this day the festival of Chanukkah celebrates not their later conquests, but the early successful defense of the faith and the cleansing of the Temple. In bringing to the fore, with reiterated insistence, this bad example which the Jews set, Professor Toynbee seems to forget that the immediate "example" of religious persecution came from the Seleucid oppressors; and that the world needed no example of this kind, alas, is also evident from the following:

> This enormity of intolerance and persecution in the cause of Unity has shown its hideous countenance, almost without fail, wherever and whenever a 'higher religion' has been discovered and formulated and preached [IV, 224].

Christianity included, of course.

Now, whether the Jewish revolts of 66–70, 115–17, and 132–5 fall under the "permissible" or "condonable" rubric of the Maccabean revolt, or are to be condemned *in toto* is something that cannot be answered out of hand. Each event must be examined separately and a judgment must be formed whether, under those particular circumstances, one could expect a people—even one that had followed the Way of Gentleness for over three centuries—not to explode into Violence. In the same way the morality of the establishment of the Second Jewish State must be weighed in the light of reasonable human feelings. Professor Toynbee's demand that all the Jews should always have behaved as no people has ever behaved in the past, or will behave before the millennium, is perhaps an unintended compliment. But it is overdone. The achievements of the Jewish people are considerable; to chide them, and with such vexation of spirit, for not being superhuman is a moral affectation. We shall meet it again, in stronger form, when we come to consider Professor Toynbee's attitude toward Zionism and the founding of the Third Jewish State.

Let us recall the exact words in which Professor Toynbee voices his abhorrence (we may fairly call it that) at the incidents we are discussing:

> The Maccabees inaugurated that long line of ever-fanatically militant Zealots—the innumerable Theudases and Judases of Galilee—whose violence reached its appalling climax in the Satanic Jewish *émeutes* of A.D. 66–70, 115–17 and 132–5 [V, 387].

Strong words, these; extremely edifying too. Unfortunately there seems to be a struggle in Professor Toynbee, unbeknownst to him, between Christian Pacifism and a Hellenic-Pagan admiration of the warrior *qua* warrior. For in one of those purple passages in which he pursues any promising hint no matter where it leads, he pays glowing tribute, in almost moral terms, to the same Satanic militants:

> The debris of this devoted Syriac people which took up the Hellenic challenge so gallantly and was shattered so remorselessly by the impact of Rome is drifting about the World down to this day, as the ash-dust once floated in the atmosphere and tinged the colours of the sunset on the other side of the planet, for weeks after the great eruption of Krakatoa. This pulverized social ash is familiar to us as the Jewish 'Diasporà.' The scattered survivors of Jewry are left with the cold consolation of remembering that their forefathers volunteered on a forlorn hope

and went down to destruction in a splendid failure [II, 286].

This from the apostle of the Way of Gentleness! Mr. Churchill, whipping Britain on to its magnificent war efforts in its "darkest hour," could not have done better.

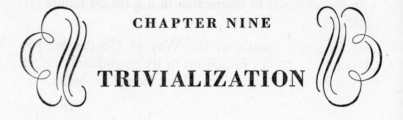

CHAPTER NINE

TRIVIALIZATION

I

Bagatelisierung is the exact but untranslatable German word for it. "Trivialization" is the nearest I can get to it in readable English.[1] I mean the denaturizing of a big thing by making it out, in a niggling way, to be an unimposing collection of little things.

It is essential to Professor Toynbee's thesis of the fossildom of Jewry and Judaism that they shall be presented as an example of continuity in spiritual and cultural sterility, and that their survival shall be attributed to factors that trivialize out of existence both inner meaning and external influence. This, we have seen, is done by simply ignoring the content of Jewry and its role in Western civilization—I refer, of course, to the Jewry of the Middle Ages and of modern times. The mechanical interplay between Jewry and the outside world cannot be entirely ignored if one is to write about the Jews at all; the description must, however, be shot through with belittling implications. All this, *en passant*, after the author has spoken of the persistent cultivation of the ethos of Johanan ben Zakkai.

Writing under the heading of "Stimulus of Penalizations," Professor Toynbee has this to say of religious minorities:

They have learnt to hold their own in any human environment in which they are allowed to exist on sufferance

---

[1] "Floccinaucinihilipilification" is better, but not so readable.

by excelling in those trades and handicrafts to which their
activities have been compulsorily confined.

The Jews, for example, have overcome the social hand-
icap which their religious idiosyncrasy entails by holding
their own successfully, as traders and financiers, in a great
variety of human environments. They have found a place
for themselves first in the Syriac and Hellenic worlds and
then in the Arabic and Iranic and Western worlds; and
during the last few centuries they have kept pace with the
expansion of Western Christendom until nowadays their
activities and interests extend, as widely as those of our
modern Western Society itself, over all the habitable
lands and navigable seas on the face of the planet [II,
235 f.].

The Ashkenazim [the bulk of European Jewry as it was
before Nazism and Communism, and the bulk of the
American Jewries] are descended from Jews who took advantage of the opening-up of Europe by the Romans and
made a Jewish perquisite of the retail trade in the semi-
barbarous Transalpine provinces. Since the conversion
and break-up of the Roman Empire, these Ashkenazim
have had to suffer doubly from the fanaticism of the
Christian Church and from the resentment of the barbarians. A barbarian cannot bear to see a resident alien
living a life apart and making a profit by transacting business which the barbarian lacks the skill to transact for
himself; and the barbarian neophytes of Western Christendom have been humiliated by the superior ability and
filled with envy by the superior prosperity of the indispensable Ashkenazic Jew [II, 241].

One may attach innocent connotations to words like
"took advantage" and "perquisite." The Jews "took advantage" of a dangerous and difficult opportunity. It was no

light thing to venture into the semi-barbarous provinces of
the Roman Empire, and it was no small service they ren-
dered in opening up the trade routes. If it was not equally
dangerous, it was not less arduous or less useful to the development of the respective societies, for the American and
South African Jewish immigrant to go peddling in the West
and "smousing" across the Veldt. "Reward" might be a better word than "perquisite," but we would let it pass (like
the phrase "religious idiosyncrasy"), were it not for passages like the following:

> The Jews of the 'Diasporà' have successfully responded to
> the human challenge of religious penalization and have
> been compensated for their Babylonish captivity among
> the Gentiles by the presence of those fleshpots to which
> their ancestors used to look back with such regret after
> Moses had led them forth into the wilderness out of the
> fat land of Egypt. The exercise of holding their own in a
> hostile human environment has not only stimulated the
> Jews of the Dispersion to activity; it has also enabled
> them, in diverse Gentile societies, in successive ages, to
> keep their footing in the market-place and their seat in
> the counting-house, and to take their tribute from the
> golden stream of commerce and finance [II, 271].

> The Hadramī in Java, the Scotsman in England, and the
> French-Canadian in the United States are all responding,
> like the Jew in the Gentile World, to the challenge of an
> alien human environment; and, like the Jewish 'Diasporà'
> again, they are being compensated for their endurance of
> this human ordeal by 'reaping where' they have 'not
> sown,' inasmuch as they are participating in the material
> prosperity which has been built up by the work of other
> men's hands in a country which is not the immigrants'
> home [II, 272].

Would it be pedantic to ask Professor Toynbee to explain—after he has unscrambled his metaphors—wherein
the "indispensable" Jew who makes "a profit by transacting
business which the barbarian lacks the skill to transact for
himself" is reaping where he has not sown? Also, is the Jew
"taking tribute" or being compensated for his "Babylonish
captivity" or is he merely being paid, however reluctantly,
for his indispensable services as distributor? Is Professor
Toynbee referring only to the unskilled European barbarians of the remote past and the role of Jewry in their society?
If so, European Jewry has as valid a stake in the prosperity
of the Western countries that it helped to develop in ancient times as the descendants of those barbarians. Would
he, again, have us think that at least in modern society the
Jew reaps where he has not sown? If so, he must look on
the trader and merchant of the modern world as a parasite
to be tolerated only when he can claim racial or national
community with his victims. This is a not unfamiliar point
of view, and Professor Toynbee is, as the saying goes, entitled to his opinion. But we must not let him express it as
it were under his breath. He is saying what the hero of
Aldous Huxley's *Those Barren Leaves* says: "Why do I
work here? In order that Jewish stockbrokers may exchange
their Rovers for Armstrong-Sideleys, buy the latest jazz records, and spend the week-end in Brighton?" It does not appear from the story that the hero of Mr. Huxley's book
would be happy to be exploited by stockbrokers of irre-
proachable English lineage.

An over-charitable reader may object: "Professor Toynbee is not reporting his own feelings, but those of the barbarians and their unregenerate descendants." I send the
reader back to the text. No such construction can be put on
Professor Toynbee's words. One begins to suspect that it is
not only the barbarian neophyte who is afflicted with envy.

These evidences of a warped attitude toward the Jewish phenomenon are important not because Professor Toynbee holds them, but because they are a stereotype; and it is fascinating to observe that the muddle-headedness and malice of the popular prejudice is reproduced with wonderful fidelity in Professor Toynbee's restatement of it. In the economy of the Western World the Jews are "parasites." They became parasites because they were excluded from productive occupations. They are highly successful parasites because they "have learned to hold their own in any human environment in which they are allowed to exist on sufferance by excelling in those trades and handicrafts to which their activities have been compulsorily confined." And so, while conceding that brutality and oppression pushed the Jews into their position, one must make the stereotyped references to the new "fleshpots" they have discovered and to their "footing in the market-place" and their "seat in the counting-house," where "they take tribute from the golden stream." We are left to infer that though the Jews were compelled to become traders, they had no right to make such a good thing of it. Incidentally, they mostly didn't; for, as Professor Toynbee himself points out (below, p. 147), they were as likely as not to be robbed of their ill-gotten gains by their un-parasitic Christian neighbors.

The above-mentioned reader will perhaps also remark that I am carrying a chip on my shoulder. That may be true, but a man with a chip on his shoulder need not have a beam in his eye; and I will ask the reader courteously, when he has finished analyzing me, to return once more to the content of the text we are examining and to deal with it intrinsically.

If we do that, we shall perhaps discover that the sentence beginning: "They have learned to hold their own . . ." is, like "the survival of the fittest," a tautology rather than an explanation. For if a barbarian or medieval people said to the Jews: "We will allow you to exist, but you must confine yourselves to trade," then they either allowed the Jews to make a living at trade or they were not allowing them to exist. And if the Jews were compelled to concentrate on trade and were permitted no other outlet, they did not have to be any cleverer than their neighbors to excel at it. We have here a description of the phenomenon; we have a picture of survival under those circumstances; we do not have an explanation.

It is also relevant to ask whether the case of the Jew in the Diaspora can in any way be compared with that of the Scotsman in England and the French Canadian in the United States (I have never met the Hadrami in Java). It trivializes the phenomenon of the Diaspora to set side by side with it and its two-thousand-year record of martyrdom and endurance the rebuffs and discomforts suffered by Scotsmen in England and by French Canadians in the United States for two or three generations—after which the latter invariably assimilate. It is a trivializing of the ghastly phenomenon of anti-Semitism to put it into the same class—as one must, after such a lead—with Dr. Johnson's half-facetious prejudice against Scotsmen. One has not heard of wild pogroms, of autos-da-fé, of mass expulsions and mass expropriations, in the history of the Scotsmen in England or the French Canadians in the United States.

II

I must now refer the reader to my observations (above, p. 101) on the differences of tone in the treatment Professor Toynbee accords certain subjects in the early six volumes and in the later four volumes: differences that do not add up to a correction, or retraction, or confession of error, but which would seem, to unwary readers, to provide him with

some sort of covering against the worst effects of his pronouncements. We have just seen that Professor Toynbee
speaks in the earlier volumes of the indispensability of the
Jews in the economy of barbarian and semi-barbarian Europe; but that it does not prevent him, in the same volumes,
from intimating that the Jews reaped where they had not
sown. He recognizes that the Jews were compelled to live
by trade if they were to live at all, but that does not prevent
him from expressing in a spirit of agreement the classic resentment of the Gentile at their success in it. In Volume
VIII he criticizes this illogical attitude with great severity—
but does not seem aware that he can himself be accused
of it. He writes:

> At a stage at which agriculture had been the staple indus-
> try of an infant Western Society, the Western Gentiles
> had taken advantage of a majority's brute power of num-
> bers to monopolize the ownership and occupation of the
> land and had profited doubly by that economic injustice
> to the Jews when this penalized minority—duly respond-
> ing to the challenge of penalization—had made good the
> Western Society's most serious economic deficiency by
> making something of such modest opportunities for com-
> merce as were to be found in a backward agrarian econ-
> omy. And now the Western Gentiles were bent on driv-
> ing out of the commercial as well as the agricultural field
> a Jewish diasporà which had done the Western World
> the two-fold service of building up the West's once ex-
> iguous commerce into a lucrative business and thereby
> teaching their Gentile neighbors the tricks of a valuable
> trade.
>   This economic quarrel between Jews and Western
> Gentiles ran through three acts. In the first act—classi-
> cally performed in seventh-century Visigothia—the Jews

were as unpopular as they were indispensable, but the ill-treatment which they incurred through their unpopularity was usually kept within bounds by the incapacity of their Gentile persecutors to fill their places. At this stage the worst that happened to the Jews as a rule was to be compelled to hand over to the Gentiles—by way of bribes, surtaxes, fines, and other euphemisms for robbery—a substantial portion of the wealth that was perpetually accumulating in the Jews' hands . . . [VIII, 285].

The second act, "which was discreditable to the Gentiles as it was tragic for the Jews," was the displacement of the Jews by force when the Gentile world had acquired the necessary skill in trade, though not enough of it to defeat the Jews in "peaceful and honest economic competition." The third act followed when the

> now well-established Gentile bourgeoisie had become such past masters in Jewish economic arts that their traditional fear of succumbing to Jewish competition no longer constrained them to forgo the economic advantage of re-enlisting Jewish ability in the service of their national economy [VIII, 285].

Whether or not this is a generally correct picture of the long-drawn-out process—and I am inclined to think it is—there is such an astonishing incongruity between its tone and the tone of the earlier passages on the same subject that, were it not for the unmistakable style, one would not credit them to the same writer. One could, of course, speak of the intervening fifteen years of reflection and study. But where is the intimation of any awareness of change, or of error in the past? Where have we the slightest hint of: "I shouldn't have said that"?

But we shall see in due course that the shifts of ground in

relation to these subjects are only a dialectic device for the better expression of a still more implacable hostility. They are another instance of *reculer pour mieux sauter.*

III

The trivialization of the phenomenon of the Jewish Diaspora is repeated in another area of ideas. There are, Professor Toynbee perceives, various ways of responding to the "stimulation of penalizations."

> The Jewish peasant in the Yaman has much more in common with his Muslim fellow-worker on the land than with his Jewish coreligionist in the ghetto; the Jewish tribesman in Abyssinia or the Caucasus has much more in common with the Christian or Muslim tribesman round about who lead the same turbulent and predatory life in the same highlands [II, 259].

> The Jews, for example, who survive in the fastnesses of the Caucasus and Abyssinia have responded successfully to a challenge from the physical environment and have been compensated by immunity from penalization at Gentile hands. These Jewish 'wild highlanders' are as free, and as upstanding, as their Monophysite and Muslim counterparts [II, 271].

We are invited to draw our conclusions from the fact that diverse Jewish groups can and do assimilate until some of them are nearer to their respective environments than to each other, and what divides them is more important than what unites them. The fact is indisputable; but what are the relevant conclusions in connection with the equally indisputable fact that a Jewish people does still exist? It is also, for example, a fact that a group of cultivated and conscientious British colonial administrators, of the type let us

say of the late Sir Arthur Wauchope of Palestine, was closer
in spirit to a group of Roman proconsuls of the type of
Pliny the Younger than the former to London costermon-
gers or the latter to sausage-makers of the Suburra. The relevant comment is: "What is the point here? Is there no
distinctive English people, and was there no distinctive Roman people?" Professor Muller writes: "The great majority
of the peasants of southern Europe and Latin America . . .
are more akin to Moslem peasants in Anatolia than to fel-
low-Christians on Fifth Avenue" (*The Uses of the Past*,
pp. 192 f.). Professor Muller does not thence infer that
there are not two distinct and enduring bodies of Christendom and Islam.

We may go much farther. There is not the slightest
doubt that Jews in the mass can and do assimilate until they
disappear. Whether this process has gone as far as Professor
Toynbee indicates with the peasant Jews of the Yaman (Ye-
men) or the Jewish tribes of the Caucasus—both areas from
which Jews have migrated to the Jewish Homeland—does
not matter. The point to be made here, in connection with
the survival of the Jewish people, is diametrically opposite
to the one that Professor Toynbee implies. The assimilatory proclivity of the Jewish people is as ancient as the people itself, which entered history as it were trying to assimilate; the Israelites, we recalled, worshipped the molten calf
at the very foot of Sinai. We have reviewed the operations
of this proclivity throughout the First and Second Jewish
States; I shall refer to their effects in medieval and modern
times and in Israel. It is this ordinary, this universal tend-
ency to yield to the lures and pressures of the human environment, this ordinary and universal reluctance to maintain
an identity, develop a gift, accept a destiny, which makes
the survival of the Jew all the more extraordinary, adds a
touch of spice to his singular history. Jews are very much

like other people—a trite and indisputable truth not of the slightest help to us in explaining why the Jewish people still exists.

Professor Toynbee writes:

At the present time, the Jews who display most conspicuously the well-known êthos which is commonly called 'Jewish,' and which in Gentile minds is popularly assumed to be the hall-mark of Judaism always and everywhere, are the Ashkenazi Jews of Eastern Europe. . . . The 'Jewish' êthos is already less conspicuous among the 'emancipated' Jews of Holland, France, Great Britain, and the United States; and when we consider how short a time has passed since the legal emancipation of the Jews took place, and how far from being complete their moral emancipation still is, even in the enlightened countries of the West, we shall not underrate the significance of the change of êthos which is already apparent here [II, 240].

What significance is this that we are being warned not to underrate? Presumably (I can think of no other) it relates to the approaching assimilation of the Jews of the West into the body of Western Christendom in such wise that they shall become as indistinguishable from their Christian neighbors as the Jewish "wild highlanders" of the Caucasus are from theirs. And this means, of course, the total disappearance of the distinctive Jewish ethos. Professor Toynbee may properly permit himself such a conjecture in a general way; but he cannot base it, as he seems to do here, on a type of Jewish behavior which is Jewish alone and which is associated with Jewish survival. It will not surprise us to note that Professor Toynbee himself has elsewhere discounted the significance of his warning. He has written, we recall: "Johanan ben Zakkai . . . became the founder of a Jewry which survived—albeit only as a fossil—in all manner of alien and inclement environments down to the present day, and which shows no signs of succumbing to its present tribulations" (V, 75).

Our main difficulty here, it seems to me, rises from the fact that logically speaking the Jews cannot have survived—that is, if our logic is based on the data visible to the merely mechanistic observer. But it can be proved in the same way, and it was in fact proved, that neither the automobile nor the telephone could ever become, and therefore never did become, established in popular use. For as regards the automobile, no man in his senses would buy one when there were no gasoline stations (where would he go?), and no man in his senses would open a gasoline station when there were no automobiles (to whom would he sell?). Similarly, it was ridiculous to install a telephone when there was no one to speak to on it. The fact that telephones may be counted in the tens of millions, and that automobiles have —at least in America—become a positive nuisance, like rabbits in Australia, cannot be taken seriously; for logic is logic, and if the facts do not fit it, then, as the German Professor said: *"Desto schlimmer für die Fakten"*—so much the worse for the facts.

CHAPTER TEN

"GOING! GOING!—"

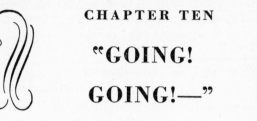

Those who know only a few words of Yiddish are apt to classify the language as a dialect of German; those with a smattering of Jewish history are apt to think that the Jewish people has survived since Biblical or at least Roman times in a sort of cataleptic trance from which it is just emerging. Or, to change the figure and take up Professor Toynbee's theory, the Jewish people became ossified; it could be pushed about from place to place, it could be hammered and chipped and scraped, but it could not be affected internally. It survived, paradoxically, because it was not alive. It could not help itself.

A little more than a smattering of Jewish history exposes the absurdity of the theory. Post-Biblical Jewish history resembles Biblical history in its rhythms of "near-obliteration and re-emergence against all probability," in its pulses and exertions of the spirit. We have reviewed briefly the hairbreadth escapes of the people from total destruction through the centuries from Sinai to the Seleucids; we have seen it repeatedly threatened, for its defections, by the direct action of God or by that of the nations into whose hands He delivered it. Every threat was overwhelming, every escape, born of a renewed will, unbelievable. Now, in another brief review, we shall see the similarity of the post-Biblical pattern; and this time the record is secular and its historicity less challengeable.

II

With the merciless destruction of the State by Hadrian in 135, the last possibility of Jewish survival was "obviously" extinguished. No "intelligent observer" would have foretold that three or four centuries hence (who would have dared to speak of thousands of years?) there would still be a Jewish people. If one put mystical expectations and wish-fulfillment dreaming on one side, the mortal prospect was as clear as day. True, large numbers of Jews were scattered throughout the Roman Empire. An accepted authority on that period, Juster,[1] estimates them at five to six millions, and if we also accept the estimate that the population of the Empire at the time of Claudius was about sixty million, the Jews would be nearly ten per cent of the total. But the Jews were scattered. They were—so the Romans complained —"everywhere." And wherever they were they no longer had, after the Hadrianic destruction, the centripetal moral force of a Jewish State to hold them together.

Even after the year 70 the Temple, the focal point of their formal worship, no longer existed; and there was no Sanhedrin to pronounce authoritatively on the laws. There had, however, been the Academy and shadow-Sanhedrin founded at Jabneh by Johanan ben Zakkai; and the Jewish State had still been a solid reality; so much so that in spite of the frightful slaughters and enslavements of 66–70, it took three Roman legions, led by the best Roman general of the time, three years to put down the Bar Kochba rebellion. But now, after Hadrian, though schools continued to function in Palestine (for a time before and after Hadrian, clandestinely), there was no local mass of population to give their rulings social momentum. The collection of funds

[1] Jean Juster: Les Juifs dans l'Empire romain (Paris, 1914).

for the upkeep of the Temple had, apart from the pilgrimages to it, played a great role in the unification of Diaspora Jewry—something like the collection of funds for the Jewish Homeland today. The collections went on—but it was the Romans who made them, for the benefit of the Roman treasury, and for the upkeep of the Jupiter Temple, which had replaced the Jewish Temple in Jerusalem, now renamed, in tribute to the destroyer, Ælia Capitolina.

It could also be argued reasonably that even before the destruction of the State there was no chance of Jewish survival (as there *never* had been!). As always, there was at work in Palestinian Jewry the ancient, the "natural," impulse to assimilation and apostasy. Professor Erwin R. Goodenough, of Yale University, has, with immense diligence and scholarly objectivity, collected in four large volumes (more to follow) the evidences of Jewish approximation to the pagan world in the use of religious symbols during the age under discussion. They constitute proof positive that Judaism could not survive. Not that Professor Goodenough says so, but then, he shares with us the advantage of a long hindsight.

But whatever Palestinian Jewry meant to Diaspora Jewry before the destruction of the Temple, and then of the State, it obviously meant much less after. The large aggregations of Jews in the countries and cities of the Empire—one million in Egypt, fifty or sixty thousand in Rome alone (I am again quoting Juster)—had a correspondingly large inertia of existence. But whatever could be said of the centrifugal forces working on Palestinian Jewry could be said more pointedly about these Jewries. The Jews of Alexandria, who made up one third of that populous city, knew neither Hebrew, the language of the Bible, nor Aramaic, the language of the Palestinian and Babylonian Jews. They spoke Greek.

The greatest of them, Philo, knew no Hebrew and used the Jewish Bible only in Greek translation for his commentaries and his neo-Platonic interpretations, and in such fashion that, as Professor Toynbee puts it, he

> sowed the seed from which [his] fellow citizens and fellow philosophers [the Christians] Clement and Origen were to reap so rich a harvest within two centuries of Philo's day; and it was perhaps from the same quarter that the author of the Fourth Gospel gained his vision of the Divine Logos with which he identifies his Incarnate God [V, 539].

Whether Professor Toynbee is right in this description I do not know; but Professor Goodenough has showed me medieval drawings of Philo as a Christian saint behung with crosses!

There was not much hope, then, in Alexandrian Jewry (which in fact disappeared, we do not know exactly how, in the next few centuries); and very little in the Jews of Rome. They too spoke neither Hebrew nor Aramaic, but Greek or Latin, and presumably were given even more to the use of non-Jewish religious symbols.

Meanwhile, in devastated Palestine, the schools obstinately continued their work. First came the systematization of the Oral Law in the Mishnah, that fascinating compilation of laws, ritual, rulings, and moral aphorisms which, with the Talmud, has remained an important ingredient of every thorough Jewish education until this day. Then, round the Mishnah, there grew up both in Palestine and in Babylon immense bodies of commentary and reinterpretation known respectively as the Jerusalem Talmud and the Babylonian Talmud, the latter of which became predominant. But the Mishnah and Talmud were written (at first only memorized) in Hebrew and Aramaic respectively; and, unlike the Bible, they were not available in Greek or Latin translation. Thus, since there was little knowledge of Hebrew or Aramaic among the Jews of the Roman Empire, these revitalizing works, like the early Midrashim, could not spread their influence westward.

It was eastward that the tide of influence spread from the crippled Jewish community of Palestine in those centuries, and Babylonian Jewry reaped the harvest it had sown five or six centuries earlier when it had re-established the Jewish State. Then in the year 425 the fading Patriarchate and shadow-Sanhedrin of Palestine gave up the ghost. By that time the Roman Empire was in dissolution. The Dark Ages were setting in; the Roman roads were falling into disuse, the cities into decay (in the Middle Ages the inhabitants of Rome believed that the immense ruins of the Forum pointed to the story of a vanished race of giants). The schools closed, the territories of the disrupted Empire became a shifting patchwork of warring, semi-barbarian principalities. The tide of Semitic conquest rolled from the East over the African dependencies of Rome, and at the western end of the known world turned northward into Spain. It was "obvious" that at least in those portions of the Roman Empire, chiefly European, which did not fall to the Arabs, Jewry would never survive.

What do we find in the tenth and eleventh and twelfth centuries? The Hebrew Mishnah and the Aramaic Talmud are being studied assiduously in southern France and in the northern Rhine territory! Great commentators have arisen, the greatest of them being Rashi; it is his Commentary, not Philo's, that has become standard for all Jewish students. The teachers and their schools bespeak, of course, Jewish communities, and the simpler people are the tonal background, *des Basses Grundgewalt,* to the music of the schools.

The commentators write in Hebrew; the folk learns by translating orally from the Hebrew and Aramaic into its own vernacular. Jewry is still there.

How did it come about? We do not know the details. We only know that it needed an immense effort of the will. We see the results, and they are not such as we associate with "fossils."

For centuries the emissaries of Babylon were the teachers of Western Jewry; for there were millions of Jews beyond the eastern borders of the old Roman Empire. They had their communal organizations, their academies, and their intestine struggles; they had their faithful ones and their schismatics and their apostates; and they had their sense of mission. They were determined that when their hour would come, and their community would be destroyed, the torch would have been passed on. So it was. When Babylonian Jewry disappeared, Spanish Jewry and the Jewries of Provence and of northern France were already carrying on.

III

Each of these separate Jewries was in itself an inherently improbable phenomenon. If one looks with the eye of a contemporaneous outsider at the external and internal conditions under which these Jewries lived, the notion of a long-continued existence for the Jewish people as a whole seems preposterous. Babylonian Jewry, the most powerful of the ancient exilic Jewries, moved from crisis to crisis. A change in the Persian dynasty, conquest by the Moslems, could and often did mean a period of persecution; then the persecution would relax, but one never knew for how long. Babylonian Jewry sank and rose again before it was finally extinguished as a force in Jewish life. It is almost unneces-

sary to speak of the Christian persecutions of the Jews or
of the precariousness of Jewish life in any European country during the Middle Ages.

One feature of Jewish survival must be repeatedly stressed.
The common notion that medieval Jewry was a monolith
that did not begin to crumble before it was struck by the
storms of modernity is false to recorded history. Apostasy
and simulated apostasy reproduce in post-Biblical history
the story of the ancient defections against which the Prophets thundered—with this difference, that now only individuals left Judaism of their own will; when masses went over,
it was under the threat of death or expulsion. In 576 the
Jews of Clermont were given the choice of baptism or exile;
five hundred of them chose baptism. What proportion of
the Jewish community they constituted, and how many of
them remained Jews in secret, and for how long, and how
many of them afterwards returned to Judaism openly, we
do not know. Outbursts like these were sporadic until the
time of the Crusades, when they became endemic. At Ratis-
bon an entire community was forced into the Danube,
where the rite of conversion was performed over it by a
priest. In Bohemia similar compulsions were used. At Blois,
in 1171, the community split up under attack; some preferred death to baptism, others chose to live as Christians.
When the Jews of Spain were given the choice of baptism
or expulsion, in 1492, tens of thousands accepted Christianity, if only to the outward eye. The story of Jewish scholar-
ship in the Middle Ages is speckled with the names of
apostates, some of whom lent themselves to the persecution
of their kinsmen and former coreligionists. I am sorry Professor Toynbee has not devoted a little attention to the
phenomenon of the compulsory baptisms. Concerning the
idolatrous Jews of the early time, he writes, as we may remember:

we see the Prophets of Israel and Judah offering themselves as martyrs in protest against the truancy of a paganizing faction who were seeking an escape from intolerable
miseries in a deliberate repudiation of the Chosen People's priceless peculiar heritage, with the base intention
of purchasing some relief from pressure at the cost of re-
merging the potter's half-shaped vessel into the still
shapeless common clay of the unregenerate Gentiles
[above, p. 77].

Of course one can no longer speak of "unregenerate Gentiles" as applying to medieval Christianity, or of a "paganizing faction" as applying to the Jews who converted to it
in order to escape from intolerable miseries. Circumstances
do alter cases, and so perhaps the purchase of relief under
these circumstances was no act of baseness. Perhaps it is
the others—the ones who accepted death or expulsion—who
can be accused of behaving basely or, at any rate, with a
fossilized obduracy that justifies the treatment they received.

There was always a section of the Jewish community
which was attached to the faith more or less loosely; and
thus, exactly like the Biblical Jewish communities, those of
the Middle Ages were forever throwing off into the outside
world contingents drawn from the decaying elements. One
might speak of these as emigrant groups. Just as a strong
people on its own soil may send out, generation after generation, sons and daughters who become assimilated into other
lands, so the medieval Jews—and still more the modern—
yielded up, generation after generation, to persuasion or
compulsion, their tribute of "emigrants."

In all ages the complaint arises that the sacred customs
and the sacred tongue, which hold the people together, are
vanishing. Of French and Spanish Jewry the historian Cecil
Roth [2] tells us, in an amusing and instructive essay:

[2] *Personalities and Events in Jewish History* (1953).

As for the Jewish observances, they were on the downward grade. Eminent rabbinical authorities in France in the period of the Second Crusade give evidence that, fifty years before, the practice of fixing the *mezuzah* on the doorposts had been virtually unknown; while in Spain a visiting scholar found to his horror that the most complete ignorance prevailed with regard to the custom of wearing phylacteries [p. 4].

And of seventeenth-century Italy:

[In the Venetian Ghetto] relations with the outside world, whether amatory, social, or literary, were close and constant. Rabbis had begun to speak of Jesus as one of the Jewish prophets, while Gentiles on their side flocked to hear the sermons in the synagogues. Pietists complained how Hebrew culture was neglected in favour of Italian. Ignorance of the sacred tongue was so far spread that there was a movement for prayers in the vernacular. The spirit of reform was rife. There was a strong current of opposition to the Talmud and talmudic literature. Works were written attacking Jewish tradition, evoking a whole literature in Hebrew, Italian, and Spanish in its defence. The ceremonial laws were not infrequently neglected. . . . We even find the phenomenon of the card-playing rabbi, more concerned with explaining Judaism to the Christian than with teaching it to the Jew. Literary and intellectual life, though centered in Hebrew studies, was by no means confined to them. We find vernacular playwrights, apologists, astronomers, mathematicians, and economists vying in activity. From that day to this it is doubtful whether so suprisingly modern an atmosphere has ever at any other time prevailed in Jewish life [p. 3].

Going back farther, Dr. Roth does, however, find an equally striking parallel to modern conditions in the Jewish community of Alexandria:

In this setting, a life indistinguishable in its essentials from that of this most modern city [New York] of the modern world was evolved. It was an age when Hebraic culture was in utter decadence. The last word in human knowledge seemed at this time to have been expressed in the current Greek philosophy, with which Hebraism had to be reconciled if it were to retain any permanent value. The use of Greek alone was fashionable. In order to have a chance in the world, Jewish literature had to be produced in the vernacular. Modern phenomena, such as religious reform, social climbing, assimilation, and scientific anti-semitism were rampant. When spirituality sought its material expression, it was much in the same way as today. The synagogues were huge. I cannot help thinking that the trustees of certain recent structures in New York must feel a little envious when they read of that extraordinary Alexandrian place of worship so vast that the beadles had to signal with flags in order to indicate to the worshipers that the time had come to say Amen. . . . We are informed that there were many who forgot their Judaism from one year's end to the other, recollecting it only on the occasion of the Day of Atonement, when they crowded the synagogues and sought pardon for their sins . . . [p. 7].

We have seen that Alexandrian Jewry disappeared. Was that the end of Egyptian Jewry? By no means. By the ninth century we find a flourishing community in the Fayoum, whence the great Saadia Gaon went to Babylonia as president of the Academy of Sura. And of course there was a schism in the Fayoum community; a large group, the Ka-

raites, rejected most of the tradition and—again of course—
it disappeared from Jewish life in the course of time. Two
centuries after Saadia Gaon, when Spanish Jewry was in
decline, and most Jews became Moslems to outward appearance, Maimonides, born at Córdoba (1135), found refuge
with the Jewish community of Egypt under a more tolerant
Moslem rule, and in a congenial atmosphere did his work as
philosopher, codifier, physician, and adviser at large to
Diaspora Jewry. In the capacity of adviser, we may note,
one of his most vexing problems had to do with Jews who
in times of religious persecution pretended to apostatize,
and when the persecution relaxed, wanted to revert.

Pretense is a form of practice, and if hypocritical practice
does not make perfect, it does affect the personality. The
great majority of Jews who became Marranos, or crypto-
Jews, retained of their Judaism, after many generations,
nothing more than some queer customs, whose origins were
understood by others than themselves—namely, the Jews
who had refused to pretend apostasy. I think that if the
word "fossil" has some use here, it is as a description of the
vestigial Judaism of the Marranos.

There were two great apostatizing movements among the
Jews after the close of the Middle Ages and before the modern Emancipation. One cannot speak of them as direct responses to persecution, though they were the result of cu-
mulative weariness with exile conditions. Nor did they start
with a program of apostasy; on the contrary, their attraction
lay in the Jewish Messianic pretensions of their leaders. But
the following of a false Messiah has always been the prelude
to the abandonment of Judaism. In the case of Sabbatai
Zevi (1626–76), the deluded Jews were all pietists to begin
with, and yet that they were moved by assimilatory longings
is shown by the history of the movement. The case of Jakob
Frank (1726–91) is more complicated; it is, in fact, some-

what pathological. In both cases, however, we have instances of decay within that Jewish field which is commonly thought of as a model of solidarity. Thousands of Sabbatists went over to Mohammedanism voluntarily, thousands of Frankists to Christianity.

And yet, as the modern world opens, Jewry and Judaism are still very much on the scene. A fascinating historical drama is revealed. The auctioneer is Time, the buyer Oblivion. The peoples come up on the block, one after another, the hammer is lifted, the established formula is intoned: "Going! Going! Gone!" But there is one people that appears on the block regularly, and over it the words "Going! Going!" have been repeated again and again; again and again it has looked like a sale: but the third word has never been pronounced over it.

CHAPTER ELEVEN

POSITIVELY
THE LAST
APPEARANCE

I

To the foregoing I can hear a reader, let us call him the Adversary, say: "All this may be true. It is even possible that the Jewish people has, since its beginnings, survived by fission, by throwing off regularly its weak and decaying elements; it is possible that these everlasting internal struggles were like the fever condition, which used to be mistaken for the disease itself, whereas it is in fact the evidence of the patient's capacity to fight the disease. But suppose fission is no longer possible because the entire body is being pulverized. Suppose that the modern world has confronted the Jewish people with a situation so different from anything it has known in the past that the old technique is meaningless. After all, the most tedious of aging actors, who has repeated his 'positively the last appearance' till the public has lost hope, does in the end fold up.

"The Jewish losses of the past," the Adversary continues, "by drift, or sectarianism, or apostasy, free or compelled—Alexandria, the Karaites, the single and mass baptisms, Sabbatism, Frankism—are trifling compared with the mass defections that have set in during the last century and a half, and particularly during the last two or three generations. For what is happening now resembles nothing that has happened hitherto. The modern world is not nibbling at the periphery of the Jewish people; it is seeping through to the heart of it. Compulsory education in the public schools, replacing the *cheder*, universal literacy in the language of the surrounding people, movies, radio, TV—how can any scattered minority cult stand up against this kind of inexorable penetration? We are dealing now not with defections, but with the total inner transformation of Ashkenazic Jewry, that Jewry which in numbers as well as spirit has for the last few centuries been the main carrier of Judaism. I therefore refer you again to Professor Toynbee's crucial statement on this subject: 'The "Jewish" ethos is already less conspicuous among the "emancipated" Jews of Holland, France, Great Britain, and the United States; and when we consider how short a time has passed since the legal emancipation of the Jews took place, and how far from being complete their moral emancipation is, we shall not underrate the significance of the change of ethos which is already apparent here.'

"Further, I ask you to remember that the Polish and Russian Jewries of forty years ago, in which the ethos was strongly embedded, are no more. Even they, you have said in your second chapter, were split into contending blocs as no Jewish community of the Middle Ages ever was—and this is not to speak of the considerable percentage of Jews who did not contend but merely drifted away. Your Western Ashkenazic Jewry is now on its own; there will be neither reinforcement nor example from East European Jewry. I am going to assume that the 'moral emancipation' lagging behind the legal will proceed apace, that the mad relapse of the Hitler episode, like the mad relapse of the Second World War, is the last. I make the assumption because discussion is impossible on any other ground; for if the world does not relax those hatreds of which anti-Semitism is both a part and a precipitant, there will be nothing to talk about.

You are not going to tell me, I hope, that if atom, hydrogen, and cobalt bombs wipe out humanity, the Jewish communities are going to be miraculously spared.

"Nor are you going to deny that 'the "Jewish" ethos is already less conspicuous' than it was forty, fifty, a hundred years ago. Let us take American Jewry as our example. It is fairly typical of a Westernizing Ashkenazic community, even though its comparative youthfulness gives it some special features. In any case, with its five or five and a quarter millions, it outweighs in numbers and influence all the other Ashkenazic communities combined. I shall not press too hard the statistics of peripheral defection, because you will answer that this is the classic feature of Jewish life. Nevertheless, I cannot pass them by, because this is a very wide periphery, and its area may be larger than the core. Synagogue and temple attendance, enrollment in Jewish courses of one kind or another, frequentation of Jewish centers, circulation of Jewish books among Jewish readers, are all, on the most optimistic estimate, indicative of communal anemia. The use of Yiddish, the last great linguistic vehicle of Diaspora Judaism, is in rapid decline. The Yiddish theater of thirty years ago is dead; the Yiddish newspapers are admittedly on their last legs. Figures on intermarriage are not available, but it is generally felt that they are high. We do not know, either, the percentage of Jews who go through the years without a single gesture of Jewishness beyond the circumcision of a son, an annual Kaddish for a deceased father, and provision for burial in a Jewish cemetery; but here too the percentage is very high. However, I put all this on one side to look, instead, at the quality of America's professing and acting Judaism, which, even if it is a minority Judaism, might still have volume enough to constitute the significant historical factor—if it were a genuine Judaism.

"It is here, within this sector, minority or majority, that

the picture is really discouraging for you. We have here a Judaism in which the fundamental awareness of 'historic peoplehood-in-God' is at a very low ebb; correspondingly, the awareness of a meaningful difference between the Jewish ethos and the ethos of Christianity is at a minimum. And yet it is not the pull or solvent of Christianity which constitutes the major danger to Judaism; it is rather the pull into a universal religiously characterless secularism on a primitive rationalist basis; and its effects are best studied among the 'loyal' Jews, those who are forever fulminating against the 'disloyal' Jews as 'deserters' or 'indifferentists.'

"The vast majority of these 'loyalists' think of themselves as good Jews, and therefore as propagators and perpetuators of Judaism, if they attend synagogue services, join Jewish lodges, support Jewish community chests, contribute toward the building of Israel, send their children to Hebrew classes, observe the Passover and Chanukkah and other festival ceremonials, light the Friday-night candles, and help to expose anti-Semitism as un-American. Or rather, they think of Judaism as *consisting* of these activities.

"I need not tell you that while Judaism cannot exist without such activities, such activities can—and here do—flourish in the absence of the Jewish ethos. What best reveals that absence among the huge majority is the general anxiety to regard the activities as counterparts of similar activities in the non-Jewish world, *and as nothing more.* 'The Christians have their church, we have our synagogue or temple; they have their Christmas, we have our Chanukkah; they Easter, we Passover; they priests and ministers, we rabbis; they the Elks, we the B'nai B'rith. The only difference is in the attitude toward Jesus. Was he the Messiah or only a great human prophet?—and there are many Christians who take the latter view.'

"But, as I have said, what is most indicative of the decline

of the Jewish ethos is the secularization of the very concept
of religion. There are many rabbis who find their justification of Judaism in Westermarck and Malinowski and Mar-
garet Mead and Ruth Benedict. They talk, as rabbis, a professional technical language drawn from anthropology,
sociology, psychology, and social service. They explain Jewish needs in terms of 'ego-satisfaction,' of 'the father motif,'
'*rites de passage*,' and the couvade. They find more comfort
in the literature stemming from *The Golden Bough* than
in the Bible; indeed, they tend to regard the Bible as an
illustration of the views set forth by Frazer and the later
anthropologists rather than as the unique utterance of a
people's struggle to hold on to God.

"Often enough, however, such rabbis stand out almost as
an intellectual élite; for over against them are large numbers
of rabbis who are merely executive secretaries of Jewish
Rotarian Associations with Hebrew names which are rep-
licas of the exotic flourishes in use among Shriners. For such
rabbis the religious element in their vocation is the stand-
ardized covering or trade-mark for the secular functions that
absorb most of their energies. The religious services are in
reality adjuncts—indispensable, to be sure, as patents of re-
spectability and propriety—to a wide range of social services
in behalf of the members of the community. All of these
services conform to the over-all purpose of soothing the
members of the community or congregation, who must be
helped toward the feeling that in their Judaism they have a
harmless, unobtrusive, and undisturbing pattern of religious
conformity, such as every decent American ought to have;
and it is of the utmost importance that their non-Jewish
neighbors shall understand this feeling, and share it. The un-
acknowledged motif behind the Jewish-Christian good-will
movement is, for the large majority of its supporters: 'All
this religious business in and for itself—it's really of no im-

portance'; and for the rabbis I am discussing, this unac-
knowledged motif is the key to the character of their
ministry.

"In the homes of most professing Jews the tone and substance of the spiritual and intellectual life cannot be distinguished from the tone and substance in non-Jewish
homes. The same books are read—when any reading is done;
the same movies are liked or disliked; the same radio and
TV programs are switched on; the same pagan rage for
sports grips the male members of the family, the same rage
of fashions the female members; the children of school age
discuss the same problems, follow the same patterns, speak
the same bobby-sox slang; there is the same interest or lack
of interest in politics; there is, however, an ancient and conspicuous emphasis on charities. Certain words and allusions would be unfamiliar to non-Jewish ears; certain organizations are supported of which non-Jews only hear. The
only psychological—not spiritual—difference, and this ex-
tends to non-professing Jewish homes too, is the presence of
an unrelaxing uneasiness as to what is being said about the
Jews in the non-Jewish world.

"The most instructive of the symptoms I have left to the
end. In how many professing Jewish homes will you find
the ethics of personal relationships, the problems of right
and wrong behavior, being discussed in the framework of a
Jewish ethos? I am not thinking of occasional abstract dis-
cussions, but of day-to-day contacts, the almost hourly deci-
sions; of parents-and-children relationships, problems of
obedience, freedom, sexual latitude, social obligations, and
so on. Where such matters are actually discussed, that is, in
'intelligently' conducted homes, what are the terms of reference? You will agree that these will not be found in the
Jewish Bible, and not in the Talmud; nor in the kind of
advice which Chassidic Jews sought from their 'rebbis.' The

terms are those of the latest psycho-therapeutic fad, and if the rabbi is consulted, he is expected to make only the regulation obeisance to a Jewish ethos; the substance of his insight must come, or seem to come, from a familiarity with the most recently most popular psychoanalytic school.

"I do not from all of this make the deduction that the term Judaism is about to disappear from the world, and that there will not exist, even for centuries, 'Jewish' communities, perhaps in considerable numbers, in the so-called Diaspora and in Israel. There may never be many actual conversions. In a world in which religion has become a courtesy rather than a conviction, it is a discourtesy to raid Churches. Only uncouth enthusiasts go proselytizing; the tolerant and cultivated Jew or Christian will not permit himself to imply that the other man's belief is an inferior one, which is what every proselytizer must do. The merging of identifiable Jews with the general population will proceed slowly. But what identity the identifiable Jews will present is the core of the question. However else it can be described, the co-ordinates of the Jewish ethos will be altogether irrelevant."

Thus the Adversary, who is a composite of all the pessimists I have encountered. Perhaps I should not say pessimists, because while some of them were bitterly regretful, others spoke frankly with satisfaction. But however they felt about it, such is the substance of their diagnosis and prognosis; and if they had read A *Study of History*, they might have added: "Whether or not 'fossil' is the right description for Diaspora Jewry in the past, it will certainly not be unapt for the Jewry of tomorrow."

II

I cannot argue with this description. So much of it is sound that the unsoundness is a matter of degree. Nor can

I argue with the prognosis. There is no way of proving that Judaism, in the sense of that original ethos which admittedly still lingers in some part of the Jewish people, will survive for a long time to come. We have no guarantee from God that this particular Jewish people will forever carry the ethos He entrusted to it; on more than one occasion, He threatened to transfer the burden to another people, to be newly created. In that sense, of course, Judaism would survive; but we are talking of the Judaism associated with the historically recognizable Jewish people.

But while not "arguing," I would enter a cautionary note. I do not think that anyone believes the Jewish ethos to be dead, with no part of the Jewish people still faithful to it. There may be a great deal of argument as to the particular group or groups in which that ethos still lives. There always has been. There may be some argument as to the irretrievability of all those non-Judaistic "professing" Jews. For while the Alexandrian Jews disappeared, the Babylonian Jews who between the fourth century before the Christian era and the second century of it were apparently weak in their Judaism did not. The Jews of the first and second and third centuries in Italy were to all appearances assimilating like the Jews of Alexandria; in the fifth and sixth centuries Judaism was re-rooted in them. It cannot be denied that modern Western Jewry faces conditions utterly unknown to Jewries of the past; but the behavior of the Jewish people has been so unpredictable for such a long time that we must be more than usually cautious in pontificating about its future.

In diagnosing the condition of Jewry at any time, the history of the case and the visible symptoms have always been in baffling contradiction. If there is anything wrong with the foregoing description of the condition of American Judaism, it is, therefore, the absence of the element of time. It is a static description. It is a snapshot, and one cannot take a snapshot of a process. The latencies, the hidden dynamism, of the Jewish people remain concealed in a purely contemporaneous picture.

Thus, for instance, my personal observation of American Jewry over the last four decades leaves me with the strong impression that there has been a perceptible deceleration in the rate of defection from Judaism, both in the formal and in the intrinsic sense of the word. Forty years ago one would have foretold from the rate of flight that in the sixth decade of the twentieth century even the formal association with Judaism would be far weaker than it is today. It seemed most unlikely then that many of the grandchildren of the immigrants would be voluntarily regrouping themselves in synagogues and temples in order that their children—the fourth generation—should not be as empty of Jewish information as the parents. It was freely foretold that the forms of Judaism would die out with the immigrants, or at the latest with their children. Such were, in fact, the symptoms. That the grandchildren would be leading the great-grandchildren back in the direction of the great-grandparents was unforeseeable. I am, admittedly, speaking here of the forms: the grandchildren who want their children to be Jewish do not, for the greater part, know what Judaism is. But that they want *something* that is not to be found by outright assimilation is obvious: and if the prognosis in the area of the formal was so wildly wrong, it may also be wrong in the area of the intrinsic.

I have found in that third generation, with which I am well acquainted by continuous and widespread contact, a homesickness for a home they cannot identify, a dissatisfaction with the emptiness of the formalities they practice, a growing doubt about the efficacy of the spurious Judaism described in the first section of this chapter. Various explanations of this condition may be offered, and among them, in my opinion, the Zionist movement occupies the first place. Many will disagree with me. They will give the first place to the reaction against Hitlerism, or perhaps to the rise of the State of Israel, rather than to the intrinsic values of the Zionist movement. Others speak of a general religious trend, long-range or evanescent, in which Jews have also been caught up, and in which it is difficult to distinguish between superstition and religion. I do not deny the role of these factors, and even while stressing the primary importance of Zionism and its spiritual content, I would observe that the process now unfolding in American Jewry is classical, that all large Jewish communities have passed through at least a first cycle of rejection and return. Zionism has therefore speeded up, not created, the process. What matters, however, is that while there is still widespread alienation from the ethos of Judaism, much of it is now the confused alienation of disorientation, not the result of that programmatic flight and rejection that characterized the children of the immigrants. In short, I suggest that now, as in the case of many communities of the past, there exists the possibility of a substantial reintegration with Judaism.

I have reserved the treatment of Zionism, that most spectacular phenomenon of contemporaneous Jewish life, for the next chapter but one. I have not done the Adversary an injustice in omitting the subject from his statement. He dismisses it contemptuously, and by implication, when he includes contributions toward the building of Israel among the manifestations of a spurious Judaism. He would agree with Professor Toynbee's analysis of Zionism, also set forth in the next chapter. He would not, I believe, agree with Professor Toynbee's denunciation of the State of Israel. Why I hold this belief will be made evident in the next chapter but two.

CHAPTER TWELVE

THE ETHOS AND
TECHNIQUES OF
SURVIVAL

SOMETHING must be said, before we come to Zionism and Israel and Professor Toynbee's statements on them, regarding the nature of the Jewish ethos we have been discussing and the forms associated with its perpetuation.

When we are told that a group or a people met a challenge with an affirmative response, we learn what took place, but not why. When Professor Toynbee says that the challenge had to be severe but not crushing, we have a tautology. We come down to the unhelpful truism that this particular group or people had the character to make this particular response. Where did it get that character? We can surmise that it acquired its character in making an affirmative response to an earlier challenge. Where and how did it acquire the original character?

If it is an evasion, almost a flippancy, to say that the Jews survived by learning "to excel in those trades and handicrafts" to which they were limited (for it does not tell us why they survived as Jews), it is also an evasion, though not a flippant one, to say, as Professor Toynbee does, that the Jews survived by "their persistent cultivation of the êthos which Johanan ben Zakkai bequeathed" to them. It amounts to: "The Jews remained Jews by retaining their Jewish character."

What is that ethos of Johanan ben Zakkai? It is of course the ethos of Pharisaic Judaism, which derived from Prophetic Judaism. But the word "ethos" is not quite sufficient. Judaism is not only an ethos. Judaism is an outlook on life which is associated and interwoven ideologically with the history of a people. Let me put it in a simple way. If somewhere in China today an individual were to work out for himself all the ethical and theological principles of Judaism, and live up to them, would that make him a Jew? My answer is no. He would be as good a person as any Jew, and better than most Jews; but he would not be a Jew until he had associated himself with the fellowship, and had accepted the responsibilities and instrumentalities of that fellowship.

By the instrumentalities I mean not only a ritual; and, as to the ritual, we must remember that the Jewish ritual is the expression of the history of a people that, when faithful to Judaism, sees history as a manifestation of God's will. Judaism cannot be separated from the Jewish Bible, the Mishnah, the Talmud, the commentators, the Kabbalah, Chassidism, the exile, the Restoration, the total fact of the Jewish experience: it cannot be separated from these and restated in the form of a series of ethical and theological theorems. From time to time in the popular press there appear articles on the beliefs of Jews, most of them written by Jews. These efforts to transpose the key of Judaism into the key of a religion of a different order are usually a testimony to the amiability of the editors who encourage them and to the goodwill-mindedness of the writers who make them. Certainly there are things that the Jews believe; but before these can be understood, one must establish the character of the Jewish people in its peoplehood. When that has been done one may proceed to inquire: "What do Jews *know* and believe?" For in the case of the Jew, to accept certain tenets of faith as abstractions, without a knowledge of the Jewish people and an informed self-identification with it, does not constitute true and reliable membership in it.

What, then, is the Jewish people? It is a continuing association of individuals, now some thirty-five hundred or four thousand years old, working out an experiment in the relationship to God. It is partly a hereditary association, though not on principle or by deliberate choice. Proselytes of any race are accepted. On the other hand, it would seem that only a limited number of proselytes can be accepted; beyond that number the relationship between the faith and peoplehood would break down. This looks like exclusion on principle. For suppose the hypothetical Chinese were joined by hundreds of thousands or millions of others, all ready to join the association. What connection could *they* have with the faith and ritual centered on peoplehood and the Restoration? The question is unanswerable; and it is unanswerable precisely because it approaches the Messianic area of ideas. Judaism in Jewry is an experiment in time; when the Messiah will have come, when all peoples will have accepted the faith, the experiment will have been successfully concluded. We shall be beyond history, and we cannot picture to ourselves in secular terms the post-historic condition of mankind.

Until that conclusion approaches, the experiment cannot be detached from the people and its modes of expressing the faith. Neither is it the kind of experiment in which one can at successive stages put the details of the previous stages in the files with the notation: "Facts A, B, and C have been definitely established." The early stages are continuously present as contemporaneous experiences. One must always be reliving the Bible and the later records of the people. A knowledge of them is therefore indispensable to the contin-

uing of the experiment. How the people reacted to the consciousness of the One God three thousand years ago, and
two thousand years ago, and one hundred years ago is, as
knowledge, part of the faith and part of the present reaction. Imperfection in that knowledge is imperfection in
one's Jewish identity.

Of course that knowledge can never be perfect, for man
cannot be perfect. There are, moreover, two general types
of knowledge, that of the scholars and that of the folk. In
neither of them is purely cerebral knowledge enough, for I
am not speaking of an academic acquaintance with certain
remote events (facts filed away), which an outsider and un-
believer may also acquire. The knowledge must be of the affective kind which amounts to a renewed participation in
the events—what Thomas Mann called "the recurrent festival of presentness." Thus folk-knowledge, when tinged with
this self-identification, is truer than scholar-knowledge
from which it is absent. There can, of course, be a combination of the scholarly and affective, and that is best.

The affective element in Jewish knowledge is kept alive
by a ritual in which the events are plastically embedded and
their meaning and circumstances brought near to us and
into us. The Passover ceremony of the Seder contains the
injunction that every man, woman, and child participating
must feel that he or she in person was liberated from Egypt,
and the ceremonial is designed in the spirit of that injunction. The celebrants relive the Exodus. The legend form of
this injunction puts it thus: all the unborn generations were
present at the giving of the Law from Sinai, and every unborn Jew uttered the words: "*Naase v'nishma*"—we will do
and we will obey. The millennial insistence on the retention of Hebrew at least for prayer and sacred study is another aspect of the technique of intimate self-identification
with the total Jewish experience. The retention of the har-

vest festivals geared chronologically to the Palestine seasons, and ignoring the seasonal realities of the lands in which the Jews actually live, is still another. The regular Jewish prayer for "the former and the latter rains" in climates where such things are unknown is one more. Certainly to one who watches these rituals from the outside, or who performs them perfunctorily, the impression is of petrification, or of fossilization. How incorrect that impression would be with regard to believing Jews we may see from the fact that all these practices kept the people alerted, as it were, for the Restoration and for a resumption of life in Palestine. The Seder foretold the Return; the harvest festivals and the prayers for "former and latter rains" made easier the adaptation to the Palestinian landscape and seasons; the retention of Hebrew, if only in prayer, made possible—though with an effort—its revival as the language of daily intercourse. It is true that not all observant Jews were to go to the new Jewish State, but all of them maintained a kind of training for it. Thus a whole army is kept in training and only a part of it goes into battle.

But, if one may so put it, the most important part of the ritual is *study*: and the difference between Jewish and other study is clarified once for all when we remember that for others a knowledge of the history of their people is a civic duty, while for Jews it is a sacred duty. It is considered God's will not only that we shall be good, but that we shall know what He did to us and what we did about Him. The view is that we cannot, in fact, know what He wants us to do without that knowledge of what happened between Him and us, between Him and the world, and among all three of us. There is a sense in which Jews consider *all* knowledge sacred, and all study—unless it leads toward apostasy—a religious exercise.

These techniques and methods—or whatever other names

one might choose—are as inseparable from the ethos as the form is from a work of art. It therefore follows that to state the ethos in other terms is very difficult, if not impossible; Judaism is livable rather than describable. And yet the ethos is distinct enough. It is based on the One God who made everything, the universe and man, light and darkness, good and evil. His relationship to man, His special and crowning creation, is direct, and forbids diminution or confusion by the interposition of intermediaries. It will not tolerate, either, the shading away of the Singularity by the suggestion of any special Emanation carrying with it the actual nature of the Divinity. Where such deviations occur in Jewish thought they are considered dangerous, and are not in the main stream of Judaism.

Just as the relationship will not suffer diminution by intermediaries, so it cannot be consistent with the delegation of moral authority to men or to things. The moral laws are not derived from political or social expediency. Man shall be good not for the health of the State but because it is God's will, transmitted by the Prophets. The moral laws shall not be deduced from sociological or anthropological study; they do not have to be, and in fact they cannot be; for they are not relative things. If the crimes of Clapham are indeed crimes, and are nevertheless considered chaste at Martaban, Clapham has not been cleansed thereby, whatever the grounds on which Martaban is considered chaste. We must desire peace not because wars between nations never settle anything—a doubtful proposition anyway; nor because, as Professor Toynbee says, they are usually civil wars between members of the same Society—the existence of Societies in his sense is a debatable proposition too. We must desire peace because it is God's will. Morality is not an "enlightened egotism," and the industrial enterprise which declared in an advertisement that it was trying to cut

down accidents because they made for "bad public relations" was not on the right track. Nor is morality a philosophic system. Every effort to seek elsewhere than in God
the ultimate authority for goodness and peace is a form of
idolatry, not the less so when it is a "scientific" search.

This does not mean that idolators and atheists cannot be
good people, any more than that professors of God cannot
be bad people. Nor does it mean that belief, any more than
unbelief, is always total. ("We called the chessboard white,
we call it black," says Bishop Blougram to Mr. Gigadibs.)
Within the range of Judaism, as of Christianity, are to be
found formal unbelievers who derive their ethos from
sources that they challenge, and sometimes the sincerity of
the challenge is a tribute to the power of the ethos.

Now I must repeat that the Jewish people associates the
striving toward its ethos with its history, and does so the
more strongly because no people among which it lives considers its own history a sacred drama. There have of course
been Christian philosophers who have seen history at large
as the unfolding of God's will; but their peoples study
God's will on Sundays, their own, and world history, the
rest of the week. Thus when a Jew considers his American-
ism or his Englishhood a substitute for Judaism and a re-
placement for his feeling of participation in the Jewish
peoplehood—which is what vast numbers of Jews actually
do—he secularizes himself out of his Jewish identity.

The refusal to give up its peoplehood-in-God is another
way of saying "the cultivation of the ethos of Judaism." To
the Jews the world did not seem "serious" because its vic-
tories and defeats, its glories and tragedies, were not being
enacted in the consciousness of a sacred purpose. Its wars
were extensions of the frivolities of the racecourses and the
jousting lists. In this Jewish outlook we find the clue to

that continuity of identity through the centuries which we are seeking.

That the Gentile world was, even with all the brilliance and attractiveness of its most creative periods—not excluding the most modern—a frivolous world, a "vanity," remained a deep-rooted feeling in those Jewish masses which clung to their peoplehood. They did not feel that the Jewish people in ancient Palestine had done well, had "behaved" better than any other people. On the contrary, they repeatedly admitted that it was because of their sins that they had been exiled from their homeland. But the two episodes of the First and Second States had been serious; they had contained the kind of effort at working out the relationship with God that was not to be found in the histories of other states.

Thence the longing to make the third attempt remained in the people, deeply worked into its religious identity, and constituting the most powerful of those "techniques" which, without looking on them as explanations, we may observe in the Jewish survival. That the Jewish people could not perish because it had to "make good" in Palestine became for its faithful elements an integral part of the ethos. For, per contra, the idea that the Jewish people should perish in exile or remain there till the end of time carried the inescapable implication that its history, thus truncated or permanently suspended without the proper rounding off or dénouement, could not have been sacred.

In this complex of views and beliefs it endured century after century, to the growing astonishment and finally the awe (not unmixed with exasperation) of the surrounding world; and the longer it endured the more obvious was, of course, the conclusion that it was not enduring for no reason. Nor could that reason be a trivial one, like the reason for the survival of certain biologic species, the turtle or the oyster, for example, which have found safety in arrested evolution behind a mechanical carapace. For the endurance of the Jewish people is a continuous exertion of the will in the face of adversity, of creative ingenuity in the midst of change.

We need not speak of the courage it needed to die for one's faith at the stake, or to become for its sake a wanderer in a hostile world. More impressive in its way was the ability to stand up to the choreography and *décor* of humiliation which the Middle Ages added to their economic and physical maltreatment of the Jew: the ghetto, the yellow badge, the spitting ceremonials, the insults, the naked foot-races, the blood libels, the accusations of poisoning the wells. Hundreds of thousands of little people accepted the verdict of an ever-renewed malevolence without a thought of purchasing security and comfort by defection. And escape was so easy, so simple! The "racial" rejection of the Jew was unknown in the Middle Ages. It was all a matter of belief. The Churchmen were eager to win souls; the conversion of the Jews was an ideal; and there were prelates of a genuine Christian disposition who, protecting the Jews in times of popular bloodthirstiness, made the offer of Christianity in a spirit that was particularly tempting. The answer of the faithful was No. The Jewish people had a task to complete and would not quit in the middle.

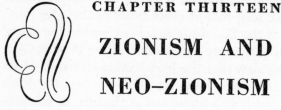

CHAPTER THIRTEEN

ZIONISM AND
NEO-ZIONISM

I

Iт is a pity that we cannot dispense with the word Zionism. It is of recent coinage, and gives the phenomenon to which it refers a false appearance of recentness and simplicity. A true definition of Zionism shows the phenomenon to be old and complex.

Zionism is the activation by wordly means of the Jewish longing for the re-creation of the Jewish State in Palestine. Zerubbabel, Nehemiah, Ezra, and the other exiles who returned to Judea to create the Second Jewish State after the destruction of the First by Babylon were Zionists. The False Messiahs of the exile, of whom Sabbatai Zevi is the best-known, were also Zionists. It follows from this definition that from the point of view of the preservation of Judaism, Zionism can manifest itself destructively as well as constructively; and the Zionism of the nineteenth and twentieth centuries, which I shall call neo-Zionism, has to be assessed accordingly.

Professor Toynbee takes the view that Zionism is not only inconsistent with orthodox or traditional Judaism and its ethos, but is the death of Judaism. He restricts the word "Zionism" to that which I have called neo-Zionism, and, even so, puts its beginning only as far back as 1897, the date of the first Zionist Congress; but under my definition he would have to maintain that the Zionism of Zerubbabel and his contemporaries was also contrary to the Jewish ethos, and destructive of it; and he does so maintain at times, though we have seen that at other times he includes most of the period of the Second Jewish State within the range of effectiveness of the true Jewish ethos of the Way of Gentleness. It is his view that the Jewish ethos demands of its adherents, the orthodox Jews, that they wait for the Messiah to restore the Jewish State; and in the first six volumes of A *Study of History*, published by 1939, he assumes that contemporaneous Jewish orthodoxy is represented by the group of the *Agudath Israel*. In the eighth volume, published with the seventh, ninth, and tenth in 1954, he concedes that the *Agudath Israel* is a minority among the orthodox (VIII, 298).

We find, however, the usual confusion even in the citing of the *Agudath Israel* as Jewish witnesses against the unJewishness of neo-Zionism. Before 1939 Professor Toynbee could write, correctly:

> . . . the strictly orthodox *Agudath Israel* at this day look askance at the Zionist movement and are holding rigidly aloof from any participation in the work of building up a material Jewish 'national home' under a British mandate in post-war Palestine [V, 76].

But even at that time the position of the *Agudath Israel* was equivocal in the new conditions facing the Jewish ethos; and Professor Toynbee himself is critical of the implications of its orthodoxy. He writes:

> At its lowest the practice of Non-Violence may express nothing more noble or more constructive than a cynical disillusionment with the fruitlessness of a Violence which has been previously practiced *ad nauseam* without having produced the intended results. . . . Alternatively Non-Violence may express a conviction that Man's divinely al-

lotted role in the economy of the Universe is to adopt a patiently passive attitude towards a mundane scene on which it is God's exclusive prerogative to execute His Divine Will through His own action—which would be hampered, and not assisted, if Man were to presume to intervene in what is wholly God's business. Such is, for example, the conviction that underlies the Non-Violence of the *Agudath Israel*. This second philosophy of Non-Violence is as pious and as scrupulous as our first is unprincipled and cynical; but at the same time it resembles the Non-Violence of Disillusionment in being unconstructive [V, 588].

Of course if Judaism is a fossil and the Jewish people fossilized, the orthodox *Agudath Israel* must necessarily be "unconstructive." Nevertheless the *Agudath Israel* must in its orthodoxy be the carrier of that "êthos of Johanan ben Zakkai" which Professor Toynbee holds in such high regard. I do not understand why he holds an unconstructive ethos in high regard, and why he seems at various times eager for the preservation of a fossil (namely, the Jewish people) which on the whole he finds rather unprepossessing. Perhaps he only means that he would rather have the fossil persist as a fossil than see it convert itself into an ordinary people. That is, indeed, what he says more than once (see below). On the other hand, he may not really mean anything. In any case, he had discovered by 1954 that the Mizrachi neo-Zionists, more numerous than the *Agudath Israel*, are also orthodox Jews, and have been working for the re-creation of the Jewish State.

Having made this discovery, he delivers himself of the opinion that the Mizrachi "embraced Zionism without admitting that this was incompatible with orthodoxy" (VIII, 298). Rushing in where Gallio feared to tread, he here (as elsewhere) enters the Jewish theological court, gives us the pros and cons (VIII, 298–301), and leaves unchanged his pronouncement in favor of the *Agudath Israel*. Unfortunately he neglects to note in 1954 that his last Jewish prop has been removed since 1939. For the *Agudath Israel* has not only accepted the principle of the Jewish State, thereby letting him down—obviously without advising him—but takes an active part in its political life, has representatives in the Knesset (Parliament) of Israel, and continues to fight for the preservation of orthodoxy; Professor Toynbee thus remains almost the sole surviving true interpreter of the ethos of Johanan ben Zakkai.

I say almost because there does exist in Israel today a very small group, the *Neturei Carta*, which is still opposed on super-orthodox grounds to the idea of the Jewish State. Its supporters do not believe that Judaism is compatible with present-day governmental functions. They wish to see the Jewish State liquidated as a state. It is possible that Professor Toynbee has not heard about them; it is also possible that they do not suit his book, for they are anything but quietists. On the contrary, they are unbelievably noisy and activist in their opposition to Jewish activism.

But even in his championship of Jewish orthodoxy Professor Toynbee cannot resist the temptation to make a sneering allusion (in the spirit of Gibbon's famous attack on Christianity, though, I need hardly say, without anything like Gibbon's mastery of style) to the beliefs in which that orthodoxy is grounded.

The Assyrian, Neo-Babylonian, Seleucid, and Roman warlords, whose crushing military superiority might appear, to an unenlightened eye, to be the natural explanations of Israel's and Judah's calamities, remained naïvely ignorant of the bizarre fact that, in the sight of Jewish

seers, they had been the unintentional and unconscious
agents of a One True God who had been employing
them, without deigning to make them privy to His coun-
sels, to punish His Chosen People for their sins with an
eye to forgiving and restoring this Chosen People when a
sufficient experience of suffering should have brought
forth fruits meet for repentance in Jewish hearts [VIII,
299].

Since he elsewhere describes (as we have seen) the reaction
of the Jews, and particularly of their seers, to their calamities in the eighth century before the Christian era as one of
the highest expressions of spirituality, we must credit one
of these two utterances to his inveterate incapacity not to
espouse a point of view when espousing it supplies him with
a rolling period.

II

His opposition to neo-Zionism is, however, total and consistent; that is to say, he condemns it from all the contradictory points of view which he adopts from time to time. He
regards it as a purely secular phenomenon of particular un-
holiness, a mixture of the worst features of European nationalism and race delusion; above all, it is to him the systematic effort of the Jewish people (or that part of it which
is Zionist and pro-Zionist) to achieve assimilation by another name. In this opposition to Zionism Professor Toynbee displays what may be called a standard or permissible
partisanship. It is when he comes to the State of Israel and
groups its creators with the Nazis that his position becomes morally and intellectually impermissible. I shall deal
first with his ideological objections to neo-Zionism. He
writes:

The ultimate aim of the Zionists is to liberate the Jewish people from the peculiar psychological complex induced by the penalization to which they have been subject for centuries in the Gentile World. In this ultimate aim, the Zionists are at one with the Assimilationist School among the 'emancipated' Jews in the enlightened countries of the West. They agree with the Assimilationists in wishing to cure the Jews of being 'a peculiar people' [II, 252].

The Zionist view is, he says, that

> . . . to be a Jew is to be a human being whose social environment is Jewry. It is an essential part of the Jew's individuality that he is a member of the living Jewish community and an heir to the ancient Jewish tradition. . . . Thus, in the Zionist view, the emancipation *and assimilation* of the Jew as an individual is a wrong method of pursuing a right aim. *Genuine assimilation* is indeed the true solution for the Jewish problem and ought therefore to be the ultimate goal of Jewish endeavors. . . . If they are to succeed in becoming 'like all the nations,' they must seek assimilation on a national and not on an individual basis . . . they must try to assimilate Jewry itself to England and France . . . [II, 253].

Then, assessing the results of the Zionist movement till 1933, he adds:

> Though the Zionist Movement as a practical undertaking is only half a century old, its social philosophy has already been justified by results. In the Jewish agricultural settlements that have been founded in Palestine within the last fifty years, the children of the ghetto have been transformed out of all recognition into a pioneering peasantry which displays many of the characteristics of the Gentile European colonial type in the New World. The

Zionists have made no miscalculation in their forecast of
the effect which the establishment of a Jewish national
home in Palestine would have upon Jewry itself. The
tragic misfortune into which they have fallen, in company with the Mandatory Power, is their inability to arrive at an understanding with the existing Arab population of the country . . . [II, 253 f.].

The captivation of the Irish by Nationalism, like the captivation of the Jews by Zionism, signifies the final renunciation of a great but tragic past in the hope of securing
in exchange a more modest but perhaps less uncomfort-
able future [II, 425].

. . . the Turkish legatees of the arrested Ottoman Civilization are today content—like the Zionist legatees of a
fossilized Syriac Civilization next door and the Irish legatees of an abortive Far Western Christian Civilization
across the street—to live henceforth in comfortable nonentity as a welcome escape from the no longer tolerable
status of being 'a peculiar people' [III, 49].

A note on the general tenor of these statements is in order before we proceed to an examination of the neo-Zionist
movement. We have already seen that Professor Toynbee
considers Judaism to be a fossil relic even though it perpetuates itself by the cultivation of a noble ethos. Now we learn
that to lose the fossil status means for the Jews "the final
renunciation of a great but tragic past." That the preservation of this past conferred some distinction on the Jews is
apparent from the "fact" that in Zionism the Jews (like the
Turks in their new nationalism) have chosen to live *"henceforth* in comfortable nonentity." They must accordingly de-
cide whether they will remain a worthless and unsightly
archaeological curiosity of distinction or become contented
nobodies. This is a hard choice, partly because it is quite

unintelligible and partly because "comfortable" is not a very accurate description of the Israeli part of Zionism. Professor Toynbee foresees with confidence that nothing of high value will ever come out of the State of Israel (or the new Turkey), just as he is confident that no high values have come out of the Jewish people in the last two thousand years. What can one do in the face of this double omniscience, historical and prophetic?

III

Neo-Zionism, like the Zionism of the past, is a battlefield on which the ancient struggle proceeds for the perpetuation of the Jewish ethos. Some observers have the feeling that this is the end of the struggle: the Jewish ethos will not survive. This is a prejudgment. The contrary feeling, which I share, that the Jewish ethos still has a long future before it, is also a prejudgment. However, if any faithful guardians of the Jewish ethos still exist they must, according to Professor Toynbee, be sought among the Jewish opponents of neo-Zionism; as neo-Zionism today means support of the State of Israel, they must be sought among the Jewish opponents of the State of Israel. These opponents are, first, the *Neturei Carta* in Israel, a fringe freak movement that no one takes seriously except as a minor nuisance; second, the American Council for Judaism, which is extreme Reform and assimilationist; third, the Jewish Communists, who are equally assimilationist, but deny any religious affiliation with Judaism, and in any case cannot even be relied on to be consistent opponents of the State of Israel. Lastly, there are the Jews who wish to disassociate themselves from the Jewish people without passing through intermediary assimilationist stages. In short, Professor Toynbee's estimate amounts to the statement that the Jewish ethos is already dead. This is a legitimate point of view; but Professor Toynbee does not voice it in so many words, whereas he does in various places imply that the ethos of Johanan ben Zakkai may be relied on to keep the Jewish people alive for a long time to come. We are again at a loss as to what he wants to tell us in the final account.

IV

The foundations of the neo-Zionist movement were laid somewhat more than one century ago by extremely ortho-dox Jews who held to the belief that the Jewish State should and could be restored only by the Messiah. This apparent contradiction is resolved only if we think of the Jewish peo-ple in dynamic rather than static terms. During the exile of eighteen hundred years, pious Jews, those with the strong-est Messianic belief, thought it a supreme piety to go to live in the Holy Land, at least for their closing years. It was also an act of piety in the Jewish world at large to support such residents in the Holy Land. The intention of these actions was a-political; the settlers in the Holy Land did not dream of re-creating the Jewish State; but they did believe that their presence in the Holy Land and the enhanced efficacy of the prayers they offered up there would hasten the com-ing of the Messiah and therefore of the Restoration. We have here what looks suspiciously like political pressure on the Messiah, for completely a-political pressure could have been exerted just as efficaciously outside of the Holy Land.

Going to settle in Palestine was a mundane, not a supra-mundane act; so was the supporting of the settlers; and whatever the supra-mundane effects, the mundane are un-deniable. For throughout the exile the Jews maintained in Palestine a moral garrison, a perpetual reminder of the Jew-ish claim. Sometimes the garrison was very small; in the time of Saadia, in the tenth century, it consisted of one thousand families; in the time of the Safad Kabbalists in the seventeenth century it was considerably larger. Let it also be stressed that whatever the numbers of the Jews in Palestine, they considered themselves there as of right, their invisible passports and visas having been issued by God Himself. It was *their* land, even though He had given it temporarily into the keeping of others; and this view was shared by all orthodox Jews throughout the world.

Thus if the number of pious Jews who wanted to settle in the Holy Land had run into tens of thousands instead of hundreds, the phenomenon would have been applauded by all pious Jews even though no Messiah was proclaimed and no intention was declared of re-creating the Jewish State. The emphasis was on orthodoxy. Not that orthodoxy was reliable either; for orthodox Jews by the thousand followed Sabbatai Zevi the Zionist into apostasy; and when Professor Toynbee asks: "What about the *soi-disant* messiahs?" the answer is that there is no foolproof system of human beliefs. The orthodox can be led astray as well as the lax. Our basic question here is whether the activation of the Jewish longing for the Restoration stands in contradiction to the Jewish ethos and religion, and the answer of all orthodox Jews today, with the exception of the *Neturei Carta*, is no.

Let us examine the elements in that longing. I have already referred to some of them. The Restoration was considered necessary and inevitable because continued Jewishness became meaningless without it, the pattern of faith was dislocated. The proposition that the drama of revelation which was Jewish history and which had opened in the Holy Land would find its dénouement elsewhere was unthinkable. Where it had begun in temporary failure, there it had to end in success.

The strength of this feeling expressed itself in the notion that the Holy Land, too, was in exile. It was in exile by separation from the Jewish people not less than the Jewish people by dispersion from it; for the land was not merely a passive stage, but also a participant in the drama. It was even suggested that the Shekhinah, the Divine Essence, was likewise in exile, suffering with the people and the land. Thus the people developed in Judaism the ritual that I described in the last chapter as a continuous preparedness for the Return.

A furious debate is still going on in the Zionist world as to whether the designation of Zionist (neo-Zionist) applies to a Jew who does not go to settle in Israel. Did the classic Messianism of the exile mean that all orthodox Jews wanted to see a Jewish state restored in order that they might go and live there? Let us once more be on our guard against oversimplification. We know that while the Second State was still in existence there were more Jews outside than in it. Palestine could not then, any more than Israel can today, even after Hitler, take in the entire Jewish world population. When the Second State no longer existed, the concept of a Restoration as a Divine Act consummating Jewish history posed a question of a different order. With the coming of the Messiah the world would no longer be the world we know; human actions too would be of a different order; going to live in the Jewish State would mean something not definable in pre-Messianic terms. When the emphasis shifted from the tradition of a Messianic Restoration to the equally valid tradition of mundane action independent of, but not contradicting, the belief in the Messiah, orthodox Jews and others might doubt the practicability of the neo-Zionist enterprise—many of them did—and the inertia of exile might hold them back. Nevertheless the "training" still continued among orthodox and semi-orthodox Jews.

It continued because it was woven into the total symbolism of Jewish belief, and even among Messianists it consisted of something more than abstract symbolism. Complete unworldliness, if it exists at all, is much rarer than complete worldliness. It was a worldly as well as an otherworldly mourning that Messianic Jews expressed in their passionate lamentations for the Destruction and their passionate prayers for the Restoration. The exile was the sign of God's displeasure; it was also a bitterness of the flesh. They wanted God's forgiveness; they also wanted relief from intolerable pressures. But even in interludes of comparative comfort they felt the exile in worldly as well as unworldly terms. It was a shameful thing to belong to a people without a homeland; a Jewish state was necessary to the proper worldly status of Jews everywhere. Thence arose the idea, so often urged in neo-Zionist propaganda, that the creation of the Jewish State meant the solution of the Jewish problem everywhere. Of course it could not mean that. The Jewish problem will only be solved when the demonological anti-Semitism that A *Study of History* perpetuates will have disappeared from the Gentile world; even then there may continue to exist the general problem of minorities, in which Jews will be involved along with others; and even then Professor Toynbee's jarring allusions to the parasitism of Jews and other minorities will be helpful to demagogues. But the illusion that the re-creation of the Jewish State is the panacea for the troubled relations between Jews and Christians had its roots in the Messianic belief.

From the Messianic belief, too, stemmed the feeling that the world could never be a good place as long as a Jewish state in Palestine was not part of it; and this feeling came to be shared by many Protestants, particularly among Anglo-Saxons, for whom the Restoration had to be the prelude to the right ordering of the world. Religious in origin, and largely so in later development, this feeling among the Protestants also spilled over as a kind of folk outlook into less religious areas.

V

Neo-Zionism arose at a time when the modern world was beginning to create in the Jewish people the conditions described by the Adversary in a preceding chapter. Direct and indirect assimilation was taking place on a scale recalling ancient Alexandrian Jewry, but its forms were more varied and complex. There were baptizing Jews, converted or careerist—mostly the latter; there were Jews who repudiated Judaism in the bourgeois rationalist liberal mood characteristic of the nineteenth century; there were Jews who entered revolutionary movements, and among these were blocs that combined revolution with Jewish secular-cultural nationalism. And of course there were countless Jews who simply slipped away.

Most characteristic of the modern era was the "inexorable penetration" of the citadels of faithful Judaism by the new forces described by the Adversary. The rise of compulsory education in most European countries—not excluding Russia and Romania—threatened the existence of the *cheders*, the Jewish elementary schools. The Jews, who had for so many centuries lived, as it were, in colonies (the word is used by the historian Simon Dubnow), saw their separatist life coming to an end. The old techniques for the propagation of Judaism were not equal to the new situation. As Jews were emancipated, obtained the vote, participated in the affairs of the host country, absorbed its culture, and shared in its political activities—and this became increasingly the case even with the ghetto—the development of the specifically Jewish side of the individual by the old methods became more and more difficult. Hence arose the types of "professing" Jews accurately described, again, by the Adversary.

It was not that the Jewish ethos was incompatible with the functions of modern citizenship. To say that would be tantamount to declaring the Jewish ethos to be immoral, a point of view not worth arguing with. It was rather that the pedagogic system of Judaism, which had arisen in and was fitted to a separatist life, was unsuited to an intermingled life. Something drastically new was needed.

In the early and middle part of the nineteenth century there began a movement toward Palestine on the part of extreme orthodox Jews, Russian followers of the Gaon of Vilna, and Hungarian Chassidim, followers of the "Chatam Sofer." They were assisted first by German and Dutch Jewish communities, and later by Sir Moses Montefiore, himself an orthodox Jew, and by scattered groups of Jews in France and America. These were the Jews who began the modern city of Jerusalem outside the old walls and, later, the first modern agricultural settlement, Petach Tikvah. There was observable at the same time, outside the Jewish world, a renewed interest in the idea of the Restoration as a practical, immediate, mundane enterprise. (For details see Nahum Sokolow's *History of Zionism*, 1919.)

Once more, let it be noted that these pious Jews did not think of themselves as the vanguard of a Jewish state. But their action was taking place in a very different setting from that of the medieval settlers in the Holy Land. They were fleeing from a Europe that was to all appearances becoming more habitable for Jews; and they were being assisted by Jews who, however deluded, believed that their emancipation in Europe would proceed rapidly from the political to the moral. The impulse behind this movement, the real beginning of neo-Zionism, long antedating the appearance of Herzl and the first Zionist Congress, was the folk feeling that the something drastically new which was needed in Jewish life was a specific Jewish center in the Holy Land, such as had not existed hitherto since the Destruction, from which Jewish influence, not denaturized by assimilative infiltration, might radiate to the Diaspora.

In other words, neo-Zionism was an instinctive countermove on the part of the Jewish people against the threat of assimilation presented by specifically modern conditions. Later on, toward the end of the nineteenth century, the philosophy of the "radiating center" was made articulate and systematized in a "secular" neo-Zionism, of which Achad Ha-Am was the first exponent and Chaim Weizmann, like most of his colleagues, a protagonist. The word "secular" must be taken here in a special sense. The neo-Zionism of the east European Jews has always been largely religious in intent even when secular in terminology. The ethos of Judaism was deeply embedded in it. It would be absurd to say of Weizmann, Bialik, Achad Ha-Am, Shmarya Levin, Menachem Mendel Ussisskin, and the other east-European Zionist leaders (I will not speak of the rabbinic leaders) that they were irreligious. They did discard some of the symbols and terms of accepted orthodoxy; but in effect they were looking for new symbols and terms for the teaching of the original God-inspired ethos.

Can the pious Jews of the early period of neo-Zionism, the followers of the Gaon of Vilna and the "Chatam Sofer," be called neo-Zionists? Let us consider. By their practical efforts in Palestine, by their unconscious recognition of the need for a new technique of survival, they assisted the Zionist movement. If they later turned violently on the "secular" and the genuinely secular neo-Zionists, it was not because these wanted to settle in Palestine or help Jews settle there, but because they did not follow the ritualistic observances, did not use the old terminology, and did not subscribe to the Messianist formula of the Restoration. As in medieval times, had tens of thousands followed the original

neo-Zionists to Palestine, but with the right ritual and terminology, they would have been welcomed instead of opposed.

It is difficult, again, to define in terms of neo-Zionism the
assimilating and semi-assimilating Jews who began giving
their financial support to the Jewish Homeland when it
became a burning, practical issue. They, like the early pietists who settled in Palestine, did not aim at a Jewish state
and did not want one; but they have been just as useful in
the creation of the State of Israel. They were drawn into the
building up of Jewish Palestine by inescapable philanthropic
duty, and again, like the orthodox, they have made their
peace with the idea of the Jewish State. Another inevitable
change has taken place. The steady raising of funds for
Palestine and Israel, though accompanied by a minimum of
intelligent pedagogic effort (Hadassah, the Women's Zionist Organization, with its significant influence on the Jewish
home, is a notable exception), has awakened in numbers of
semi-assimilating American Jews an interest in more than
their philanthropic duty; the humanitarian appeal had stim-
ulated a longing, still vague and uninformed, but of mounting intensity, for the fundamentals of Judaism. This is the
parallel to which I have already referred between the Diaspora's payment of Temple dues in the Second Jewish State
and the Diaspora's participation today in the support of Israel. Here too, as I have mentioned, is one of the explanations, perhaps the most important, of the restless groping
among third-generation American Jews for the heritage of
the Jewish people.

VI

Neo-Zionism became a battleground when non-orthodox
Jews, with the Jewish ethos, but without some of its symbols

and dogmas, entered the movement toward Palestine. To
what degree these were irreligious or secularist I shall discuss
shortly. The conflict deepened when a purely European nationalism, such as Professor Toynbee mistakenly ascribes to
neo-Zionism as a whole, and a flatly irreligious and anti-religious element (coming much later) also entered the movement.

Some of Professor Toynbee's observations (and one need
not agree with his blanket repudiation of modern nationalism, which has been creative as well as destructive) apply to
part of the secularist-nationalist elements in neo-Zionism;
what he does here, however, is what the New Testament
(with Professor Toynbee following suit) has done with the
Pharisees: ignore everything that does not fit in with a negative picture. There are large numbers of neo-Zionists who
certainly want the Jewish people, or that part of it which
will settle in Israel, to become "like all the nations," and
who see it becoming just that. They do not, I think, subscribe to the prophecy that the new nation will be a "comfortable nonentity," but they want to be done with "the peculiar people." There are neo-Zionists who find a delicious
excitation in the sight of Israeli soldiers, the Israeli flag, and
in the thought of Israeli ambassadors, ministers, and representatives in the United Nations. This excitation is not to
be confused with a feeling of satisfaction in the possession
of certain necessary instruments of governmental action. It
is that miserable passion which, always sinful, has now become doubly sinister, as well as ludicrous, in a world which
is struggling against the impulse to self-destruction. For
them the purpose of Zionism has become the creation of
"the Fighting Jew," whose existence is in itself the fulfillment of the only Zionism they can understand. Comically
enough, they want to become "like all the nations" when
the nations no longer want to be like themselves. The best

moral elements in humanity are moving away from the mob psychology of nationalism; these neo-Zionists are only just catching up with it. They think they are entitled to their fling, and whether in Israel, or in America, or elsewhere, they are determined to have it; they are going to get drunk while the rest of the world is trying to sober up, and they want the whole neo-Zionist movement to be drunk with them. They think of this as "justice to the Jew," and "our turn has come at last."

Opposite these atavisms, which are not so much fascist as pre-fascist, or proto-fascist, stand the anti-religious groups that are concentrated in the Communist and pro-Communist movement. Their philosophy is familiar, if not intelligible, to anyone, anywhere, who has read, or tried to read, the *Daily Worker* of London or New York, or *Pravda*, or *L'Humanité*. Should these be called "nationalists"? A discussion of their views has more psychological than political or historical interest, and would be largely irrelevant here.

I have been careful to point out in the last paragraph but one that we are dealing with "part of the secular-nationalist element in neo-Zionism." I shall be challenged by those who believe that secular nationalism is vicious through and through, and that all secular nationalists are mobsters. Here one can open an endless debate. One can also debate endlessly whether the Jewish ethos can exist outside of orthodox circles. I shall content myself with a brief statement of opinion.

We may begin by returning to the question: can atheists be moral? I have answered: certainly. My quarrel with atheism is not that atheists must be bad people, for some of them have been very good people, but that, besides being wrong, they practice what they cannot effectively preach, goodness being unteachable in atheism. Let us take the converse: can believers be bad people? We know they can, and these cannot effectively teach what they do not practice. In other words, we are dealing with human inconsistency. It is correct to say, I think, that moral atheists and immoral believers do not even understand what they believe.

The Bible does not deny that there can be goodness in idolaters. One only has to remember Ruth, the sailors in the Book of Jonah, Ebedmelech, the two Abimelechs in the stories of Abraham and Isaac. Idolatry and atheism resemble each other in that they preach relativism in morals; thus, when the idolater and the atheist have an innate goodness and practice it, they nevertheless block the channel for its transmission to others.

The Jewish ethos still exists most intensely in orthodox circles, but in orthodox circles will also be found participants in that mob nationalism which is an utter contradiction of the Jewish ethos. For just as orthodox Jews could err in following a False Messiah, thus negating their orthodoxy, so some can and do negate it in succumbing to the lure of mob nationalism. "Thou shalt not follow a multitude to do evil" (Exodus xxiii, 2). The Jewish ethos, again, will be found among the secular-nationalists, and among Jewish agnostics and atheists, and the question for me is how long it can continue to exist there if it does not revert to a form of orthodoxy in belief, whatever the forms of symbol and ritual and dogma it adopts. Secular-nationalism can be, and in many places is, consistent with purity of moral purpose and action, and my objection to it (as to atheism) among non-Jews as well as Jews lies in its ultimately fatal pedagogic impotence.

Professor Toynbee asks:

. . . how was a God-fearing Jewry to reconcile itself with a secular Zionist movement that numbered agnostics among its leaders, and whose programme had been in-

spired, not by the messianic visions of post-Exilic Jewish
prophets, but by the blue-prints of a Western Gentile Nationalism whose prophets had been a King Louis XI of
France, a King Henry VII of England, and the Florentine
publicist Niccolò Machiavelli? [VIII, 300].

This brings us to the heart of the present discussion. We
have seen that a God-fearing Jewry has in fact reconciled itself to a Jewish state—that is, unless the Mizrachi never was,
and unless the *Agudath Israel* has ceased to be God-fearing—without reconciling itself to the present leadership of
Zionism and Israel. But what is the nature of the agnosticism of the "agnostic" leaders, and what is the true character of the secularist branch of the movement?

I have already touched on these phenomena in their extreme manifestations of the right and left, pointing out that
they constitute, in the sum, a minority of the Israeli people.
They are not representatives of the solid body of so-called
Secular Zionism.

If I think of recent secular Zionist leaders and teachers
who are no longer among the living—of Herzl, Achad Ha-
Am, Weizmann, Sokolow, Jabotinsky, Shmarya Levin,
Chaim Nachman Bialik—I am not able to fasten on a single
one of them the label of Agnostic or Atheist in the usual
sense of either word, as it could be fastened, for instance, on
a Voltaire, a Bradlaugh, a Huxley, or an Ingersoll. The men
to whom it properly belongs are to be found only in the
Communist-Zionist (strange yoking of words!) group. As to
the leaders I have just mentioned by name, they no doubt
varied in the degrees of their faith in God, and the least believing was still in some sense a believer. Of Herzl and Jabotinsky it may be said that they became the patron saints of
the most secular branch of secular Zionism outside of the
Communists; but I am not sure that the followers have not

outrun their masters. It should be borne in mind that these
two men did not receive the traditional Jewish education in
their childhood, and that Herzl acquired very little knowledge of Judaism later, and none at all of Hebrew. Jabotinsky
as an adult made good the deficiency as far as the language
was concerned. The others were steeped in the tradition;
their knowledge of Judaism was both folkist and academic,
and it was a knowledge of emotional participation. Their
ethos was Jewish.

Their nationalism was not that founded by Louis XI of
France, Henry VII of England, and Niccolò Machiavelli. It
was the nationalism I have described as felt by the simple
Jewish masses. It was interwoven with the Bible—all of
them had a deep love of it, and read it continually in the
original—and with a sense of a non-secular meaning in human history. It was not based, like the nationalisms of the
modern Western countries, on the economic developments
of territorial units. It had its economic argumentation in relation to the Jewish position, but it had not grown with
the internecine European struggle for markets; it had not
followed the line from feudalism to mercantilism, from
mercantilism to capitalism. It adapted itself to these stages
in the European scene; it did not imbibe post-medieval European nationalism any more than it had imbibed the tradition of medieval chivalry. How far Professor Toynbee is
from understanding this is revealed by the account he gives
of his contact with Weizmann:

To the author of this Study the spiritual and political
duress under which the Ashkenazim have had to live their
life in 'the Pale' was brought home by the following two
anecdotes which were recounted to him in 1919, during
the Peace Conference of Paris, by Dr. Chaim Weizmann
in order to explain why this great statesman and scien-

tist—the most distinguished member of the Ashkenazi community in his generation—had become a convert to Zionism.

The first anecdote was this. In Dr. Weizmann's boyhood, at Vilna,[1] there was a young Jewish sculptor of great promise who was expected to become one of the historic exponents of the Jewish culture. The young man's promise was fulfilled, but Jewry's hope was disappointed; for the *chef d'œuvre* in which this Jewish artist eventually gave expression to his genius was a statue of the Russian Orthodox Christian Czar Ivan the Terrible! Under the duress of 'the Pale,' Jewish genius had been perverted to the glorification of Jewry's oppressors. It was as if the *chef d'œuvre* of Jewish literature in the second century B.C. had not been the Book of Ecclesiastes or the Psalms but some panegyric, in the Isocratean manner, upon Antiochus Epiphanes. . . .

Dr. Weizmann's second anecdote was an incident which had happened to himself as a grown man before his migration from Vilna [*sic*] to Manchester. A piece of urgent business made it indispensable for him to break the Russian law then in force, under the Czardom, by trespassing beyond the eastern boundary of 'the Pale' in order to have a personal meeting with a friend in Moscow. As a precaution against the vigilance of the Russian police, it was arranged beforehand that Dr. Weizmann should travel from Vilna to Moscow in a train arriving at nightfall, do his business in his friend's house during the night, and return to Vilna by a train leaving Moscow before dawn; but this arrangement fell through. For some reason, the friend whom Dr. Weizmann had come to see was unable to keep the appointment; and Dr. Weizmann found on inquiry that there was no return-train to Vilna earlier

---

[1] Dr. Weizmann never lived in Vilna.

than the train which he had been intending to take. How should he pass the night hours? To engage a room in a hotel would be tantamount to delivering himself up to the police. Dr. Weizmann solved the problem by hiring a cab and driving round and round the streets of Moscow until the hour of his train's departure. 'And that,' he concluded, 'was how I had to pass my time on my one and only visit to the capital of the Empire of which I was supposed to be a citizen!'

Such anecdotes as these sufficiently explain the êthos of the Ashkenazi immigrants from 'the Pale' into the more enlightened countries of the modern Western World . . . [II, 242 f.].

Do they indeed? And do they also "sufficiently" explain to Professor Toynbee why Dr. Weizmann had "become a convert to Zionism"? I think that even as a feature article in a popular newspaper this piece of writing would not pass muster. The fact is, of course, that Dr. Weizmann never had to "become a convert to Zionism" anymore than Johanan ben Zakkai had to be "converted" to the Way of Gentleness. He grew up in Zionism even as Johanan ben Zakkai grew up in Pharisaism. Dr. Weizmann writes in *Trial and Error*, his autobiography:

In my early childhood Zionist ideas and aspirations were already awake in Russian Jewry. My father was not yet a Zionist, but the house was steeped in rich Jewish tradition, and Palestine was at the center of the ritual, a longing for it implicit in our life. Practical nationalism did not assume form till some years later, but the "Return" was in the air, a vague, deep-rooted Messianism, a hope which would not die [American edition, 1951, p. 11].

If Professor Toynbee merely wishes to say that persecution in general explains the ethos of the Ashkenazi Jews, he is, in my opinion, still wrong. Many peoples have been persecuted, though none as persistently as the Jewish people, one obvious reason being that none has stood up to persecution—and in exile, at that—as long as the Jews. Persecution is *one* of the factors that have contributed to the Ashkenazi ethos; other factors I have described at some length.

That "the ultimate aim of the Zionists is to liberate the Jewish people from the peculiar psychological complex induced by the penalization to which they have been subjected for centuries in the Gentile World" is misleading part-truth. Partially true, and misleading, is also the statement that the Zionists "agree with the Assimilationists in wishing to cure the Jews of being 'a peculiar people.'" All Zionists (and non-Zionists) want to see the stigmata produced by persecution in exile removed from Jewish life, but this is not the creative side of Zionism; it is regarded as a curative effect to be produced by the affirmations of Zionism. Further, the Jews can be "a peculiar people" without being "penalized" as a minority: they were a peculiar people in ancient times. Only those who have no knowledge of Judaism regard the "peculiarity" of the Jews as having been created by persecution. Professor Toynbee may have that view, or may be implying it here; it may be one of the reasons behind his use of the word "fossil"; but he errs in that just as—and for the same reason that—he errs in thinking that experiences or stories of persecution "converted" Weizmann to Zionism.

That there are Zionists and Israeli Jews who aim at total assimilation in the sense here intended by Professor Toynbee is undeniable. But when were there *not* numbers of Jews who wanted total assimilation? What is it that the Prophets fought if not assimilation—and that in the Jewish State itself? Certainly Jews who believe that merely living in a Jewish state and speaking Hebrew constitute Judaism or guarantee the existence of a specifically Jewish people are assimilationists; even as Ahab and Jezebel, and Jeroboam the Second, and Manasseh, who all lived in a Jewish state and spoke Hebrew, were assimilationists. To say that Israel is assimilationist because there are Israelis who are indifferent to or contemptuous of Judaism and the Jewish ethos is like citing the Hasmoneans as the true and effective representatives of Judaism in their time; or, for that matter, the defaulting members of the Pharisaic movement.

I have said that the New Testament description of the Pharisees is accurate for part of the Pharisaic body round the time of Jesus. The Talmud itself, in Tractate Sotah, classifies the sinners among them, and stories are told elsewhere of Pharisaic leaders whose arrogance and quarrelsomeness belied the principles of their school. For it was not likely that, having exposed in their most sacred book the shortcomings of the Patriarchs, Prophets, and Kings, the Jews would hesitate to record those of their later teachers. We know, too, that there were among the Pharisees warlike spirits, supporters of the Zealots; but we also know that the majority was faithful to the original and continuing pacifist spirit of Pharisaism. Such divisions in ethically oriented movements are universal. For rough parallels we may glance at the history of Christian Orders founded for charitable purposes and then attracting and developing internal power groups. This is what happened with the Knights Hospitalers of St. John, with the Teutonic Order, and with others which, in spite of the deviationists, never lost, and sometimes almost wholly recovered, their original character.

We shall find the same pattern in the Chassidic movement, one of the periodic renewals of the Jewish ethos. It began among the humble and unlettered, the founder himself being a comparatively unlettered man who lived in great poverty. Those who gathered about him, the earliest Chassidic teachers, were men of religious genius whose impress on the movement can never be erased. But within two or three generations Chassidism had its wealthy prelates, its dynasties, its rank superstitions, its snobberies, its un-Chassidic and un-Judaistic mob following. Nevertheless Chassidism remains a creative force, and has found its own renewal in a restatement of its legends and principles and spirit. Until forty or fifty years ago, Jewish scholars and historians of the modern school often reported on it in a negative, partisan spirit of total condemnation, after the manner of the New Testament reporting of the Pharisees; today it is finding recognition as it gathers strength. Neo-Zionism must be seen in this context and in the general context of the everlasting Jewish struggle.

I cannot help wondering what picture Professor Toynbee has in his mind of the Jewish people at the time when they were raising themselves spiritually "head and shoulders," as he says, above the surrounding peoples of ancient Syria. Does he see a nation consisting mostly of saints and visionaries and God-seekers? He speaks of the existence, in the most glorious epoch—the Prophetic—of a base "truant minority." I have indicated that this minority may in fact have been a majority. I do not know what proportion of the Israeli population is "total assimilationist," nor do I wish to imply that we have in Israel today the equals of the ancient Prophets. I do know, from long and continuous contact, that the struggle round the Jewish ethos continues today as it has continued from the first evidences of the emergence of a pagan nationalism.

What has the internal political history of the Jewish settlement in Palestine, and then the State of Israel, been, if not precisely that struggle? In the days of the Arab Terror, when the great majority of the Jews of Palestine adopted a policy of *Havlagah*, of self-restraint, suffering, and opposition to reprisals, what was it but the ancient Jewish ethos exerting itself against the Way of Violence? When the dissident groups in Palestine broke out against *Havlagah* and engaged in one of those vendetta wars which are always ascending and widening spirals of destruction, what was it but the ancient paganism against the Jewish ethos? In the days of the Jewish Terror against the British, when on the walls of Tel Aviv and Jerusalem and Haifa the dissidents chalked the words: "Down with Pétain-Weizmann," what was it, again, but the ancient internal struggle, now expressed in the symbols of the Sternists and Revisionists on the one hand, and of Weizmann and his colleagues, representing a majority of the Jewish population, on the other? And even today, in the opening period of the State, when provocation has been increased beyond human endurance and reprisals have become almost standard, the struggle is still on, with a deep and instinctive recoil in the majority of Israelis against the reflex actions to which they have been reduced. Of this new situation, however, more in the next chapter.

VII

A note on Professor Toynbee's treatment of the revival of Hebrew as a spoken language. He cites four other instances of what he calls "linguistic Archaism" in the modern Western World: the Norwegian, the Irish, the Ottoman Turk, and the Greek. He writes:

Our fifth instance . . . is the reconversion of Hebrew into a vernacular language of everyday life on the lips and in the ears of the Zionist Jews from the Diasporà who have settled in Palestine; and this is the most remarkable case of all the five . . . [VI, 70].

This statement is preceded by a satirical reference to the little peoples which, in new-found freedom, or in renaissance, are seeking to re-establish cherished languages, their own. He speaks of

> the laborious and ludicrous expedient of fabricating the 'mother-tongue' that they are determined to possess, in the temper of a *nouveau-riche* who furnishes himself with portraits of appropriate ancestors [VI, 63].

Ignorant of the values to be found in the languages the four other peoples are attempting to revive, I will confine myself to the meaning of the rebirth of Hebrew, with the preliminary observation that in this general question the Toynbeean statistical, over-all method of classification is peculiarly inept and impertinent; each case must be examined separately. Laborious the re-establishment of Hebrew certainly was; it certainly had and has its ludicrous moments— there are always comical episodes in the learning of a language; and Professor Toynbee, with ostentatious shyness, pleads with Greek scholars not to make fun of the Greek poem he has written as a preface to A *Study of History*. (What did he want to do that for?) But those who know from the inside the Judaizing effect that the revival of Hebrew has had on some segments of the Jewish people will be puzzled by Professor Toynbee's metaphor of the "*nouveau riche.*"

Myself an indifferent Hebraist, I was led by the Zionist movement to establish living contact with the language of the Prophets, and if I have indeed to some extent recaptured their message in the original, I am again indebted in a great measure to this contact. *Nouveau riche?* Here is a national heritage considerably older than the English of Professor Toynbee or even the Greek with which he adorns his opus. He calls the revival of Hebrew the most remarkable

of the five instances of "linguistic Archaism," but does not
tell us why; and I cannot guess whether he knows as little
about the other four as he knows about the fifth. But certainly one section of the Zionist movement was drawn to
Hebrew by a spiritual impulse akin to that of Isaiah and
Amos, and this is not less true because there are Hebrew-
speaking atheists and agnostics—as there were, of course, in
the days of Isaiah and Amos. Let us note, too, as one of the
fantastic features of this complex movement called Zionism, or neo-Zionism, that many Hebrew-speaking agnostics
and atheists, even on the extreme left, cannot rid themselves
of the Prophetic Books. I have heard them again and again
driven for self-expression to the moral intuitions of the Hebrew Prophets, whom they frequently quote at length by
heart while contemptuously denying any intellectual community with them. Is this the Devil quoting Scripture or is
it a spiritual anchor to windward? Which is more significant, their quotations or their disclaimers? We may be sure
of one thing: the apostates of the time of Isaiah did not
go about repeating his moral pronouncements with the passion (and the intellectual confusion) of many Israeli unbelievers.

There were purely practical reasons for the revival of Hebrew as the language of the new homeland which was to
gather its inhabitants from the four corners of the earth.
Yiddish predominated among the newcomers until recently,
and yet it was the Yiddish-speaking neo-Zionists who converted themselves, with a painful effort, into Hebrew-speaking Israelis. They felt that no particular language of the exile, whether Yiddish, or Ladino, or any other, had the right
to impose itself on other exile languages. It is an astonishing fact that the—at one time—fanatical opponents of Yiddish in Palestine were Yiddish-speaking neo-Zionists who
were tormenting themselves into the use of Hebrew. As a

unifier of the fragmented Jewish groups who came into Palestine, Hebrew was strategically indispensable.

There were other reasons of a psychological practical nature not so easily formulated. Yiddish, though it had become a wonderful vehicle for Judaism, was specifically an exile acquisition. Its perpetuation in Palestine would have been a perpetuation of exile tradition in the land of freedom. In a strange pattern of cross-purposes the old-time Messianist neo-Zionists of Palestine clung to Yiddish as the language of daily use, retaining Hebrew as the medium of religious and scholastic expression, while the new "secular" non-Messianist neo-Zionists insisted on the Biblical tongue for everyday purposes. Within Palestine, the struggle between Yiddish and Hebrew represented the wider struggle between those orthodox Jews who wanted Jews to come to Palestine with a Messianist outlook and the other Jews, orthodox and non-orthodox, who had a worldly approach to the Restoration. Today, with Hebrew triumphant, the hostility toward Yiddish has subsided, and an affectionate regard for this great achievement of the exile is in the ascendant.

But the most powerful reasons for the cultivation of Hebrew were of a spiritual practical nature. There was felt to be a profound impropriety in a reunion of the Jewish people and the Holy Land which did not also include a reunion with Hebrew, the language in which the spiritual self-consciousness of the Jewish people had crystallized with this landscape as background. That secularists and even leftists and avowed unbelievers, as against a dwindling group of the super-orthodox, should have shared this feeling with orthodox Jews is another of the fascinating oddities of neo-Zionism; and this is what gives a special coloration to the "secularism" of a great many Zionists. It is a secularism tinged with a corrective nostalgia for the tradition.

Of all this Professor Toynbee glimpses nothing. Nor does it ever occur to him that in re-establishing Hebrew as a living language the neo-Zionists have opened to the world a pathway to the original sources of the faith of the Western World. But I am forgetting. Professor Toynbee is allergic to this "old-fashioned Syriac oracle."

VIII

A *Study of History* is issued under the auspices of the Royal Institute of International Affairs, of which, we learn on the title pages of the ten volumes, Professor Toynbee is Director of Studies. We learn further that the Institute "is an unofficial body, founded in 1920 to encourage and facilitate the scientific study of international questions." Also: "The Institute, as such, is precluded by its rules from expressing an opinion on any aspects of international affairs; opinions expressed in this book are, therefore, purely individual." The Institute is thus absolved from responsibility for the views Professor Toynbee expresses on Jewish and other matters; but it still remains responsible, I suppose, for retaining him at least since 1933 as Director of Studies— scientific studies, at that. Nor is this a purely academic responsibility, as we shall see.

Professor Toynbee has written:

> The tragic misfortune into which they [the Zionists] have fallen, in company with the Mandatory Power, is their inability to arrive at an understanding with the existing Arab population of the country . . . [above, p. 189].

Let us set side by side with this innocent statement two statements from the autobiography of Chaim Weizmann, first President of the State of Israel, whom Professor Toynbee admires so much and understands so little. Looking

back to 1919, when England had been in occupation of
Palestine for a year, Weizmann wrote in 1947:

> On the whole the spirit governing officialdom was not
> conducive to co-operation between ourselves and the Brit-
> ish or between ourselves and the Arabs [op. cit., p. 224].
> I tried to find an answer to a question which was to oc-
> cupy me for the remainder of my life. Why, from the very
> word go should we have had to face the hostility or at best
> the frosty neutrality of Britain's representatives on the
> spot? . . . And why was it an almost universal rule that
> such administrators as came out favorably inclined turned
> against us in a few months? [ibid., p. 258].

The early years of British obstruction to Zionist work in
Palestine may be charitably ascribed to the unprecedented
nature of the task; and some of the obstruction, from beginning to end, to divided opinion among the British. But
the later years should have produced a crop of sympathetic
administrators. They never did; sympathetic administrators
were always few and far between. Granted the difficulties
and perplexities added by the approach of the Second
World War, granting more than is morally permissible to
England's Imperial needs, there was still room for enormous
improvement in the attitude and insight of British official-
dom. If no improvement took place, we have the right to say
that Professor Toynbee had his share in promoting the
tragic misfortune he laments, as well as another—the Zionist
quarrel with Britain. One realizes with a shock what views
on Zionism, on Judaism, and on the values in the Jewish
people the Director of the influential Royal Institute of International Affairs must have imparted not only to the public, but to the young men of "Chatham House," who in
their turn exerted an influence on the formulation and administration of British policy in Palestine. How much un-

derstanding would they bring to the problem, and how much promote between Jews and Arabs? What could they be expected to understand of the tidal spiritual wave that carried the Zionist movement?

The Zionist quarrel with Great Britain is over, and Jews prefer now to remember that there were great spirits in England whose generous insights helped launch the enterprise and acted as a deterrent on those who did their best to wreck it. But there was, fortunately, something more than a group of men at the top; there was, in England as in America, that wider sensitivity to the religious folklore connected with the idea of the Jewish Restoration. There were, in this sensitivity, overtones of the tradition of fair play and of simple compassion for the underdog; but dominant was a kind of awe in the face of a phenomenon beyond the range of commonplace understanding, and therefore doubly connected with the religious sense. It must never be forgotten that such emotions, deriving from the Bible, have played their part not only in the survival of Jewry despite millennial persecution, but also in the re-creation of the Jewish State in spite of overwhelming difficulties.

It is heartening to think of *this* response to the appeal of the State of Israel, and to turn from the narrowness of Professor Toynbee's approach to the largeness of view expressed by the American writer Lewis Mumford:

The binding force of an ethical force based on purpose has been dramatically confirmed in the history of the Jews: its practical consummation in our own time perhaps merits our special note. Scattered to the four corners of the earth, the Jews, during the long period of the Dispersion, still retained their faith in a divine promise: in the restoration of Jerusalem, in the advent of a Messiah, and finally, in the prophecy of Isaiah, of the coincident coming of a day when the nations will no longer war against one another, but join together in ways of peace.

All these purposes may well, at many grievous times during the last two millenniums, have seemed delusional projections: the reactions of desperate souls to unfortunate political and social conditions: reactions bearing every mark of a collective neurosis. By holding to these purposes, the Jews kept together as a people under conditions that would have ground any less hopeful nation out of existence: that itself would constitute a pragmatic justification of purpose. But these goal-seeking people have done more than hold together, while their conquerors and oppressors, given to ephemeral satisfactions and immediate aims, vanished. Today the Jews have performed the incredible feat of returning as a unified political group to their native home in Palestine. Thus a collective purpose, working over an almost cosmic stretch of time, has brought its own fulfilment. By that fact, every contributory ceremony and ritual and prayer, every hardship and sacrifice, has been retrospectively justified. The mere existence of Israel today is a testimonial to the dynamics of purposive development. If the Greeks had had such a vision of life, they might have left an even deeper impression upon modern man. [*The Conduct of Life*, 1951, p. 139.]

Here the perspective is properly broadened far beyond the limits of Jewish interest. The creation of Israel is perceived as an event in the history of civilization; and such it was felt to be by millions of gentiles of varying degrees of religious consciousness. There are perhaps signs in the air that the author of this passage again struck the right note in reminding us "of the coincident coming of a day when the nations will no longer war against one another, but join together in ways of peace."

CHAPTER FOURTEEN

SUPPRESSIO
VERI

I

Thus far, in speaking of the treatment of Jewish values in *A Study of History*, I have referred to the confused and the hostile. In evaluating the treatment of events attending the birth of Israel these mild strictures will no longer suffice. We are dealing with contemporaneous events. What is more, we are going to deal with a report on these events which has been issued under the editorship of Professor Toynbee himself; and it is in his ignoring of the largest part of this report, parallel with his use of a tiny part which fits in with his intemperate criticism of the Jews, and his failure to cite other reports to justify his invidious choice of material, that Professor Toynbee exhibits a partisanship of the most violent order.

II

The Survey of International Affairs is a publication issued, like Professor Toynbee's *A Study of History*, under the auspices of the Royal Institute for International Affairs. This body, as we have noted, was "founded in 1920 to encourage and facilitate the scientific study of international questions." Its Director of Studies, we have also noted, is Professor Toynbee himself; he is also the editor of the *Surveys*, in one of which a Mr. George Kirk gives his version of the events attending Israel's achievement of independence.

It is in my opinion a biased version. I did not expect anything else. It did not surprise me that, in an earlier account, Mr. Kirk had written:

> Zionists were apt to compare the discrimination against Jews in the Diaspora with that against 'colored' people; but once in their 'ancient homeland' they themselves behaved as a *Herrenvolk*. [*Survey for 1939–46*, Vol. II, *The Middle East and the War*, 1952, p. 250, n.].

It did not surprise me because I had learned to regard the *Surveys* not as "scientific" studies, but as slanted pronouncements with a general conformity to the group view of the "Chatham House" membership or following. I have therefore chosen Mr. Kirk's account as being the least open to the suspicion of pro-Jewish or pro-Zionist bias; and in giving below a résumé (almost entirely in quotations) of this account of the events under discussion, I am willing to accept it at face value as the basis of my charges against *A Study of History*. (The account is entitled *The Middle East 1945–50*, and was published in a 1954 volume. Mr. Kirk refers throughout to "the Zionists," for which read "the Jews of Palestine.")

I begin with an observation that occurs in the middle of the account. The rest, except for the closing excerpt, is in chronological order.

> The Secretary General of the United Nations had optimistically told the Palestine Commission [UNSCOP—United Nations Special Commission of Palestine] at its first meeting on 9 January [1947]: 'You are entitled to be confident that, in the event it should prove necessary, the Security Council will assume the full measure of responsibility in implementation of the Assembly's resolution' [p. 257].

The resolution that later had to be implemented was that of November 29, 1947, which, by a vote of 33 to 13, called for the partition of Palestine and the setting up of a Jewish state.

> During the four months that had elapsed since the departure of the United Nations Committee from Palestine, there had been sporadic attacks by Arabs on Jews which had been checked by Haganah reprisals . . . [p. 251].
> The Haganah was mobilized for self-defence, the Zionists complaining that the British security forces were not doing enough to protect Jewish lives and property. Almost certainly they were now doing less than their strict duty in the matter, for the temper of the British soldiers in Palestine had been affected by the fact that they had lost 127 killed and 331 wounded at the hands of Jewish terrorists between the end of the Second World War and 20 October 1947 . . . [p. 252].

The general fighting increased:

> Both sides committed shocking outrages in Haifa and Jerusalem as the new year came in [1948] . . . [p. 253]. Frontal attacks upon Jewish settlements were almost invariably costly failures for the Arabs, but they evolved a more effective, if more protracted strategy of reducing the outlying settlements by attacks upon the road communications by which they were supplied with provisions and munitions; these attacks were bloody affairs in which neither side was accustomed to give quarter or return prisoners . . . [p. 254].
> At the beginning of April the Zionists were still seriously challenged by the 'Arab Liberation Army,' which had by this time publicly received the blessing of the Govern-

ments of the Arab states and had been reinforced to a strength of between 6,000 and 7,500 men, preponderantly Syrians and 'Irāqīs, with an Egyptian contingent at Gaza. The Arab forces were based, with a large measure of British tolerance, on localities within the territory assigned to the Arab State by the resolution on partition . . . [p. 260].

[On April 9] . . . an I.Z.L. (Irgun Zvai Leumi, Revisionist) and Stern Group force about 200 strong attacked the Arab village of Dair Yāsīn. . . . The I.Z.L. afterwards claimed to have suffered appreciable casualties in the house-to-house fighting that followed; but of Arabs some 250 were killed, about half of them women and children. . . . The Arabs retaliated in their turn by intercepting on the outskirts of Jerusalem a Jewish convoy bound for the isolated Hadassah Hospital and the Hebrew University on the strategic Mount Scopus ridge, and killed some seventy-seven doctors, nurses, and university teachers and students . . . [pp. 260 f.].

[The Arab Legion of Transjordan] . . . after taking part in the occupation of the Kfar Etsion group of Jewish settlements isolated in Arab territory 12 miles south-west of Jerusalem, intervened to defend what remained of Arab Jerusalem, and began shelling the Jewish New City. In the first fortnight of fighting they inflicted upon its 100,000 civilians some 1,200 casualties, of whom 450 were killed, and slow paralysis was threatened by the cutting of supplies and reinforcements . . . [pp. 271 f.].

On 17 May, three days after the open intervention of the Arab states, the United States delegation had submitted to the Security Council a resolution, under Article 39 of the Charter, ordering the belligerents to cease fire within thirty-six hours. However, the chief British delegate, Sir Alexander Cadogan, questioned both the desirability of invoking Article 39 (with its attempt to define an aggressor against whom sanctions might be taken) and the practicability of applying a stand-still order in the present fluid situation . . . [p. 272].

I have left for the end of my quotations from the Kirk Report a passage that occurs in the middle, in order that the reader may be able to contrast it more easily with Professor Toynbee's statement on the "expulsion."

The beginnings of the Arab mass flight went back to an early stage in the Arab-Jewish fighting. As early as 27 January the High Commissioner had confirmed a 'steady exodus' of Arab middle-class families who could afford to leave the country, taking with them cars and considerable quantities of household goods. In March Zionist sources estimated that 20,000–25,000 Arabs had already left Haifa and 15,000–20,000 Jaffa; and the Arab irregulars' use of conveniently situated Arab villages as bases for attacks on Jewish localities, and the consequent Jewish reprisals against such villages, had caused a substantial flight of Arabs from villages on the fringes of Jewish territories to safer places. A subsequent Zionist assertion that 'many weeks' before the Dair Yāsīn massacre the Arab Higher Committee had 'called on the Arab population to leave the country en masse' should be treated with reserve in the absence of positive evidence to corroborate it; but there can be no question that the publicity which the Arab press and radio gave to the massacre at Dair Yāsīn for the purpose of attracting sympathy greatly accelerated the demoralization and flight of non-combatant Arabs. At this stage of the fighting the Jewish attitude to the Arab flight was ambiguous, since, while there is clear evidence that the civil authorities at Haifa tried to tranquillize the Arab population, the Jewish combatants there and elsewhere made skilful use of psychological warfare to break their opponents' morale, and the effect upon the civilians was only what was to be expected. At a later stage, the Israeli armed forces did not confine their pressure on the Arab civilian population to playing upon their fears. They forcibly expelled them: for example, the population of 'Akka (including refugees from Haifa) in May [1948]; the population of Lydda and Ramla (including refugees from Jaffa) in July; and the population of Beersheba and western Galilee in October [pp. 263 f.].

III

Such is the account prepared by Mr. George Kirk for the *Survey of International Affairs* and published under the auspices of the Royal Institute for International Affairs and *under the editorship of Professor Toynbee.* I accept it, as I have said, at its face value for the purpose of the present discussion.

How does it compare with Professor Toynbee's observation in A *Study of History* on the relations between Jews and Arabs during the relevant period? What I am about to say will leave the reader incredulous. A comparison is difficult because, as far as A *Study of History* is concerned, no assurance had been issued by the permanent official of the United Nations that the Security Council would "assume the full measure of responsibility in the implementation of the Assembly's resolution"; there had not been, "during the four months which had elapsed since the departure of the United Nations Commission from Palestine" any "sporadic attacks by the Arabs which had been checked by Haganah reprisals"; there had not been any Zionist complaints "that the British security forces were not doing enough to protect Jewish lives and property"; nor could it be said that "almost certainly they were now doing less than their strict duty in the matter"; there had not been "shocking outrages" on both sides as the new year came in; there had not been unsuccessful frontal attacks by the Arabs on Jewish settlements, followed by "a more effective if more protracted strategy of reducing the outlying settlements by attacks upon the road communications by which they were supplied with provisions and munitions"; there had not been an invasion by the "Arab Liberation Army," based, "with a large measure of British tolerance, on localities within the territory assigned to the Arab States by the resolution of partition . . ." (that is, within the borders of territory subject to British administration under Britain's still unexpired mandate); there had been no intervention by the British-subsidized Arab Legion; there had been no shelling by the Arab Legion of the open city of Jerusalem, there had not been 1,200 casualties—including 450 deaths—among its 100,000 civilians; there had not been a threat of "slow paralysis . . . by the cutting of supplies and reinforcements" (that is, there had been no attempt to deprive the civilian population of Jerusalem of food and, what is worse, water, in an effort to reduce the city). *None of these things are mentioned in Professor Toynbee's account.* The reader is, I suggest, incredulous, perhaps even aghast. "But that is impossible," he exclaims. "Such things are not done even by propagandists of a hired press, let alone by the Director of Studies of a British Institute for scientific study operating under Royal patronage. He cannot wholly have ignored the report of his subordinate or colleague!" And as it happens the reader is right! Professor Toynbee has not wholly ignored Mr. Kirk's report: he has taken from it the single item of the massacre of Dair Yasin— and has linked it to his version of the "expulsion" of the Arabs in a manner unwarranted by Mr. Kirk's account. (Of

this, more below.) Thus, from a reading of Professor Toynbee's observations, one obtains the impression of an utterly
unprovoked universal uprising of the Jews against the de-
fenseless and peaceable Arabs, an outburst of murderous
cruelty in the worst traditions of savage peoples. This impression he deepens by his comments. He writes:

> On the morrow of a persecution in Europe in which they
> had been the victims of the worst atrocities ever known to
> have been suffered by Jews or indeed by any other human
> beings, the Jews' immediate reaction to their own experi-
> ence was to become persecutors in their turn for the first
> time since A.D. 135—and this at the first opportunity that
> had since arisen for them to inflict on other human be-
> ings *who had done the Jews no injury*, but who happened
> to be weaker than they were, some of the wrongs and suf-
> ferings that had been inflicted on the Jews by their many
> successive Western Gentile persecutors during the inter-
> vening seventeen centuries. In A.D. 1948 some 684,000
> out of some 859,000 Arab inhabitants of the territory in
> Palestine which the Zionist Jews conquered by force of
> arms in that year lost their homes and property and be-
> came destitute 'displaced persons' [VIII, 289 f.].
> The Jews in Europe in A.D. 1933–45 had been the vicari-
> ous victims of the Germans' resentment over their mili-
> tary defeat at the hands of their Western fellow Gentiles
> in the war of A.D. 1914–18; the Arabs in Palestine in A.D.
> 1948 became in their turn the vicarious victims of the Eu-
> ropean Jews' indignation over the 'genocide' committed
> upon them by their Gentile fellow Westerners in A.D.
> 1933–45. This impulse to become a party to the guilt of
> a stronger neighbour by inflicting on an innocent weaker
> neighbour *the very sufferings* that the original victim had
> experienced at his stronger neighbour's hands was per-

haps *the most perverse* of all the base propensities of Human Nature; for it was a *wanton* endeavour to keep in perpetual motion the sorrowful wheel of *Karma* to which Adam-Ixion was bound and from which only Love and Mercy could ever release him [VIII, 291].

It would be an affectation, and it is perhaps impossible, to comment with moderation on this sanctimonious pretense at historical (and, indeed, cosmic) objectivity by the Director of Studies of the Royal Institute for International Affairs. There is not a sentence in the quoted passages which does not affront the intelligence and outrage the moral susceptibilities of an informed reader.

Sentence No. 1): To speak of the fierce struggle between the Jews and Arabs as a persecutory reaction of the former to the Nazi extermination of Jews in Europe is not merely mendacious, and not merely intellectually contemptible; it is a calculated effort to divert attention from British responsibility, which the writer elsewhere admits in uneasy mitigation. That the Arabs had done the Jews "no injury" is an impression that Professor Toynbee can only have derived by forgetting large parts of this and of other reports that he has edited; and I will not speak of the history of Arab assaults on Jews in 1921, 1922, 1929, 1932–3, 1936–9. It is, to say the least, extraordinarily disingenuous to use the phrase "who happened to be weaker than they" as contrasting the Arabs with the Jews. Such was not the belief and hope of the attacking Arabs in those days; it was hardly the belief of the desperate Jews; it was undoubtedly not the belief of the British and of the British Delegation to the United Nations when Sir Alexander Cadogan, opposing the American resolution "three days after the open intervention of the Arab States . . . questioned both the desirability of invoking Article 39 (with its attempt to

define an aggressor against whom sanctions might be taken)
and the practicability of applying a stand-still order *in the
present fluid situation.*" We may be quite sure that if Sir
Alexander Cadogan (or his chief in London, Foreign Sec-
retary Ernest Bevin) had foreseen the pattern in which the
fluid situation was ultimately going to congeal he would not
have questioned "the desirability," etc. It was, again, fear of
the outcome which prompted the American proposal.

No. 2): ". . . of the territory in Palestine which the Zionist Jews had conquered by force of arms . . ." Of the territory that the Jews had conquered by the sweat of their brow
and by means of the contributions of world Jewry, of the
territory that had been converted from noisome swamp and
uninhabitable desert into fertile orchards and grain-fields,
and of the cities they had built, not a word; of the threat to
those hard-won possessions—as well as to the lives of the
Jews—posed by the invading armies, which were advancing
with the avowed intention of "pushing Israel into the sea,"
not a word; of the complicity of the Palestine Arab population, whether intermingled with the Jews or living apart, in
the plan of invasion and conquest, not a word; of those
Arab populations within Mandated Palestine which lent
themselves ("with a large measure of British tolerance") to
the plan, not a word. And I have yet to deal with Professor
Toynbee's other references to the "expulsion" of the Arabs.

No. 3): What took place in Palestine in "A.D. 1948" was
not an outburst of indignation over the genocide committed upon the Jews of Europe, deflected against the Arabs; it
was a passionate outburst of longing to bring into Palestine
the survivors of the genocide and an upwelling of determi-
nation to see that by additional immigration the homeland
into which they were welcomed should be a place secured
for the future by numbers and stability against such attacks as were now being launched on it.

No. 4): That the Jews inflicted upon the Arabs *"the very suderings"* which they [the Jews] had experienced at the hands of the Germans is a monstrous and unforgivable untruth. With this too I shall deal later. And that the furious reaction of the Jews to the Arab attacks was "wanton" is of a piece with the shameless perversity of Sentence No. 1.

IV

I must preface my remarks on Professor Toynbee's treatment of the "expulsion" of the Arabs from Israeli-held Palestine territory with renewed reference to the Blurring Effect. Its purpose, we have seen, is to create the impression of an affirmation out of a number of statements that cancel out logically but not psychologically. The thesis is stated, then modified out of validity, then mentioned again without the modification, then referred to tangentially as *chose connue*. . . . In writing on the "expulsion" of the Arabs, Professor Toynbee interweaves semi-retractions and modifications in respect both of this subject and of that of the resemblance between Jewish treatment of the Arabs and the Nazi treatment of the Jews. We have just heard him refer to *the very sufferings*. . . . We shall now hear him retract. We shall then, in the same passage, see him introduce a sort of "nevertheless"; and in the end there remains only the association: *"Jew is to Arab what Nazi is to Jew."* In a footnote to page 290, Volume VIII, we read:

The cold-blooded systematic 'genocide' of several millions of human beings in extermination camps, which had been the worst of the Nazis' crimes against the Jews, had no parallel at all in the Jews' ill-treatment of the Palestinian Arabs. The evil deeds committed by the Zionist Jews against the Palestinian Arabs that were comparable

to crimes committed against the Jews by the Nazis were
the massacre of men, women, and children at Dayr Yāsīn
on the 9th April, 1948, which precipitated a flight of the
Arab population, in large numbers, from districts within
range of the Jewish armed forces, and the subsequent deliberate expulsion of the Arab population from districts
conquered by the Jewish armed forces between the 15th
May, 1948, and the end of that year—e.g., from 'Akkā in
May, from Lydda and Ramlah in July, and from Beersheba and Western Galilee in October. When Nazareth
was captured in July, most of the population seems to
have been allowed to stay. On the other hand, the Arabs
who were expelled from 'Akkā in May included refugees
from Haifa, and those who were expelled from Lydda
and Ramlah in July included refugees from Jaffa, in addition to the local Arab population. The massacre and
expulsions, between them, were responsible for the exile
of all those Palestinian Arab 'displaced persons' (to use
the current euphemism), from the territory conquered by
the Israelis, who fled from or were driven from this territory after the 9th April, 1948. The expulsions seem to
have accounted for about 284,000 out of the total of
about 684,000 Palestinian Arabs who became 'displaced
persons' from first to last, including those who had already been evacuated by the British mandatory authorities or had already fled on their own initiative or had
already lost their homes as a result of military operations
between the outbreak of hostilities in Palestine in Decem-
ber 1947 and the massacre on the 9th April, 1948.

The Arab blood shed on the 9th April, 1948, at Dayr
Yāsīn was on the heads of the Irgun; the expulsions after
the 15th May, 1949, were on the heads of all Israel.

If, on behalf of Israel, it were to be pleaded that these
Jewish outrages in A.D. 1948, even reckoned *pro rata*, were

dwarfed in quantity as well as in heinousness, by the Nazi atrocities in A.D. 1933–45, it would have to be taken into account, on the other side, that the Jews had had much more experience than the Germans had had of the sufferings that they were inflicting. If the Nazis were debarred from filing the plea that they knew not what they did, the Jews were debarred *a fortiori*.

That last sentence is a gratuitous piece of cant; the Jews did not file, never suggested filing, a plea that they knew not what they did. They were driven by an agony of necessity, and upon this agony there came into play the rages and brutalities that all wars engender. This pious snuffle of Professor Toynbee's is one of the repetitions that fasten into the reader's mind the suggested, withdrawn, resuggested formula: "Jew is to Arab what Nazi is to Jew."

But we return to Mr. Kirk's report, which, on the subject of the expulsions, opens as follows:

The beginnings of the Arab mass flight went back to an early stage in the Arab-Jewish fighting. As early as 27 January [1948] the High Commissioner had confirmed a 'steady exodus' of Arab middle-class families who could afford to leave the country, taking with them cars and considerable quantities of household goods . . . [above, p. 221].

Who were these "middle-class families" who began to move out of Palestine in large numbers shortly after the passing of the Partition Resolution by the United Nations? They were the Arab leaders—merchants, professionals, landowners, money-lenders—who had been the main support of the Mufti and the Arab Higher Committee during all the years of Britain's mandate over Palestine. Some of them had incited the Arab workers and peasants to murder and pil-

lage since the time of the Balfour Declaration. Now they
packed up and moved, and the Arabs of the villages and the
countryside watched the processions of laden automobiles
streaming toward the Egyptian and Syrian frontiers. Mr.
Kirk accuses the Jewish combatants of making "skilful use
of psychological warfare to break their opponents' morale"
(an unheard-of crime!). He adds: "The effect upon the
civilians was only what was to be expected." What effect
does he think was produced upon the civilians by the sight
of the thousands of leaders getting away from the scenes of
the troubles they had helped to precipitate, taking their
movables with them? Of course these leaders had every
hope and intention of returning later, when the "Arab
Army of Liberation" should have done its work and oblit-
erated the Jewish cities and settlements; and, as during the
days of the war, when Rommel was nearing Alexandria, and
Palestine was the next step, they could look forward to a
sharing of the booty according to prearranged schedules.
Mr. Kirk's grave warning that one must take with reserve
the "subsequent Zionist assertion that many weeks before
the Dair Yasin massacre the Arab Higher Committee had
'called on the Arab population to leave the country en
masse'" has more than a touch of driveling pseudo-impor-
tance. I do not know whether the Arab Higher Committee
ever issued such a call, and I do not put it past Zionist propagandists to have invented it and fathered it on the Arabs.
What puzzles me here is the question of what the members
of the Arab Higher Committee and the other Arab leaders
said to the Arab villagers and fellahin among whom they
may have stopped here and there outward bound; and what
they said to their hosts in Alexandria and Cairo and Damas-
cus and Beirut; and what they sent by way of answer to any
messages that may have reached them from their followers
in Palestine. The more I ponder the question, the more it

seems to me that the only thing they *could* have said was: "Let us vacate the battlefield so as to give our brave liberators from the Arab lands a free hand. When it's over we will return. . . ." But this is a digression. I return to Professor Toynbee.

Throughout he ignores the Arab uprising against the Jews; and he begins his note on the massacre and expulsions by ignoring Mr. Kirk's account of the sequence of events. Farther down he refers vaguely to those Arabs "who had already fled on their own initiative," without even hinting that at the outset these consisted of the well-to-do classes to which the Arabs looked for leadership, and that their flight occurred long before the Dair Yasin massacre—and if Mr. Kirk does not choose to draw the inevitable inference from the fact, Professor Toynbee is unable to do so, because for him it does not exist. He seems to place the number of Arabs actually expelled by the Jews at less than half of the total number of refugees (284,000 out of 684,000), but there is not even a hint of the direct and indirect responsibility of the Arab leadership. There is not a word of condemnation for the men who, whether they proclaimed it or not, whether they planned it or not, executed a strategic military withdrawal in which a considerable part of the population was involved when it followed suit. Every disaster that came upon the Arabs is made the consequence of Jewish malevolence.

It is not a question of clearing the Jews of their share of the blame. Once war is unleashed and human beings begin to kill one another systematically, crimes will be committed, injustices inflicted, for which the miserable tradition of history provides a certain latitude. No one can say how much of the Jewish expulsion of the Arabs from Palestine falls within it. When one reflects on the intentions of the Palestinian Arabs toward the Jews, on their co-operation with the Arabs of the invading countries, on their readiness to act as a massive fifth column against the emerging Jewish State sanctioned by the United Nations, one must hesitate before pronouncing judgment. The massacre of Dair Yasin certainly does not fall within the latitude mentioned; but even this abomination—an isolated incident—had a setting that Professor Toynbee withholds from the reader in what he calls A *Study of History*; and his use of it in the continuous bracketing of Jews and Nazis disqualifies him from pleading in any court the cause of the wronged Arabs. Only this remains to be added—the most tragic sentence in all of Proust: "It is necessary that even those who are right should be wrong also, so that Justice may be made an impossible thing."

CHAPTER FIFTEEN

SUGGESTIO FALSI

I

In the preceding chapter we have seen how, in dealing with the struggle over the birth of Israel, A *Study of History* made use of the device of *suppressio veri* in the service of *suggestio falsi*. In the persistent bracketing of Nazi-Jew and Jew-Arab relationships it is *suggestio falsi* that takes the lead; but here, as there, the Blurring Effect is heavily employed as it rises, in its anti-Jewish prejudice, to a climax of poisonous innuendo mingled with pseudo-prophetic indignation.

In Volume VIII, pages 272–312, he gives us in a section entitled *The Modern West and the Jews* (quoted above, pp. 146 f.), a rapid survey of the development of relationships between the Jews and the Western World, leading up to what he calls the fourth act, which is the Nazi attempt at the extermination of Jewry. He then begins the subsection *The Fate of the European Jews and the Palestinian Arabs*, A.D. 1933–48 with the following words:

> The peculiar horror of this fourth act lay in the unprecedented wickedness of the malefactors and unprecedented sufferings of both innocent Jewish victims and an innocent Arab third party [VIII, 288].

Let us note carefully the implication of this opening. "Unprecedented sufferings" is made to apply equally to what happened to the Arabs of Palestine and to the Jews of

Europe. This is *suggestio falsi* at its slyest. Only the heart-
less will make light of the sufferings that have come upon
the Arabs of Palestine—in no small part through the folly
and cruelty of their kinsmen in the neighboring states; but
only a reckless partisan will talk, here, of "unprecedented"
after the word has been used to characterize the experiences
of the Jews under the Nazis. The effect is, of course, the
Blur; for thus the impression is left that what the Jews suffered was the killing of a certain comparatively small number, and the expulsion of the rest; or else that the vast
majority of the Arabs were exterminated and a minority permitted to escape. Yet this was not all that the Jews suffered,
as we shall observe below in touching on the Nazi action
against them; and I must add the miserable reflection that
as far as the Jews are concerned the murder of a certain
number of them in a given territory, and the expulsion of
the rest, are far from unprecedented; these have, indeed,
been regular occupational hazards for many, many centuries.

After a comparison with the persecutions suffered by the
Jews in fourteenth- and fifteenth-century Spain and Portu-
gal, Professor Toynbee continues:

> The full measure of the Nazis' depravity is not given in
> the bare statistical statement—appalling though these fig-
> ures are—that, within a period of no more than twelve
> years, they reduced the Jewish population of Continental
> Europe, west of the Soviet Union, from about 6½ million
> to about 1½ million by a process of mass-extermination
> which was so unprecedentedly systematic and cold-
> blooded that the new word 'genocide' had to be coined to
> describe what was in effect a new crime. In the operation
> of the destructor-plants in which the Nazis' victims were
> asphyxiated, the maniacal sadism of the men and women

in command was less appalling than the criminal docility
of the hundreds and thousands of subordinates who duly
carried out their monstrous instructions, and the moral
cowardice of the German public, who took good care to
avoid acquainting themselves with the atrocities that
their husbands, sons, brothers, and even their sisters,
wives, and daughters, were committing in their name. . . .
But the Nazi Gentiles' fall was less tragic than the Zion-
ist Jews'. On the morrow of a persecution in Europe
. . . the Jews' immediate reaction to their own experience was to become persecutors in their turn [etc. VIII,
288 f. Rest of passage quoted above, p. 224].

The sentence I have italicized is one of the most remarkable utterances on the Jewish tragedy to come from the pen
of a public figure in a democratic country; and as this particular public figure presents himself in the double role of
scientific historian and moralist, one is inclined to call it,
like the crimes of the Nazis, unprecedented. Unprecedented
—but not quite unequaled, for a little farther on Professor
Toynbee does even better when he writes:

On the Day of Judgment the gravest crime standing to
the German National Socialists' account might be, not
that they had exterminated a majority of the Western
Jews, but that they had caused the surviving remnant of
Jewry to stumble [VIII, 290 f.].

Now what is the man driving at? The one charitable interpretation that can be put on these last words—charitable,
that is, to Professor Toynbee's idealism, if not to his intelligence—is that before 1933 Zionist Jews and Jews at large
had been following the path of rectitude, and here, under
the Nazi assault, they had turned aside from the path; and
this impairment of the character of the Jews was a graver

crime on the part of the Nazis than the extermination of a
majority of the Western Jews. If such is Professor Toynbee's sentiment, we must admit that it is one of almost
stupefying nobility, even though he entertains it at someone else's expense. But such cannot be his sentiment, for
his opinion of Jewry in the Diaspora is predominantly
negative. The alternative interpretation to which we are
driven by elimination is that if the Nazis committed a grave
crime in exterminating five million (the number is actually
six million) Jews, they committed an even graver one in
having caused the Palestinian Arabs to suffer what they did
at the hands of the Jews. To this alternative interpretation
we are also directed over and over again by Professor Toynbee's opinion of that Zionist movement which had been at
work in Palestine for many decades before Hitler had been
heard of; and as if to make sure that we shall not give him
the benefit of the more charitable interpretation, he once
more summarizes his evaluation of the Zionist movement a
little farther on:

> The Zionists' audacious aim was to invert, in a new life of
> their own making, all the distinctively Jewish character-
> istics enshrined in the diasporà's traditional life. They set
> out defiantly and enthusiastically to turn themselves into
> manual labourers instead of brain workers, country-folk
> instead of city-dwellers, producers instead of middlemen,
> agriculturists instead of financiers, warriors instead of
> shopkeepers, terrorists instead of martyrs, aggressively
> spirited Semites instead of peaceably abject non-Aryans;
> and this Nietzschean revaluation of all traditional Jewish
> values, for destruction as well as for construction, for evil
> as well as for good, was directed toward the horizon-filling
> narrow-hearted aim of making themselves sons of a latter-
> day Eretz Israel in Palestine that was to be 'as Jewish as'

England 'was English,' instead of remaining the step-sons of a New York, London, Manchester, and Frankfort that were not more Jewish than Bombay was Parsee or Ispahan Armenian [VIII, 310 f.].

"For evil as well as for good": but it is not easy, from the tone of this passage, to discover where Professor Toynbee sees good, especially as all these revaluations move toward a "horizon-filling narrow-hearted aim" to become terrorists instead of martyrs, defiantly, deliberately! We suspect that even in becoming "aggressively spirited Semites instead of peaceably abject non-Aryans" the Jews have offended him. But it was certainly an error on his part to have included Frankfort in the list of places where Jews could have remained as stepsons; for most of the Jews of Frankfort, and Berlin, and Warsaw, and Lodz, and Cracow, and a hundred other places did not remain there, and did not become stepsons anywhere else; they became charred remnants, and gaseous exhalations, and soap.

In one of those tortuous semi-concessions which on the surface create an impression of over-all objectivity, Professor Toynbee writes:

There was neither justice nor expediency in the exaction from Palestinian Arabs of compensation due to European Jews for crimes committed against them by Western Gentiles. Justice required that the debt to Continental European Jewry which the Western World had incurred through the criminality of a Western nation should be assumed by a defeated Germany's victorious Western adversaries; and expediency pointed in the same direction as justice; for the victorious Western countries between them did possess the capacity—for which Palestine's resources were quite inadequate—of absorbing the European Jewish survivors of the *Furor Teutonicus* without seriously deranging their own domestic social equilibrium [VIII, 307].

It is obvious, indeed, that the victors in the war against Germany could have absorbed the Jewish survivors of the *Furor Teutonicus* without undue internal derangement; and Professor Toynbee knows as well as we do that there was never any prospect of their doing so. When, however, he prefaces his statement with the irrelevant and nasty aside that the long-deferred fulfillment of the promises of a Jewish National Home by the very nations he is talking about was devoid of justice and expediency, and was an exaction from the Arabs of compensation for Germany's crimes, he falls into a tangle of misunderstanding from which no human intelligence can extricate him. It is enough to point out that he regards the promise made under the League of Nations Mandate, with the authority of the nations he is referring to, as null and void; and while thus encouraging them to dishonor their pledges in one enterprise, he expects them to display their honorable intentions in another. If, moreover, the gravest crime standing to the Nazis' account, graver than their extermination of a majority of the Western Jews, is that they caused surviving Jewry to stumble in the matter of the Palestinian Arabs, what crime stands to the account of the victorious Western nations which did not open their doors to this surviving Jewry, but left it heartlessly to its own devices?

Professor Toynbee speaks with high indignation of the "moral cowardice of the German public, who took good care to avoid acquainting themselves with the atrocities" being committed against the Jews. The Germans were not the only ones to avert their eyes. The trick of pretending that nothing too dreadful was going to happen to the Jews was already being practiced outside of Germany on the eve of the Second World War. Writing of the St. James Conference of February–March 1939, Chaim Weizmann has this to say:

> Lord Halifax was strangely ignorant of what was happening to the Jews of Germany. During the St. James Conference he came up to me and said: "I have just received a letter from a friend in Germany, who describes some terrible things perpetrated by the Nazis in a concentration camp the name of which is not familiar to me," and when he began to grope for the name I realized it was Dachau he was talking about. He said the stories were entirely unbelievable, and if the letter had not been written by a man in whom he had full confidence he would not attach the slightest credence to it. For five or six years now the world had known of the infamous Dachau concentration camp, in which thousands of people had been maimed and tortured and done to death, and the British Foreign Secretary had never heard of the place. . . . It is difficult to say whether this profound ignorance was typical for the British ruling class, but judging from its behavior at that time, it either did not know, or else it did not wish to know because the knowledge was inconvenient, disturbing, and dangerous [op. cit., pp. 404 f.].

If a knowledge of Dachau before the time of the gas chambers and crematoria was unwelcome because it was inconvenient, disturbing, and dangerous, a knowledge of Auschwitz, Belsen-Bergen, Treblinka, and others in 1941–4 was even more so. For those were the days when it was considered essential to the victory over Germany that boatloads of refugees should at all costs be prevented from reaching the shores of Palestine.

Even more disheartening than this motivated ignorance in a time of admitted stress is the unwillingness of the world to know and consider, now that we have the opportunity to study the past, what took place between the Nazis and the Jews. Decent human beings shrink from the notion that they belong to the same species as a Hitler, a Himmler, a Frank, a Streicher, and their thousands and tens of thousands of underlings. We want to forget; and it is only because of this willingness that Professor Toynbee could permit himself the unheard-of vilification of lumping the Jews of Israel in their actions against the Arabs with the Nazis in their actions against the Jews.

However distasteful it may be, I find it necessary in the face of such a wild and monstrous charge to say something of the Nazi-Jewish *physical* actualities before I touch upon the equally revolting, almost unbalancing record on the psychological and sociological side. I quote from *Harvest of Hate* (original French, *Bréviaire de la haine*) by Léon Poliakov, based on the official documents of the Nuremberg and other trials of Nazi War Criminals (Jewish Publication Society of America, Philadelphia, 1954).

I begin with the occupation of Poland, which, the reader may remember, was taking place when I first read *A Study of History* in 1939. This was before the German adoption of a policy of extermination.

The SS set the example, though they were far from holding a monopoly. There were certain classic procedures. Cutting off the beards and earlocks of Jews was a widespread entertainment; it was also the thing to be pulled about in a cart by a victim. How many Germans sent their families photographs preserving these deeds for posterity! Another amusement consisted of breaking into a Jewish apartment or house and forcing young and old to undress and dance, arm in arm, to the sound of a phonograph. Following this with rape was optional, as one risked being tried for the "crime of race defilement." Staider spirits, combining business and pleasure, seized pedestrian Jewesses in the streets in order to make them clean their quarters or barracks (business) with the victims' underwear (pleasure) [p. 41].

Between the adoption of a policy of extermination and its scientific implementation the mass killings were crude and unsystematized. We read:

Most of the time the extermination squads worked as follows: After going into a place, they would have the leading Jews pointed out to them, in particular the rabbi. These Jews they would charge with organizing a Jewish council. A day or so later the council would be notified that the Jewish population was to be registered for transfer to a "Jewish territory" being organized in the Ukraine or some other region. The council would then be ordered to call the Jews together; in the larger localities this was also done by posting notices. Given the haste of the operation, the order was on the whole pretty well obeyed by the inhabitants, who were still ignorant of German methods. (Later, when the last ghettos in White Russia and the Baltic countries were being closed down, the victims had to be rounded up by force in indescribable manhunts.) The Jews were crowded into trucks, or freight cars, and taken a few kilometers out of town to some ravine or anti-tank ditch. There, after being stripped of their money, valuables, and often even their clothing, men, women, and children were shot on the spot.

This was the usual procedure, though every action group and squad had its preferred methods. Certain squads forced their victims to lie down and fired a pistol point blank into the back of their necks. Others made the Jews climb down into the ditch and lie on top of the bodies of those already shot so that the pile of corpses steadily mounted. Still others lined the victims up along the edge of the ditch and shot them down in successive salvos; this was considered the "most humane" and the "most military." . . . Sometimes only a few hours elapsed between the time the notices were posted and the execution.

The Germans preferred warmer seasons for carrying out the executions. A report from Group A complained about the difficulties of the work. "The cold has made the executions more difficult. Another difficulty is the fact that the Jews are scattered all over the territory. The long distances, bad roads, lack of trucks and gasoline, and inadequate numbers of men strain our forces to the limit." Later the author of the report promised to finish with the Jews of the region within two months "if weather conditions permit" [pp. 122 f.].

The transition from primitive to scientific slaughter was made piecemeal, the old continuing side by side with the new for some time.

Shooting was not the only method the commandos used. On the shores of the Black Sea there were mass drownings; at Bachtchissarai . . . the drowning of 1,029 Jews during the period July 1–15, 1942, was reported. There were cases of Jews being burned alive, especially at Minsk, in White Russia. Finally, in the Spring of 1942, mobile gas chambers, designed and manufactured in Berlin and disguised as gas trucks, made their appearance all over Russia. A complaint from SS Lieutenant Becker on May 16 reads: "The gas is generally not used in the right way. To get things over with as soon as possible, the driver presses the accelerator to the floor. This kills people by suffocation instead of making them gradually doze off.

My directives have proved that, with the correct adjust-
ment of the lever, death comes quicker and the prisoners
sleep peacefully. There are no more of the contorted
faces or defecations there used to be" [p. 124].

It became apparent that the extermination of six million
human beings was not a task to be left to the haphazard in-
genuities of squad leaders.

Techniques had to be discovered, and these . . . proved
very difficult to perfect. . . . An industry for the slaughter of human beings had to be organized in detail. Added
to the problems of exterminating so many people were
the problems of deportation [p. 113]. [But] German technical genius made it possible to set up an efficient and ra-
tionalized industry of death within a few months. Like
other industries it had its department of research, improvement, administrative services, a business office, and
archives . . . [p. 182].
. . . we shall consider only the chief establishment where
extermination was systematically carried out, and pass by
those other murder methods which were used almost everywhere, of which mass shooting was always the leading
one. The morbid ingenuity of the Nazis devised dozens
of different individual and collective techniques: the
quicklime method . . . used particularly in Poland; in-
jections of carbolic acid into the heart, used in most con-
centration camps; or the one which made the Mauthau-
sen camp infamous, which consisted of throwing the
victims from the top of a quarry. But these represented an
exercise of local initiative, the refinements of individual
sadism. What concerns us here is the more or less official
method commanded from Berlin by the officials charged
with the job of genocide. This method, employed in specially prepared places, resulted in the death of the over-

whelming majority of the victims of Nazism; the exact figures can never be finally established. The method chosen was asphyxiation; by carbon monoxide in the four large Polish camps (Chelmno, Belzec, Sobidor, Treblinka), and by prussic-acid fumes at Maidanek and in the huge Auschwitz installations in Upper Silesia [pp. 182 f.].

Finally, as to the personality of the participants in this work:

The men of the action groups sought to distinguish themselves in the service of Greater Germany; they aspired to be "hard," and competition in savagery played a considerable role. "Paper soldier" was the scornful nickname with which Commando 6 of Group C dubbed Corporal Matthias Graf, who was in charge of the intelligence section of his group, and never had—and never sought—an occasion to take part in the massacres. . . . Such a milieu bred complete monsters, real legendary ogres. There was, for example, the police constable who afterwards at Lwow used to kill Jewish children to amuse his own children; or another who used to bet that he could cut off the head of a ten-year-old boy with a single saber stroke [p. 131].

The attitude displayed by the leading members of the action groups in the course of their trial at Nuremberg several years later, throws light on the astonishing confusion that reigned in the Nazi mind. Among the twenty-two accused were a university professor, eight lawyers, a dental surgeon, an architect, an art expert, and even a theologian, a former pastor. All pleaded guilty; not one expressed the least regret; at most they mentioned the harsh necessities of war and the fact that they were acting under orders. And yet in their defense they referred to the same values of Western civilization that they had

trampled underfoot for years. Their witnesses and lawyers praised their honesty, their familial virtues, their
Christian feelings, and even their gentleness of character
[p. 132].

It is with this inferno of human degradation, the stark
realities of which outrun the maddest imaginings of Dante,
that Professor Toynbee classes the actions of the Jews of Israel against the Arabs who had engaged them in war. And
still the iniquity of the identification is not revealed in its
fullness until we have taken in the larger canvas of the Nazi
policy on the Jews.

II

The war that the Nazis declared on the Jewish people is
undoubtedly the only one of its kind in human history. Various attempts have been made to analyze Nazi anti-Semitism in more or less "reasonable" and familiar terms; it has
been described as prejudice exploited in a bid for domestic
political power by demagogues who may or may not have
shared it; as a deflection of frustrated rage upon an innocent
and easily available victim (suggested by Professor Toynbee); as a concealed rebellion born of a secret hatred of
Christianity and Jesus the Jew; as a cunning maneuver in
the international field, aimed at the demoralization of the
democracies. All of these elements were certainly to be
found in it, but no combination of them suffices to explain
the convulsive seizure of horror, loathing, and fury which
the mention of Jews or Judaism precipitated among a considerable number of Germans. The word "pathological" has
been used. It is an escape word. It classifies and dismisses
without explaining or even describing. The paroxysm was
not directed toward an "understandable" goal—even in the
sense that lunatics may be regarded as having such goals. It

was not a question of getting rid of all the Jews in Germany or in Hitler-conquered territories, whether by expulsion or extermination. There was no limitation of objective, no point at which the spasm could be expected to be spent —one reason being that the furious urges were in some ways contradictory.

They wanted to make the entire earth uninhabitable for Jews; they wanted to make the name of the Jew such a byword for infamy and repulsiveness that no people would harbor him. They wanted also to reach back into the history of the Jew and to expose his past as a prolonged calamity for the human species. At the same time they wanted to permit some Jews to remain alive, but in a condition of degradation so hideous and at the same time so indecently comical to look upon that their hatred could continue to feed upon the spectacle and find therein its justification.

The pronouncements of the German leaders on the Jews read like the incoherent ravings of the demented. The head of the great and civilized German State delivered himself as follows:

> If the Jews were alone in this world, they would suffocate as much in dirt and filth, as they would carry on a detestable struggle to cheat and ruin each other, although the complete lack of will to sacrifice, expressed in their cowardice, would also in this instance make the fight a comedy [*Mein Kampf*, Reynal and Hitchcock, 1939, p. 416].

But, astoundingly enough, this wretched, subhuman species is a power against which the whole world must arm.

> If, with the help of the Marxian creed, the Jew conquers the nations of this world, his crown will become the funeral wreath of humanity, and once again this planet,

empty of mankind, will move through the ether as it did thousands of years ago [ibid., p. 84].

And, in connection with the First World War:

> If, at the beginning of, or during the war, 12,000 or 15,000 of these Jewish corruptors of the people had been plunged into an asphyxiating gas . . . the sacrifice of millions of soldiers would not have been in vain [462nd ed. of *Mein Kampf*, 1939, quoted by Poliakov, op. cit., p. 198].

These ravings, and scores of others like them, appear in the source-book of the Nazi movement, written at the beginning of Hitler's career, and issued in some millions of copies and made compulsory reading in Germany after his accession to power. I wonder if anything like them can be found in the considered statements of any other head of a government since such statements were made permanent in writing. I wonder if any other civilized people has voted into power, or permitted to come into power, a character so obviously and criminally deranged. It cannot be pleaded, on behalf of the Germans, that they did not know the man before his book had become a part of the educational system of the country, which was after his accession. It sold well between 1924, when it was written, and 1933; and Hitler's campaign speeches were shot through with the same obsessive and delirious preoccupation with the Jewish subject. (It is well to observe, in passing, that the gas chambers were in his mind as early as 1924.) I repeat here carefully what may have sounded in another place (Chapter 1) like a piece of rhetoric: namely, that Hitler's investiture with the Chancellorship "was proof enough that the German people had passed into a maniacal condition uncontrollable from within" and should have been the moment for international intervention. This time it will be pleaded that the foreign powers, at least, could not have known the man. How ironical that millions of dollars and pounds are spent to spy out the secrets of the atom bomb of the physicists while the placing of a human atom bomb at the heart of civilization, in the form of a maniac lifted to power by maniacs in the open light of day, is ignored by the gatherers and sifters of "intelligence." Some of this "ignoring," we know, was motivated by a low cunning that found its ghastly and bloody nemesis. The world was not big enough for the spoon one needed to sup with this devil.

To what extent did Hitler succeed in infecting parts of the democratic world with his diseased condition or in re-infecting it with a sickness already virulent enough long before his coming? There can be no scientific answer to that question. One only remembers—I again refer the reader to Chapter 1 above—the desperation of those Jews who, let us say in sheer self-defense, tried to warn the world of the larger meaning of the phenomenon of Nazi anti-Semitism, and the counter-warnings with which they were answered; one remembers also the timidity of many prominent Jews, who trembled to hear the protests of other Jews, and agreed with the cunning ones that it was impolitic to irritate the alligator while he was devouring his victims; and I personally remember overhearing in a club car a conversation in which reference was made to a speech on Hitlerism by the late Stephen S. Wise, and a curt, irritated dismissal of the subject in a phrase that sums up a popular attitude of those days: "It's only the Jews squawking again." It sticks in my mind together with the phrase I saw chalked on walls in Paris in August 1939: *"Mieux vaut Hitler que Blum"*—better Hitler than Blum. I was sure Professor Toynbee would not agree with that preference. But today, in the light of his opinion of the Jews of Israel, and recalling that Léon Blum was favorably disposed toward the creation of the Jewish State, Professor Toynbee might be inclined to substitute: *"C'est plus ou moins la même chose"*—it's six of one and half a dozen of the other.

The soul of the Western World was redeemed by groups of men and women who did understand what was afoot. Before and during the Second World War there were thousands—and some among them were Germans—who risked at first their standing, then their freedom, and later, in many cases, their lives, in protest and counteraction; and if ever there was in this world atonement for blindness or indifference on the part of hundreds of millions, it was made by the Western nations between 1939 and 1945. Still, we must make the sorrowful observation that the immense expiation has not been followed by a proportionate clarification. The Jewish Question still remains the touchstone of the condition of the Western World—and who can assert that the response is satisfactory today? How can it be when molders of public opinion equate these two relationships: "Nazi-Jewish" and "Jewish-Arab"?

To what curious conclusions Professor Toynbee perverts the moral damage done to the Jewish people by Nazi anti-Semitism when he writes:

> On the Day of Judgment the gravest crime standing to the German National Socialists' account might be, not that they had exterminated a majority of the Western Jews, but that they had caused the surviving remnant of Jewry to stumble [above, p. 235].

He is in effect implying that the Nazi program for the demoralization and debasement of surviving Jewry was largely successful, for he tells us that an enraged Jewry after World War II took it out on the Arabs as an enraged Germany had taken it out on the Jews after World War I. For him, it seems, the dominant Jewish emotion was hatred, and a ferocious demand for vicarious revenge. Actually the most serious moral damage done to the Jewish people, especially in its relationship to the Jewish Homeland, resulted from a panic of compassion.

I have described the struggle that has always gone on within the Zionist movement between the creative and the destructive elements—that is, according to my interpretation of Jewish values. From the beginning the Achad Ha-Amists and the Weizmannists were the cautious builders, insistent upon quality; from the beginning they were opposed by the maximalists of quantity and speed, who were prepared to defer the qualitative achievement until later. This struggle was conducted both in the Jewish Homeland and throughout that part of the Jewish people everywhere that constituted the Zionist movement. With the rise of Nazi anti-Semitism the ideological pressure for quantitative achievement was reinforced by the cry for help from European Jewry and by the emotional response of fellow Jewries throughout the world. This was not a time for social idealism, for the higher moral statesmanship of the Jewish Restoration, for picking and choosing men and forms; it was a time for unreflecting rescue of fellow Jews; they had to be got out of the threatened area; and with the doors of other lands all but closed, there was only Palestine to look to— and the doors of Palestine had been closed by Great Britain.

Professor Toynbee is at pains to rebuke the victorious Western nations for not having admitted into their lands the Jewish survivors of the Nazi mass-murderers, thus preventing by anticipation the pressure upon Palestine. But what of the failure of the democracies to open their doors *before* the outbreak of the war, when all but the willfully blind could see what was coming? He has not a word to say about the pitiful and ignominious spectacle of the proud Royal Navy chasing boatloads of refugees in the Mediterranean before and during the war. He does not seem so much as to glimpse the madness of frustration which came upon millions of Jews who had to stand by and watch the consignment of their kin to destruction and worse than destruction in what seemed to be a world-wide conspiracy. What a good thing it would be if we could forget that the democracies had their part in creating the circumstances that caused surviving Jewry "to stumble"! But Professor Toynbee will not let us forget; he compels us to exhume the memory as testimony against his aspersions.

When, after the Second World War, it was a question of getting out of Europe those survivors who, even according to Professor Toynbee's view, could no longer remain there, the international pre-war situation reproduced itself and remained in force until the State of Israel was proclaimed on paper by the United Nations and established in fact by the Jews of Palestine. Surely the man who wrote—perhaps in an uncaught moment of absent-mindedness—of the "splendid failure" of the Bar Kochbas could have "stumbled" into a phrase of commendation for the splendid success of ben Gurion. What the United Nations gave Palestine was the right to risk everything in a last desperate gamble. Simultaneously with the acceptance of the challenge, the Jews of Palestine, now the Israelis, opened wide the gates and called upon every Jew who felt the need, to join them without delay. Two things then happened—one of them unbelievable, the other inevitable. The Israelis threw back the invading Arab nations; and the onrush of immigrants placed an intolerable strain on the economic, social, and organizational structure of the community. It is my personal opinion, which I have expressed elsewhere at length,[1] that in the joy, relief, and triumph of the moment the Israelis overextended themselves; despite all pressures, they could and should

[1] *Level Sunlight* (New York, 1953).

have limited immigration to a maximum of one hundred thousand a year instead of admitting nearly three quarters of a million in three years. They not only invited; they also cajoled; and in the wake of the systemless wild welcome there followed a deterioration of standards and ideals and forms from which it will take the country a generation or more to recover.

This is not the place for a detailed examination of both sides of the case: the one pleading that speed was of the essence because only numbers could ensure safety; the other countering that quality too was of the essence even from the strictly utilitarian and security point of view. In place here is the observation that the stampede that had been precipitated by the long agony of martyrdom in Europe and by the long agony of helpless watching everywhere else gave an immense forward thrust to the physical being of the Jewish State and a backward thrust to its moral and social being. Had there been no Hitlerism, had the pace of growth maintained a slowly mounting rate, the ideal that permeated the classical Chalutzic urge would have had a longer span in which to operate. Is there a Jew anywhere who would not have the six million of Europe still alive though it might mean that the Jewish State would still be in the making?

We have no record—there is no system for the compilation of such data—of the psychic damage that had been wrought on those Jewish survivors from Europe who poured into Israel by the hundreds of thousands from 1948 on. There is no way of computing the cost—in money, effort, discouragement, retreat from early standards—of integrating with the Israeli society the young and old whose first need was moral and psychological therapy. And I still believe that, looked on as a whole, this Israeli society is an astounding achievement. Its problems were superhuman; its failures are human; its successes have been creditable in the highest degree.

One can easily understand the readiness of an unsympathetic observer to stigmatize as revengeful rancor the leading motive in this enormous effort. To some degree this sort of imputation is natural in those who will not frankly admit the degree of their own guilt. It is incomprehensible to them that the Jews should not have emerged from this unparalleled ordeal contemptuous of a world that had betrayed them, and cynical of all moral values. And it is true that a corroding cynicism appeared here and there, and that here and there the Nazis produced the kind of Jewish individual who would justify their scurrility. The poet Segalovitch wrote in moral, not cynical, despair:

> My stomach turns when I reflect on Man,
> His vileness and the vileness of his deeds:
> And not alone the Prussian torturer,
> The manufacturer of human soap,
>
> But the two billions of the globe entire,
> Who looked on at the greatest of all murders.
> My stomach turns, my mind and body fail me;
> My words stick in my throat.

How many fell into such a mood at times? We do not know. Their number cannot have been great or the seizures enduring; it is not in this mood that an enormous constructive enterprise is furthered. How many were there whom the Nazis turned, by ingenious manipulation of deferred hopes, delegation of power, hierarchies of Jewish councils, and the rest, into monstrosities like themselves? There were some—and they too cannot have been many. They represent that quota of weaklings, cowards, criminals, and just ordinary people driven below the human level, who, whether as American prisoners in Korea or British prisoners under the Nazis, bring into sharper relief the stronger natures that endured until death without surrendering their souls. In suggesting this analogy, I should like to remind the reader that the volume and the depth of the villainies employed for more than a decade by the Nazis against the Jews have no parallel in what was inflicted on prisoners of war for much shorter periods. The survival of a sound Jewish people is perhaps in itself that people's greatest achievement in these last two decades.

And as we are talking of the failures and defects of the State of Israel, what has become of the historic "sweep" in Time and Space? At this writing less than eight years have passed since Israel was created in the midst of almost unimaginable discouragements and difficulties. At this writing the Arab States still consider themselves at war with Israel; an economic blockade surrounds Israel from all sides but the sea; the Suez Canal is closed to it; on the borders a continuous guerrilla warfare flickers; the Arab States still refuse to consider the resettlement of their refugee kinsmen within their underpopulated territories, and openly proclaim that nothing will satisfy them but the erasure of the State of Israel from the map—to King Saud of Saudi Arabia the removal of this "cancer" is worth ten million Arab lives; [2] as they once used the Arabs of Palestine in a military maneuver to facilitate—as they hoped—the destruction of Jewish Palestine, they now wish to use them for the destruction of the State of Israel. The constellation of international forces which made possible the creation of the State in 1948 has disappeared; in its place we have the constellation of the Cold War, and within it the Arab States occupy the same

[2] Address to Arab journalists at Riyadh, Saudi Arabia, January 9, 1954, reported in the New York Times, January 10, 1954.

advantageous position as they did in the constellation of the War of Nerves before 1939; and Israel is at the same disadvantage now as Jewish Palestine was then.

Is this the exact moment to pass judgment on the meaning and value of the State of Israel? How long should it take for a people to recover from the effects of such calamities as have been visited upon the Jews in the last twenty-odd years? How long should it take a people that has not practiced statehood for eighteen hundred years to set up the machinery of a state while coping with problems that would baffle governments with centuries of tradition and practice? How long should it take to create out of nothing, or almost nothing, a postal system, a tax system, a police service, a diplomatic service, a foreign policy, a democratic system of elections, an army, and, above all, a tradition of governmental forms?

We have observed earlier how Professor Toynbee, while crying down the narrowness and mundaneness of a Zerubbabel, concedes that the State which he founded lived for more than three hundred years in the Way of Gentleness. Nearly ten times eight years had to pass before Zerubbabel's Second Jewish State began to find itself with the help of Ezra and Nehemiah, and perhaps the Second State did not have to face such formidable obstacles—physical, political, and psychological—as the Third faces. Again, this is not an attempted justification of the means by the hoped-for ends. Given the Jewish situation as it was in the middle decades of the twentieth century, considering what the Jews of Europe and Palestine have gone through and what the Jews of Israel are now going through, the performance, with all its imperfections, is from the moral point of view a creditable one. If it could have been better, it could also have been expected to be much worse; the behavior of Israel in the unique, complicated, multi-sided war it has had to fight for survival stands comparison with that of the best of peoples at war. It is admittedly a miserable standard; an objective historian ought to have waited until he was in position to apply the standards of peace. That is what the Israelis are waiting for.

CHAPTER SIXTEEN

ON ALIVENESS–
IN-HISTORY

I

I CLOSE this book as I began it, on a personal note; and I have chosen to be personal for the purpose of objectivity, so that the reader may find it easier to apply his corrections to my statements of opinion. Besides, I have wanted to do something more than expose the misrepresentations of the Jewish past and present in A *Study of History,* or indicate the state of mental confusion which runs through other parts of the work; I have wanted to convey that sense of aliveness-in-history which the Jewish people has communicated to me, and to add something about its implications. And as that sense was not communicated to me alone, but to considerable numbers (albeit probably a minority in this Jewish generation), I shall, again, be writing of a historical as well as of a personal phenomenon.

How was this communication effected? By early immersion, by study—in its wider sense—and by experience. I have written: "It strikes me as quite extraordinary that simple people—none of those I knew in my childhood were learned —should be living in a continuous awareness of history." This awareness I took in, as we say, with my mother's milk. It has been deepened by what I have learned from books, persons, and movements. It has been sharpened by special incidents, many of which I must certainly have forgotten, some of which, however, have become ever-present possessions, so that I can rehearse them at will, as one does with

unforgettable passages of poetry and music. And as with
such passages, but more vividly than in their case, the incidents seem to reveal new depths with every rehearsal, as if
the years added to their resonance. The incident or experience I describe here is recent, but it has already accumulated in me a great fullness of overtones.

II

On the evening of my departure from Israel in the fall of
1951 I strolled through the streets of Rehovot in a depressed
mood of farewell. As I passed along the hedge of the public
garden on the main road to the Negev, I heard Romanian
spoken by a group passing in the opposite direction on the
other side. Though Romanian goes back to my earliest
childhood—together with Yiddish and the Hebrew of some
prayers—I paid little attention. Since the proclamation of
the State tens of thousands of Romanian Jews had been
brought in from Costantza to Haifa, their ships converging
with those that bore "returners" from Greece and Italy and
France and Morocco to meet in Israel the planes converging
from south and east with their Yemenite, Iraqi, Persian, and
Indian contingents. I had heard Romanian on the streets
of Tel Aviv and Haifa and Jerusalem. I had even heard it,
Semitized with glottal stops and throaty nasals, on the lips
of remaining Arabs of Tarshiha in Galilee. There had been
Romanian Jews, too, in the older, pre-war pioneering groups.
Thus the sound of the language did not set up reverbera-
tions in my deeper memories; it stood out only for a moment among the many languages that fringed the dominant
Hebrew.

But as I returned down the road a few minutes later I
heard the same voices again, and suddenly two of them, a
man's and a woman's, broke off and began to sing, in Yid-

dish with Romanian pronunciation, the pilgrim's chorus from *Shulamis*:

> Each man bowed beneath his gift,
> Each one with his staff in hand,
> We go marching forward swift
> To our far-off Holy Land. . . .

I stopped dead. The crowd flowing about me became, on the instant, phantom-like. The voices died out, and the road to the Negev, glittering under the arc lights, dimmed and dissolved. A lamp was kindled between two backdrops. On my right I saw Pandelli's inn and the barbershop of Todoracu, and on my left the bakery and the house of Sarah, the tinsmith's wife. Far beyond stood the synagogue in the fields and, beyond that, infinitely remote, mysterious, frightening, the *mahala*, the open country, beckoned. Against the ghostly voices of my mother and my uncle Moishe I heard the whisper of countless footsteps, and with these sounds came back the suggestion of the third backdrop of memories, antenatal, things told, vistas set in a twilight of centuries, with hurrying figures and a feeling of oppressive urgency.

They were as much of me, these indistinct multitudes, as the first *cheder* chant in the house of the *shochet* on the slope behind the main street; they mingled with the voice of the muezzin and the murmur of my father's morning prayers; they were as surely a part of that which had made me as had been those who had transmitted their images to me.

The seizure passed and the tumult of the Rehovot road rushed back on me as if a thousand doors had been opened.

In all of this there was nothing extraordinary. I made a note of the experience that night, and gave it no more thought. The extraordinary was to follow.

The next day I took plane for Rome, where for a work in
hand I spent several days among the Imperial ruins, and
from Rome I went on to Manchester. When I arrived two
weeks later in New York, there was waiting for me a letter
from Israel in an unfamiliar hand. The language was Yiddish.

> Dearest Cousin Moishe:
>   I who write you am called Shmeel, and I am the son of
> Moishe of Piçiniagu, as they called him, who was the
> brother of your father, Srul Itzig of Maçin. Know that I
> arrived here in Israel a year ago, to join my daughter and
> my sons who have lived here for many years. . . .

Here are the details of the coincidence:
Two days before I left Israel a young woman in the Haifa
accounting department of the Israel International Telephone Service came across a charge slip from a hotel in
Nahariya to one Mendel Samuel, in Manchester, England.
As she told me afterwards, she might very well have been
off duty that day, or she might have copied the entry me-
chanically. Samuel is not an uncommon name, and though
it was her father's, and had therefore been hers before her
marriage, it occurred often enough to pass without notice
among tourist Levys, Cohens, Hurwitzes, and Greenbaums
calling England, France, America, the Argentine, and South
Africa. But it happened that she was on duty that day, and
not in a routinized mood. Very possibly there stirred in her,
unperceived by her conscious mind, the memory of a story
that long, long before she was born, some granduncle of
hers, her father's uncle on his father's side, was supposed to
have migrated from Romania to England and to have settled in Manchester. More or less indifferently she mentioned the name to her father.
The following evening—the evening of my stroll in Reho-

vot—she was in Nahariya, which is forty minutes distant by
bus from Haifa, inquiring at the hotel for the person who
had called Manchester some days previously. The proprietor
had the record of the caller's name, but for further information directed the young woman to a square, green-roofed,
prefabricated house on the road running along the seashore.
It was my niece's house, where I had stayed on my visit to
Nahariya.

My niece, English by upbringing, and a recent settler in
Israel, a stranger to Maçin and Piçiniagu and the early history of her maternal grandfather's branch of the family, had
this to say, in a mixture of English and Hebrew: the subject
of the young woman's inquiry was her uncle on her mother's side; he lived in America and came often to Israel; his
father—that is to say, her maternal grandfather—had come
originally from Romania, but he had died when she, the
granddaughter, was five years old, and she knew only that
his first name had been Isaac, his wife's Fanny, and these
and these were their children. The young woman had better write to the said uncle, who was leaving the next morning for America, via Rome and Manchester. For my cousin
Shmeel, son of my uncle Moishe of Piçiniagu, I needed no
further identification.

During the warm correspondence that followed we ex-
changed the annals of the respective branches of the family
for the last fifty-one years. When we had last seen each
other I had been five years of age, he seventeen. He remembered me clearly, but my memory of him may have been
mostly hearsay; it was his father, and, above all, his father's
voice, that were clear in my mind. It was borne in on me, to
my confusion, that in more than thirty years of Zionist preoccupation and many visits to Palestine, I had never thought
of inquiring among Romanian Jews for the Weissbuchs and
Samuels of long ago. I had apparently made up my mind

that they had passed into legend. Now I was filled with a great curiosity, and I wanted from my cousin Shmeel what I could only get from him in long, rambling conversations, to which I looked forward eagerly as part of the pleasures of my next visit. I was in search not so much of persons as of a better view of the prenatal backdrop. My cousin would no doubt have stories of people born well over a hundred years ago, contemporaries of the semi-mythical Naphthali Weiss-buch (two of his sons changed their name, one to evade mili-tary duty, the other to keep him company, to Samuel), the great-great-great-grandfather of my grandchildren—Naph-thali the honey-gatherer, nicknamed Pantoul, who was born, they said, in Kolomea of Austria, migrated to Romania, there deposited a vast number of children, and in his old age made a pilgrimage to Palestine, where he died in one of the four Holy Cities. Not that it would avail me much, in brooding on a history of so many centuries, to push back the contact by another generation or two; there was only the desire to linger in the farthest zone of the recoverable past with one who was better acquainted with it than I.

The correspondence went on for eight months, and I de-veloped a great liking for my resurrected cousin. He was a simple and intelligent man, pious, but with little learning. He wrote a sound, flavorsome Yiddish, and I answered in the same language. His mind was alert, his memory keen, his interest in the family annals lively. He was as impatient for the meeting as I. I arrived in Israel on the last day of Passover 1952, three days after his death from a heart attack.

III

It may seem strange that the coincidences attending this incompleted reunion have not left a mystical impression on me. But on the other hand it seems to me that it would be

the most remarkable coincidence of all if remarkable coincidences did not turn up in life. They are perfectly natural
things, and their purpose is to keep alive our faith in the
miraculous.

The impression that this experience left on me has at
bottom little to do with the fact that my cousin's daughter
should so curiously have come across my name and mentioned it to her father; and only a little more with the fact
that on the evening she was seeking me out I should have
been reminded of her grandfather by a song I heard on the
lips of strangers passing in the dark. Far deeper is the sense
of a reinforcement of feeling arranged for me in the everlasting flux of my people's history. Death prevented me
from pushing back the personal contact with the past by
another generation or two; but the experience fulfilled its
purpose, which was to strengthen by one more vivid illustration "that sense of aliveness-in-history which the Jewish
people has communicated to me."

If I have often reflected on the experience—one of a class
of similar experiences—it has been in a spirit of rational inquiry. I have asked myself whether a strong feeling of history within one's own people makes it impossible to share
in the general sense of history; whether this kind of belonging and inclusion must lead to a proportionate not-belong-
ing and exclusion; whether, in short, this is a form of egocentricity destructive of one's all-human consciousness.

At first glance one would say that it is. But then the question arises whether one can feel history (and the contemporaneous world) at all without feeling it as something personal operating from within as well as from without; and
another question follows: whether the cultivation of the
personal sense of history is possible on a planetary basis or
even on the basis of a whole civilization. If the answer here
is no, as I think it is, we are driven to the impossible conclu-

sion that the less we are aware of any kind of history, the better.

I say the conclusion is impossible because insensibility to one's place in history is an obstacle in the right approach to the all-human scene. It is not among those who are ignorant of history, or insensitive to their place in it, that we find a benevolent interest in the destiny of our species. On the contrary, they are the ones likeliest to succumb either to cynical indifference or to gusts of mob passion; and in this they provide occasion and material for the plans of those who have a distorted sense of their place in history.

Let us, then, re-examine our first question: does a strong feeling of history within one's own people make it impossible to share in a general sense of history? By abuse (distortion) it can, and it is often abused; but without it the general sense is diffused into nothingness. The Jews have abused it as much as any other people, perhaps more, because they have more of it; but as much as any other people or, rather, certainly more than any other people, they have nurtured a tradition of universalism, of an intimate relationship with the destiny of all mankind.

That tradition is very old. If it does not go back to the earliest national consciousness, it is definitely thrown back to that period by a secondary tradition, the tradition of the tradition, which is old enough. It is, indeed, thrown back to the pre-national patriarchal time, and is implicated in the very *raison d'être* provided for the nation yet to be created. "In thee shall all the families of the earth be blessed" are the words contained in God's first communication to Abraham. The Prophets were everlastingly aware of the unity of their world, and their utterances on the gentiles, frequent and vivid, are based on a common moral law. Apart from such well-known passages as the vision of the end of things in Isaiah and Micah, or the linking in ultimate brotherhood

of Egypt, Israel, and Assyria in Isaiah, or the mission of
Jonah to Nineveh, there are entire chapters in Amos, Jeremiah, and others devoted to the respective fates of adjacent
peoples. Before the rise of the so-called literary Prophets,
Elijah and Elisha were bidden to carry their work beyond
the boundaries of Israel; and the post-Biblical history of the
Jewish people is one long expectancy of the universal Messianic redemption.

The consciousness of Jewry has always swung back and
forth between extremes of egocentricity and world-percep-
tion, and it is still the moral-intellectual problem of the Jew
to find the proper balance between his Jewish self and his
world self. That is, of course, the moral-intellectual problem of all children of all peoples. But how does one go
about the search?

Not, I think, by a deliberate suppression of the attachment to one's own, personal historical sources—when one
is aware of them—and not by making a virtue of one's un-
awareness of such sources. There is much confusion in that
stereotype admonition, with its air of large-mindedness: "Be
less an American (or Englishman, or Slovakian) and more
of a world citizen." It appeals (sometimes unintentionally,
perhaps) to a false antonym. It implies that the harmony
of the world will arise not from peoples living together on
this planet, but from the planet-wide community of bil-
lions of people-less individuals.

In this respect the moral-intellectual problem of the Jew,
despite its special features, is not different from that of
other peoples. The Jew is peculiar in that he can draw on
two sets of sources side by side, his own, and those of his
adopted country; but if he relinquishes his Jewish source he
does not thereby enrich the other. I will not say that he
thereby impoverishes it, but he does rob it of potential values that only Jews can conjure out of it. Thus, what being

American or English can mean to a Jewish-historically conscious Jew cannot be created in the mind and heart of others
than Jews; nor can it be created in the mind and heart of a
Jew who has lost affectively the thread of Jewish continuity.

Yet it is quite senseless to chide a Jew for not feeling Jewish. But on the other hand it is even more senseless for such
a Jew to make propaganda for his lack of Jewish feeling, as
if it were a positive achievement (it is in any case purely ac-
cidental). The gain it is supposed to represent—to wit, the
widening of one's horizon—is an illusion born of the diminution of one's power of sight. This is an illusion shared by
all those—of whatever origin, and in whatever setting—who
are convinced that their detachment from personal historical associations is the groundwork for a kind of universalism. Actually they are a transitional generation, and transitional generations are the raw material of new peoples; they
are not the forerunners of an undifferentiated mankind.

This is not to say that in principle peoples are eternal.
Peoples must die in order that peoples may be born, and a
people dies either by murder, or assassination, or by the inability to adapt itself to change of circumstance, or by running out of the capacity to hold on to its children. When
extinctions take place in the natural course of things, no
moral question is involved any more than in the natural
death of an individual. There is, however, a moral question
involved in the murder (by war) or assassination (slaughter
without risk) of a people. Nor does assassination always
take the straightforward form of the machine gun and the
gas chamber; equally effective is the legislative suppression
of freedom of self-expression. But whether it is outright assassination or forcible cultural subjugation, the criminal
people will always justify its action by convincing itself, or
pretending to convince itself, that the victim people has no
real right—on these or on those grounds—to existence. Some-

times it will be, with relative frankness: "They stand in our way, and our right to exist comes first." Sometimes it will be: "They stand in the way of history, of which we are the representative." And sometimes it will be a mixture of the two.

There is also a moral element involved in the intellectual attitude that dehumanizes history until it becomes nothing more than a play of "natural" forces. Certainly there are phenomena that we have to call "natural" historical forces, just as there are in the individual chemical or electrical forces; but as I do not trust the man who sees the individual as *nothing but* the crossing-point of mechanical forces, so I do not trust the historian, or the philosopher of history, who sees a people as *nothing but* the resultant of historical forces.

Imaginative schemata of the all-human drama are legitimate and useful as frameworks, as co-ordinates of analysis. They are perhaps unavoidable, for what is history without imagination? But they are not history itself. Their usefulness depends, too, on the honesty of the historian. He must draw his curves according to the record, and not shift the record according to his fancy-free curves. Where he disagrees with the record, surmising that such and such was the fact, he must say so; he must not ignore the record. He must, in fact, account for it. Even so, I, the layman, do not expect the historian to know the facts. Ranke's famous ideal: "*Ich will bloss sagen wie es eigentlich gewesen ist* (I only want to tell how the thing actually was)" is, despite the fun that has been poked at it, a sound one, as long as we know that it is impossible of realization, or that if it could be realized, it could not be proved, which amounts to the same thing. I do not expect the historian to know the truth; I only want him to be truthful.

But that does not, for me, exhaust the function of the historian. If he is something more than a compiler and copyist of the records, I want him to convey to me, out of the past of all peoples, something of that sense of organic belonging which I experience in regard to the past of mine. I want him to strengthen my respect for the reality and the right-to-be of other peoples without diminishing anything in my relationship to my own people. Or, to put it conversely, I want him to play on my immediate historical associations and to widen them. I want to learn from him how to be more myself by virtue of being more of the generality.

INDEX

A NOTE ON THE TYPE

This book is set in Electra, a Linotype face designed by W. A. Dwiggins. This face cannot be classified as either modern or old-style. It is not based on any historical model, nor does it echo any particular period or style. It avoids the extreme contrast between thick and thin elements that marks most modern faces, and attempts to give a feeling of fluidity, power, and speed.

Typographic and binding designs are by W. A. Dwiggins.

The book was composed, printed, and bound by The Plimpton Press, Norwood, Mass. The paper was made by S. D. Warren Company, Boston, Mass.